KETOCLARITY

| C O O K B O O K |

Your Definitive Guide to Cooking
LOW-CARB, HIGH-FAT MEALS

**Jimmy Moore
& Heather Rushin**

VICTORY BELT PUBLISHING INC.
Las Vegas

First published in 2019 by Victory Belt Publishing Inc.

Copyright © 2019 Jimmy Moore & Heather Rushin

ISBN-13: 978-1-628603-68-2

The authors are not licensed practitioners, physicians, or medical professionals and offer no medical diagnoses, treatments, suggestions, or counseling. The information presented herein has not been evaluated by the U.S. Food and Drug Administration, and it is not intended to diagnose, treat, cure, or prevent any disease. Full medical clearance from a licensed physician should be obtained before beginning or modifying any diet, exercise, or lifestyle program, and physicians should be informed of all nutritional changes.

The authors claim no responsibility to any person or entity for any liability, loss, or damage caused or alleged to be caused directly or indirectly as a result of the use, application, or interpretation of the information presented herein.

Front and back photography by Hayley Mason and Bill Staley

Cover and interior design by Yordan Terziev and Boryana Yordanova

Illustrations by Yordan Terziev, Boryana Yordanova, Allan Santos and Crizalie Olimpo

Printed in Canada
TC 0119

To everyone whose life has been forever changed by the power of nutrition, I am grateful for any small role I might have played in helping to make that happen for you. Never stop learning and pursuing the best possible health you can attain.

—Jimmy

To Mom,

This book is dedicated to you. You carried me through the creation of this book on your shoulders. Now we both have it to hold in our hands to remember forever. Thank you for everything you have done for me, inspiring me to work for myself, and every other way you have contributed to my life.

I love you with all my heart.

—Heather

CONTENTS

Introduction | 7

   Heather's story | 9

   Meet the keto experts | 11

   The five key Keto Clarity concepts | 14

CHAPTER 1 Eating LOW-CARB Is the Foundation of It All | 16

   Know your sensitivity to carbs | 18

   Eat mostly green leafy, nonstarchy vegetables | 20

   Try to incorporate fermented veggies | 21

   Omit whole grains and refined carbohydrates | 21

CHAPTER 2 Keto Isn't a High-Protein Diet; It's a MODERATE-PROTEIN DIET | 22

   Knowledgeably choose fatty proteins | 24

   Eat only enough protein to fulfill your body's needs | 24

   Take steps to source the best quality | 25

   Observe the kinds of proteins consumed | 25

CHAPTER 3 Welcome to the Dark Side of Eating Healthy HIGH-FAT | 26

   Kiss low-fat and fat-free goodbye | 28

   Eat a mix of mostly saturated and monounsaturated fats | 30

   Taste what healthy food is supposed to be like | 31

   Obliterate the myth that dietary fat will harm you | 31

4 **Optimize Your Diet by Choosing Mostly REAL FOOD** | *32*

Know where your food comes from | *34*

Eat mostly whole foods | *35*

Take time to savor your meals | *36*

Overwhelm your body with nutrient density | *37*

 5 **Major LIFESTYLE FACTORS That Can Impact Ketosis** | *38*

Keep to a regular sleep schedule | *39*

Exercise in the right way for your body | *40*

Tap into strategies for complementing your diet | *40*

Overcome the daily stressors that hinder health | *41*

 6 **Weekly MEAL PLANS** | *42*

 7 **RECIPES** | *60*

Why no macros? | *62*

Kitchen tools and equipment | *64*

SAUCES and BASICS | *68*

APPETIZERS and SNACKS | *100*

SOUPS, SALADS and SIDES | *138*

BURGERS and PIZZA | *178*

MAIN DISHES | *210*

DESSERTS | *268*

DRINKS | *300*

Acknowledgments | *314*

Recipe Index | *316*

General Index | *322*

INTRODUCTION

KETO: It's the hottest diet trend since the heyday of the Atkins diet a decade and a half ago and the Paleo diet after that—and keto shows no signs of slowing down anytime soon. This low-carb, moderate-protein, high-fat way of eating has taken the world by storm, promising weight loss, control of hunger and cravings, and chronic disease prevention. The proof of its effectiveness is in the tens of millions of people who have embraced the ketogenic lifestyle and are reaping the benefits while simultaneously enjoying the most decadent and delicious foods they've ever consumed on a "diet." A *Business Insider* survey conducted in December 2018 found that half of the millennials surveyed wanted to try either a low-carb or a ketogenic diet in the coming year. That's huge!

The runaway popularity of keto brings a great big smile to my face because it was something I saw had great potential for widespread influence on the nutritional health landscape way back in 2012 when I first started experimenting with it myself. My name is Jimmy Moore, and I'm an international bestselling author and longtime health blogger and podcaster. I began eating low-carb when I started the Atkins diet on January 1, 2004, and it enabled me to stop taking three prescription medications and lose 180 pounds that year. I went on to start a blog called *Livin' La Vida Low-Carb* in 2005 and then began podcasting on *The Livin' La Vida Low-Carb Show* in 2006.

Podcasting provided me with a great opportunity to meet and interview some of the best and brightest minds in the medical and research world. I talked to people who were looking into the health effects of the ketogenic diet, and that made me curious about how I was doing in my pursuit of nutritional ketosis beyond fleeting weight loss. As I continued to soak up knowledge on this subject by reading books and interviewing guests on my show, I became more and more curious about deliberately pursuing a constant state of nutritional ketosis. So, in 2012, I began self-testing with my now-famous yearlong N=1 experiment. (N=1 refers to a trial consisting of just one patient.) The results were so profound that I just knew I had to share this experience with my blog readers, who were enthusiastic about what I was demonstrating.

When Victory Belt Publishing approached me in 2012 about writing books for them while I was in the midst of my N=1 testing, they wanted to know what ideas I had. The first thing out of my mouth was "ketogenic diets." At the time, Victory Belt was well known as a Paleo publisher, producing some of the biggest and best books in that genre. While I wasn't necessarily opposed to eating a real food–based Paleo-style diet, my focus had shifted almost completely to keto because it was producing such incredible changes in most of the relevant health markers, such as triglycerides and HDL cholesterol. I knew this information could help so many people, and books would be the perfect way to get the message out.

My debut book with Victory Belt, *Cholesterol Clarity*, shined a bright light on the misinformation that people have been given about the importance of their cholesterol levels on their health. I included quite a bit of information about how the ketogenic diet improves the relevant markers, and I even teased that my next book would be all about keto. *Keto Clarity* was released in August 2014, and it took off like wildfire, with legions of people interested in learning more about the ins and outs of this way of eating.

That's when I teamed up with my friend and ketogenic recipe goddess Maria Emmerich to write *The Ketogenic Cookbook*, which went on to become my first international bestseller. In the years since, I've cowritten many other books about this way of eating, including *The Keto Cure* and *Real Food Keto*, as the explosion of keto into the mainstream began in earnest in 2017 and then blew up big. But it was *Keto Clarity*, that first book on the subject, that got it all started several years ahead of the curve. The timing was fortuitous, and the public was ready to hear more about the benefits of low-carb, moderate-protein, high-fat living.

While I was writing *Keto Clarity*, it was my baby. I literally wrote and rewrote that book more than a hundred times to make it as perfect as it could possibly be. My passion was to make it the go-to resource for beginners about the ins and outs of doing keto. I used easy-to-understand language while still honoring the science behind why keto works. When I noticed Amazon reviews that said the book was both too simple and too hard to understand, I knew I had struck the right balance for the audience I was trying to reach. That book has since been translated into more than a dozen (and counting) languages, and I couldn't be prouder of the impact it has had. To this day, I still hear stories of how that book has changed the lives of people around the world.

Some truly incredible keto authors have come on the scene since Maria and I published the first cookbook in this genre in 2015, including Carolyn Ketchum, Suzanne Ryan, Kyndra Holley, Leanne Vogel, Natasha Newton, Kristie Sullivan, Megha Barot, and Matt Gaedke. But in this companion cookbook to *Keto Clarity*, I'd like to introduce you to a brand-new voice in the keto space. Her name is Heather Rushin, and she is an incredibly talented recipe creator and photographer. Her personal story is one of triumph over a serious health issue that began when she was a teenager and was resolved when she turned to the low-carb, high-fat way of life. It's intriguing history that will make you appreciate her recipes all the more. Let's meet Heather now.

Heather's story

At the age of sixteen, Heather was sitting in her first-period math class in high school with her head down and her eyes closed because she was writhing in intense pain. Her stomach was giving her trouble, and she couldn't concentrate on her teacher's explanation of the finer points of some algebraic equation. Instead of actively participating in class, she was white-knuckling it through the intolerable churning that radiated from her stomach, and she knew something horrible was happening to her.

When she got home from school, Heather told her parents about this experience, and they theorized based on her symptoms that she was lactose intolerant. So they went to the local pharmacy and got her some over-the-counter pills to help her digest dairy. Although those pills helped curb her excruciating pain, they didn't make it go away completely.

Unfortunately, Heather continued to live with the pain for the next six years as she went off to college and grew into early adulthood.

While in college, after hearing something about a gluten-free diet, Heather decided on a whim to give up gluten for three weeks to see what would happen. Although she was not eating any bread or pasta, the pain she had dealt with since she was sixteen persisted. She also noticed weight gain that went well beyond the typical Freshman Fifteen. This marked the beginning of her fateful journey into calorie counting, portion control, and obsessively tracking all of her food, because that's what her naturally skinny roommate told her she needed to do. And so Heather's frustration with her weight and health began.

For the next decade, Heather did exactly what that college roommate said to do and tracked every morsel of food she ate, starving herself practically all the time. In reality, she was punishing her body needlessly, all in the hopes of losing weight and getting rid of the stomach pain that had plagued her for so long. She lost a few pounds here and there, but, in hindsight, it was the most miserable experience of her entire life. Heather was eating low-fat cheese crackers and anything else that had the word *lite* or *skinny* on the front of the package. Sound familiar?

A few years later, Heather got involved in a podcast called *A Real Food Journey*. The podcast featured various food bloggers, and it's where Heather heard about the Paleo diet for the first time. That propelled her to start incorporating more real, whole foods into her diet. After a short time, she noticed that her stomach pain had diminished, and she quickly regained her energy. However, despite seeing some success, she was still eating far too many carbohydrates and had not yet learned how incorporating a low-carb approach into her real food journey could benefit her.

As she was working her way through understanding how the changes in her diet were affecting her, Heather got engaged and picked out her wedding dress. When she tried on the dress after it had been altered, it didn't fit quite right. She reverted once again to her tried-and-true starvation diet to shed the 10 pounds she had regained despite eating Paleo. Fearing that every bite she took would make her fatter and fatter even though she was eating the best-quality whole foods she could, she became afraid of eating any food at all.

But Heather was starving most of the time and couldn't figure out why. She became hyper-obsessed with food—to the point that it was consuming every facet of her life. This food confusion and panic plagued her for many more years, and she suffered some mental distress as a result. Most people would have buckled under the pressure and simply given up, but Heather is a fighter. About this time, she had a fortuitous encounter with a book that talks about shifting your body from burning sugar to burning fat through a process known as nutritional ketosis. The book was *Keto Clarity*, written by Jimmy Moore (that's me!), and it was exactly what Heather had been looking for all along.

After reading *Keto Clarity*, Heather's eyes were opened to the importance of restricting carbohydrates and eating fat for energy and metabolism. It took some serious mental strength to give up her long-standing calorie-counting routine and let go of the crappy carbage that was plaguing her health. Of course, this keto thing was so brand-new to her that she had to persevere through some ups and downs to make it work; like most people who are new to keto, Heather experienced the "keto flu" in the early days when she failed to balance her electrolytes. But once she found her keto groove, it was on like Donkey Kong!

Thanks to the incredible benefits of her new ketogenic lifestyle, Heather quickly began to trust her body in a whole new way and realized that she could still consume the real, whole foods that had been part of her Paleo diet; she just needed to leave out the carbohydrate-based foods. It wasn't difficult at all for her to do. She greatly reduced the amount of carbs she was eating and began adding more dietary fats like cheese, butter, and meats to keep her body healthy and satisfied. Heather quickly discovered that eating this way was incredibly intuitive and enjoyably delicious, which made her want to experiment with creating new recipes. She didn't need to skimp on anything, and that gave her freedom in her food choices like no other eating plan had given her before. Going ketogenic was the best thing she ever tried, and now she's happily sharing her experiences on her blog, *A Real Food Journey* (www.arealfoodjourney.com), which features stunning photography and amazing keto-friendly recipes like the ones she shares in this book.

It's important to enjoy the food you eat and know that it is nourishing your body well so you can live in the moment when you're not eating. That wasn't always the case for Heather when she was a teenager enduring severe stomach pain. Now all those years of hunger, deprivation, and desperation are a thing of the past, and she is enjoying everything that life has to offer. She wants everyone dealing with health and weight issues to be able to experience this same sort of happiness, which is why she decided to join forces with me on this book that brings her story full circle. *Keto Clarity* was what inspired her to make a change in her life, and now, through *Keto Clarity Cookbook*, she will inspire countless others to get serious about their nutrition, too.

Meet the keto experts

Fans of *Keto Clarity* raved about how much they loved having input from various experts in the ketogenic community sprinkled throughout the book as "Moments of Clarity" to reinforce the messages my coauthor and I were sharing in the main text. So, for *Keto Clarity Cookbook*, Heather and I just had to include useful comments from six of the leading voices in the keto world. Many of these medical doctors, functional medicine practitioners, and researchers have come along in prominence since *Keto Clarity* was published, and we're honored to feature them and their wisdom in this book.

Will Cole, DC, IFMCP

Dr. Will Cole, a leading functional medicine expert, consults with people around the world via webcam at www.drwillcole.com and locally in Pittsburgh, Pennsylvania. He specializes in clinically investigating underlying factors of chronic disease and customizing health programs for thyroid issues, autoimmune conditions, hormonal dysfunction, digestive disorders, and brain problems. Dr. Cole was named one of the top fifty functional medicine and integrative doctors in the United States and is the author of *Ketotarian,* in which he melds the powerful benefits of ketogenic and plant-based diets.

Gus Vickery, MD

Dr. Gus Vickery is a board-certified family physician, a speaker, and the author of *Authentic Health.* He founded Vickery Family Medicine in 2005, which has grown to include multiple medical providers serving patients in three locations, including The Clinic at Biltmore, an innovative direct-to-employer clinic for the Biltmore Company. Vickery Family Medicine has received numerous awards for customer service and quality. Dr. Vickery also studied health-care delivery and founded Synergy Health Solutions, an innovative direct-to-consumer organization helping improve access and reduce costs while providing effective care. In addition, Dr. Vickery developed a holistic health curriculum that teaches people how to experience their best health regardless of their current state of health. He is an expert on chronic obesity and reversing chronic weight gain in sustainable ways. These resources led to the formation of Health Shepherds, an online health resource. Dr. Vickery speaks to organizations, audiences, and book clubs around the country, and he's committed to helping people gain resources to access their best health. Learn more about his work at www.drgusvickery.com.

Ken Berry, MD

Dr. Ken Berry is a practicing board-certified physician, an Amazon bestselling author, and a passionate advocate for health on his YouTube channel, which has more than 450,000 subscribers. Along with his online presence, he is active in his community of Camden, Tennessee, where he has been practicing at the Berry Clinic since 2003. Dr. Berry is known for his direct, no-nonsense approach to health and wellness. The second edition of his bestselling book, *Lies My Doctor Told Me,* was published in 2019. He is in the process of writing his second book, *Common Sense Keto.* He looks forward to continuing his mission to bring an end to the obesity and type 2 diabetes epidemics, along with bringing awareness to such issues as thyroid health and hormone optimization. Learn more about Dr. Berry at www.kendberrymd.com.

Ryan Lowery, PhD

Ryan P. Lowery, PhD, CISSN, is a 2014 national champion baseball player and the coauthor of *The Ketogenic Bible.* He earned BS and MS degrees in exercise physiology and exercise and nutrition science from the University of Tampa. He completed his doctorate work in Health and Human Performance at Concordia University with a focus on ketogenic dieting, exogenous ketones, and their impact on human performance. Over the past five years, Dr. Lowery has published an astounding ninety papers, abstracts, and book chapters on human performance and sports nutrition, and he's rapidly becoming one of the premier sport scientists in the United States. He has received the Exercise Science Scholar of the Year Award, the NSCA Award for Outstanding Presentation of the Year, and the National AAHPERD Exercise Science Major of the Year Award. In addition to his outstanding academic and research accomplishments, Dr. Lowery is one of the most sought-after nutrition and supplement formulators in the industry. He has worked with more than two dozen nutrition and exercise companies, including multimillion-dollar affiliate marketing companies and sports nutrition companies. In doing so, he brings a unique skill set to sourcing ingredients, assuring compliance of companies, formulating novel products, and bridging the gap between the science of nutrition and the industry of it. Dr. Lowery is currently serving as the president of a brand-new research center in Tampa called the Applied Science and Performance Institute. Learn more about Dr. Lowery at www.ketogenic.com.

Eric Westman, MD

Eric C. Westman, MD, MHS, is an associate professor of medicine at Duke University. He is board certified in obesity medicine and internal medicine, and he founded the Duke Lifestyle Medicine Clinic in 2006 after eight years of clinical research regarding low-carbohydrate, "keto" diets. He is past president and Master Fellow of the Obesity Medicine Association and Fellow of the Obesity Society. He is an editor of the textbook *Obesity: Evaluation and Treatment Essentials* (for medical professionals) and coauthor of the *New York Times* bestseller *The New Atkins for a New You* and bestsellers *Cholesterol Clarity* and *Keto Clarity.* He is also a cofounder of the companies Adapt Your Life (adaptyourlife.com) and Heal Diabetes Clinics (healclinics.com), which are based on low-carbohydrate concepts.

Tony Hampton, MD

Dr. Tony Hampton, who is board certified in obesity medicine, shares his knowledge in his clinical practice, as a blogger, as a regular speaker for the American Diabetes Association and other associations, and as an author of the book *Fix Your Diet, Fix Your Diabetes.* He leads both the Healthy Living Program for Advocate Aurora Health and the Advocate Medical Group Outpatient Beverly's Diabetes Prevention Program to give patients tangible resources to help them reach their health-related goals. His other roles include serving as regional medical director of Advocate Medical Group's largest outpatient clinic, which has more than fifty clinicians, vice chair of Advocate Medical Group's Governing Council, and chairs of Advocate Medical Group's Health Outcomes committee and Advocate Healthcare's Diversity Council. Dr. Hampton believes all clinicians should work in their practices to prioritize obesity management, which is foundational in reversing the diabetes epidemic. Visit his website at www.drtonyhampton.com.

We invite you to soak in the collective knowledge and decades of experience that these top keto experts have to share from both a personal and a patient perspective.

The information in this book is making a profound impact on real people on a daily basis. You should feel confident that keto living can and will help you become healthier than you ever thought possible. And who doesn't want that?

MOMENT OF CLARITY "People have to realize there is not a 'best' diet that applies to all people, but there *is* a best diet that applies to each individual. One person might do better eating more animal products, while someone else might thrive with more vegetables. There is always a proper balance, and our individualized approaches to eating have to honor the fundamental principles of healthy eating. Paying attention to your energy, hunger, weight changes, mood, and how your body feels after eating will help you determine which version of keto works best for you."

—**Dr. Gus Vickery**

Now that you know more about the people who are behind this book, let's get down to business. First we want to explain the five key Keto Clarity concepts that you're going to learn about in this book as you pursue better health. Then we have some scrumptious low-carb, high-fat recipes for you to make and enjoy with your entire family—and nobody will ever think they're on a diet! Are you ready to bring some more clarity into your life? Here we go!

The five key Keto Clarity concepts

We believe that there are five key concepts involved in implementing a well-formulated ketogenic diet and making the lifestyle work well for you so that you can succeed at becoming keto-adapted and experience the full range of benefits of this way of eating. We cover each of these Keto Clarity concepts in much more depth in the first five chapters of the book, but here's a quick list so that you can start thinking about them:

KEY KETO CLARITY CONCEPTS

1.
LOW CARB

2.
MODERATE PROTEIN

3.
HIGH FAT

4.
REAL FOOD

5.
HEALTHY LIFESTYLE CHOICES

Many people are talking about keto these days, but they don't always include all five of these elements. A proper ketogenic diet is defined as being low in carbohydrates to your personal tolerance level, moderate in protein to your individual threshold, and high in dietary fats to satiety. In addition, you should consume mostly real, whole foods that provide the vitamins and minerals your body needs for optimal health and make lifestyle modifications such as movement (aka exercise), stress management, and sleep optimization to complement your nutrition choices. That's it! That's keto, whittled down to its very essence. That doesn't sound so hard, right?

In *Keto Clarity*, Jimmy and his coauthor, Dr. Eric Westman, share the following acronym, and it still holds true for anyone seeking to get into a state of nutritional ketosis:

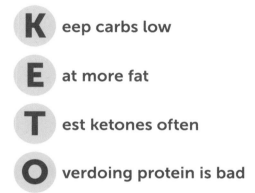

K eep carbs low

E at more fat

T est ketones often

O verdoing protein is bad

For this companion cookbook, we have created a brand-new K-E-T-O acronym for each of the five key Keto Clarity concepts to go a bit deeper into these topics. Look for the acronym at the beginning of each chapter.

Keto is not just some trendy buzzword for quick weight loss; it's a permanent healthy lifestyle change that will radically shift the trajectory of your path to health in the years to come. Embrace this way of life fully, and you'll experience robust health and healing from the inside out. If you'd like to make that happen, then let us bring a little more clarity to your keto pursuit.

CHAPTER 1:

Eating
LOW-CARB
Is the Foundation
Of It All

(K) now your sensitivity to carbs

(E) at mostly green leafy, nonstarchy vegetables

(T) ry to incorporate fermented veggies

(O) mit whole grains and refined carbohydrates

"There are no essential carbohydrates, starches, or sugars. The word *essential* here means that the human body can't make them, and we must eat them to survive. There are many essential fatty acids that we must eat routinely, or we will get sick, suffer, and eventually die. There are essential amino acids (building blocks of protein) that we must eat routinely, or we will get sick, suffer, and eventually die. There are, however, no known essential carbohydrates, starches, or sugars. This means that either we don't really need them, or the human body can easily manufacture these things from other building blocks."

—Dr. Ken Berry

The first key Keto Clarity concept is the foundation on which a ketogenic diet is based—cutting carb intake. Low-carb diets are not new to the nutritional health scene. In fact, in just the past few years, we've seen a huge surge in carbohydrate restriction being used in many popular diets, including Paleo, Whole30, and fasting (which restricts everything), all of which encourage dieters to give up primarily refined sugars and grains as the way to better health.

Before that, beginning in the early 1970s and during a resurgence in the late 1990s and early 2000s, the Atkins diet was all the rage. It encouraged people to cut down on carbs and eat more fat and protein. But these concepts weren't brand-new even then. A British undertaker named William Banting wrote a pamphlet in 1869 called "Letter on Corpulence," and it became the world's first bestselling diet book. It was all about a low-carb diet.

"Keto had its early beginnings with the Banting diet in the UK in 1863! In the twentieth century, the most influential pioneering practitioners who carried the torch and wrote popular books about low-carb and ketogenic diets were Dr. Robert C. Atkins and Jackie Eberstein, RN *(Dr. Atkins' Diet Revolution),* Drs. Michael and Mary Dan Eades *(Protein Power),* and Dr. Richard K. Bernstein *(The Diabetes Solution).* While Dr. Atkins tragically passed away and the Eades have retired, Dr. Bernstein still has a clinical practice today!"

—Dr. Eric Westman

So, given that cutting carbohydrates has been well-known dieting strategy for a century and a half, you might be wondering why there is a perception that low-carb living is new. Most of it has to do with the development of the Dietary Guidelines for Americans, which were first instituted in 1980 by the United States Department of Agriculture (USDA) and sought to codify nutritional health to present recommendations for how to eat healthily. Without having much scientific evidence to support these guidelines for eating, the government basically told Americans that dietary fat was the most evil substance in the world and that they should be eating more "healthy" foods like whole grains, beans, and pasta. This decision to promote a high-carb, low-fat diet has been disastrous, to say the least, with more obesity, type 2 diabetes, heart disease, and other chronic diseases than ever before!

"A thousand calories' worth of spinach has a totally different metabolic impact on our bodies than a thousand calories of pound cake. The first law of thermodynamics argues that calories in must equal calories out. That's true in a lab, but not in the human body. Science has clearly shown that the worst macronutrient to consume in an effort to lose weight is carbs. That's why I put the focus on reducing carbs as a much more effective tool for achieving and maintaining an ideal body weight than focusing on calories."

—Dr. Tony Hampton

Many people who hear about a ketogenic diet immediately curl up into the fetal position as they try to face the prospect of giving up bread, pasta, and sweets. The fact that people respond so emotionally and demonstrably is evidence of the addictiveness of carbohydrates. Letting go of these foods is like giving up a dog you've owned since it was a puppy or moving away from a town you've lived in your entire life. It's hard, and most people can't imagine what it's like to start, as Jimmy calls it, "livin' la vida low-carb."

But you can and should do it if you care about your state of health. If you picked up this book, then you are, at the very least, interested in making a change so that you can lose weight, feel better, stop being hungry on a diet, and improve some health condition you're dealing with. Give yourself a moment to grieve over the carbohydrates you need to cut the cord with, and then you can start going keto in earnest. Until you come to a place where you recognize that those foods are health-robbing and not health-promoting, you will remain stuck. Let them go once and for all, and then the health and healing you've wanted can commence.

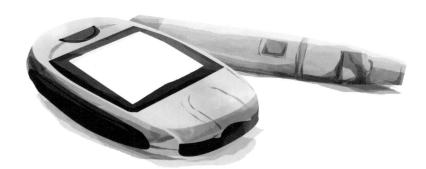

Know your sensitivity to carbs

Each of us has a highly individualized response to carbohydrate consumption. Some people can eat as much as 75 to 100 grams of carbohydrates per day and still be in a state of nutritional ketosis, whereas others have to stay closer to zero grams to see positive results in their weight and health markers. Most of the population falls somewhere in the middle of this range—it's all a matter of tinkering and testing to find what works for you.

"Carbohydrate tolerance changes throughout our lives. As we get older, we aren't as insulin sensitive, and therefore we can't handle carbohydrates the same way we could as kids. Everyone's carbohydrate tolerance varies. Some high-level bodybuilders can eat 100 grams of carbohydrates per day and still be in ketosis because they have a lot of muscle and are burning through those carbohydrates with their workouts. On the other hand, older people need to stay around 20 grams of carbohydrates due to their insulin resistance. Movement is a key part of helping to increase your carbohydrate tolerance. Even a little exercise on a regular basis can make a huge difference."

—Dr. Ryan Lowery

The best way to know your carbohydrate tolerance level is to test your blood sugar (or glucose). Once thought of as devices only for people with type 1 or type 2 diabetes, blood glucose monitors are now widely available at any pharmacy or big-box store. You can use one of these monitors to determine how your body responds to any given food. Because carbohydrates raise blood glucose the most, try testing your response to a sweet potato (or some other carbohydrate-based food) to see how your body reacts. The process is simple:

1. Test your blood sugar level before you eat (baseline reading).
2. Eat a sweet potato (or whatever carbohydrate-based food you want to test).
3. Test your blood sugar one hour after eating the sweet potato (one hour postprandial).
4. Test your blood sugar two hours after eating the sweet potato (two hours postprandial).

Here's an example of the perfect response you are looking for:

If your blood sugar starts at 90 mg/dL, a good response at the one-hour mark after eating the sweet potato is a reading that has gone up no more than 25 to 30 points—to 115 to 120 mg/dL. Then, at the two-hour mark, your blood glucose should have returned to within 5 points of the baseline reading—90 to 95 mg/dL in this example.

Here's an example of a response that indicates you had too many carbohydrates:

If your blood sugar starts at 90 mg/dL, a poor response at the one-hour mark after eating the sweet potato is a reading that has gone up more than 30 points— to above 120 mg/dL. Then, at the two-hour mark, your blood glucose hasn't quite returned to baseline and remains elevated by 15 or more points—105 mg/dL or higher in this example.

You wouldn't feel this reaction happening inside your body; the only way to know how your body reacts to the carbohydrates you consume is to test your blood sugar levels. And many people are oblivious to how their bodies respond because they don't test to see how sensitive they are to carbs. Test, test, and test some more if you want to determine exactly how many carbs are right for you on your keto eating plan.

Eat mostly green leafy, nonstarchy vegetables

Your carbohydrate intake on a ketogenic diet is comprised of mostly green leafy vegetables like arugula, collards, kale, lettuce, spinach, and Swiss chard, as well as nonstarchy vegetables like asparagus, broccoli, cabbage, cauliflower, celery, cucumbers, eggplant, green beans, peppers, yellow squash, and zucchini, just to name a few. These kinds of low-carb veggies are packed with micronutrients that your body can use when you're eating keto. They're very tasty when they are cooked in fat to bring out their flavor and help your body absorb their nutrients. (Vitamins A, D, E, and K, which are found in many of these vegetables, are fat-soluble, and you need fat in your diet in order for your body to use them.)

Of course, we must note here that while there are essential amino acids (protein) and essential fatty acids (fat), there is absolutely no such thing as an essential carbohydrate acid! The human body has no nutritional requirement for carbs at all. Shocking, right? The body can create the glucose it needs for various glucose-dependent functions from the fat and protein you consume. That's not to say there is no benefit from consuming the vegetables discussed in this section, including adding vitamins and minerals, flavor, and variety to your diet. But the human body could subsist on fat and protein if needed. So, again, why is it recommended that we eat gobs of carbohydrates? It doesn't make any sense at all!

MOMENT OF CLARITY "From my scientific perspective, 'keto' is merely a low-carbohydrate diet—much of the benefit comes from the fact that it is low in carbohydrates. Not everyone needs to count macronutrient ratios. The major message should always be to keep the carbs low!"

—**Dr. Eric Westman**

Try to incorporate fermented veggies

There is one category of carbohydrate that, while not necessarily essential from a macronutrient perspective, can provide enormous benefits to your health, and that is fermented vegetables. Foods like sauerkraut, kimchi, and fermented pickles are excellent plant-based matter than can enhance your keto food choices. Making these foods (and fermenting virtually any other vegetable) at home is best, but you can purchase commercial fermented products. Keep in mind that you won't find them in the center aisles of the grocery store with the other shelf-stable foods; the healthy bacteria for your gut would not survive without refrigeration. That's why quality brands of sauerkraut and fermented pickles, like Bubbies, are found in the refrigerated section.

Omit whole grains and refined carbohydrates

This should go without saying if you're even remotely educated about keto, but whole grains ain't healthy. Refined carbohydrates and sugars are the greatest saboteurs in your pursuit of nutritional ketosis. Eliminating them when you begin your ketogenic diet is a must. Your body simply cannot make the metabolic changes necessary to start reaping the benefits of being in ketosis until whole grains and refined carbohydrates are gone from your diet. They have disastrous effects on blood sugar and insulin levels and will cause astronomically high levels of inflammation, which is the root of all chronic disease. Let them go. You'll be so glad you did.

Now that you understand the importance of eating low-carb as the foundation for a ketogenic diet, let's take a look at a surprising aspect of keto that many people said was a game-changer for them when they read Keto Clarity. In the next chapter, we examine the importance of moderating protein intake.

MOMENT OF CLARITY "Carb consumption leads to insulin production in the pancreas. Insulin's job is to help put glucose from the foods we eat into the cells for fuel. Because our glucose storage tank holds only 1,700 calories of energy while fat storage nets 70,000 calories for fat, eating carbs makes you hungry compared with eating fat. I teach my patients to avoid excessive carb/sugar consumption over a long period to avoid insulin resistance and to become fat burners instead!"

—Dr. Tony Hampton

CHAPTER 2:

Keto Isn't a High-Protein Diet; It's a MODERATE-PROTEIN DIET

(K) nowledgeably choose fatty proteins

(E) at only enough protein to fulfill your body's needs

(T) ake steps to source the best quality

(O) bserve the kinds of proteins consumed

"Eating too much protein has been linked to an increase in mTOR, a pathway that is responsible for the activation of cancer. This is one pitfall that I find in people eating a Paleo or low-carb diet like Atkins compared with doing keto. By not focusing enough on healthy fats, they are overdoing foods that are higher in protein, and this is reflected in their overall health over the long term."

—Dr. Will Cole

The second key Keto Clarity concept relates to a common misconception that people have about keto: they think it's a high-protein diet. Actually, it's only moderate in protein, and in this chapter we explain why.

Protein is perhaps the most interesting of the three macronutrients. The amino acids that make up the protein we consume are essential to human health. In other words, if you did not eat protein, then you would die. Period. End of story. Literally.

But one of the myths about protein is that because it's essential, you need to eat a lot of it to prevent muscle loss, increase your levels of satiety, and reduce your overall calorie intake. But what if people are eating *too much* protein?

Your body can easily store the carbohydrates you eat in the form of glucose (which is stored in the muscles as glycogen); when carbs exceed the body's storage capacity, they get stored as body fat. But what about protein? Can the body store protein as well? Actually, no, it can't. The protein in a steak, for example, gets used in the areas of the body where amino acids are needed, but any extra protein that is still floating around in the body after those needs have been met has nowhere to go. So what happens to it?

That excess protein is sent to the liver to be converted into a usable form of energy—glucose—through a process known as gluconeogenesis. Don't worry about that fancy word; it just means that the liver turns excess protein into sugar. But when you're trying to be in a fat-burning ketogenic state, extra sugar is the opposite of what you want. This is why protein moderation is such a critical element of keto. Some people argue that limiting carbohydrates alone will put you into ketosis, but neglecting the negative potential impact of too much protein is a critical error many newbies make that prevents them from succeeding.

"Two-thirds of adult Americans are insulin resistant, which forces their bodies to produce five to seven times more insulin than non-insulin-resistant adults. This leads to an increase in belly fat and worse. I teach my patients to use dietary fat as their primary source of energy on a ketogenic approach, moderating protein while reducing carbohydrate consumption. By using fat as the primary energy source, insulin resistance and the increased stored body fat are reversed over time."

—Dr. Tony Hampton

Knowledgeably choose fatty proteins

We hate to break it to you, but chicken breast is not a health food. We'll give you a moment to pick your jaw up off the floor. Chicken breast is 99 percent fat-free and basically all protein. As we shared earlier, if you eat more protein than your body needs, the excess protein will be converted into sugar in your body—the exact opposite of what you're trying to accomplish on keto. So, if you're going to eat chicken on your ketogenic lifestyle, then make sure to choose the darker, fattier cuts like the wings, thighs, and legs.

Better yet, go out of your way to find the fattiest cuts of meat that give you ample fat with naturally moderate levels of protein. Pork belly is a perfect example, as is rib-eye steak. Choosing animal proteins with fat on them prevents you from overeating protein, and that fat is satiating to your body. Some people argue that you can simply add fat like butter or avocado to a leaner protein like chicken breast. However, when you do that, you still get a big bolus of protein, and it's not going to be offset by the added fat. Purposefully choosing fattier cuts will keep you in fat-burning mode so you burn plenty of therapeutic ketones.

Eat only enough protein to fulfill your body's needs

This concept is tricky for people to wrap their heads around. Since the body has no protein-o-meter to let you know when you've had enough, the trick is to choose a target amount of protein and then make that your daily goal. For example, if you choose to eat 100 grams of protein per day, then you partition your protein choices to hit this goal and not exceed it.

A 6-ounce boneless, skinless chicken breast has 54 grams of protein, so you couldn't eat more than two of them in a day without blowing way past your protein threshold. If, instead, you chose to eat three large eggs (18 grams of protein) and three strips of thick-cut bacon (12 grams of protein) for breakfast, a 5-ounce hamburger patty (27 grams of protein) with 2 ounces of cheddar cheese (14 grams of protein) for lunch, and 5 ounces of rib-eye steak (30 grams of protein) for dinner, then you would consume a grand total of 101 grams of protein. Doesn't that sound a lot more satisfying than two chicken breasts?

The most important thing is to choose fattier proteins so you don't run the risk of overdoing it on protein consumption. Those two chicken breasts come in at a whopping 108 grams of protein, and some people can eat that much in just one meal. We've just shown you how choosing fattier meats can help prevent you from going beyond your body's protein needs. The fat that comes with these proteins will fill you up for hours, whereas eating chicken breast will likely leave you feeling hungry again within one hour! Which would you prefer?

Take steps to source the best quality

The quality of the proteins you eat matters. Do the best you can within your budget to buy the most nutrient-dense proteins possible. Grass-fed meats are slightly more expensive than factory-farmed meats, but the nutrient content of grass-fed meats is far superior to that of meats produced by the farming practices that have become the norm for our food supply. Jimmy's backyard chickens provide him with free-range organic eggs anytime he wants a good source of protein (and those glorious yolks are loaded with ample fats!). Wild-caught fish and other seafood products also are excellent protein sources—for example, salmon contains healthy omega-3 fats.

The added nutrients that you get from these quality proteins help nourish your body and benefit your health markers in ways that go beyond counting macros. If you want to up your keto game, then make sure to choose the best-quality proteins when you shop for food.

Observe the kinds of proteins consumed

Many people think protein is protein, but that's just not true. The protein you get from a grass-fed rib-eye steak, for example, is a complete protein, but the protein in beans or soy is not complete. (Sorry, vegans.) Also, the kind of protein you eat matters because some proteins produce a greater insulin response than others. Whey (dairy) protein is well known as the most insulinogenic protein. And remember the two-chicken-breasts meal example we cited earlier? The reason you get hungry so soon after that meal is the insulin response of that kind of protein. In general, the fattier the protein, the less insulin your body releases. So always observe the kind of proteins you eat, because they matter.

Now that you've got a grasp on why moderating protein is critical to success on keto, let's look at another massively important element that's hard for people to wrap their heads around when they begin eating this way. Making fat the majority of your diet is still a taboo subject for most people. Don't let anyone fool you into thinking that keto is anything but a high-fat diet. In the next chapter, you'll learn why fat is an instrumental piece of the ketogenic puzzle.

MOMENT OF CLARITY "Most doctors receive very little nutrition education in medical school. Of the little they do receive, most of it focuses on promoting a fruit-heavy, grain-heavy diet containing very little meat and no saturated fat at all. This trains doctors to promote a diet that doesn't work and reinforces their perception that diet isn't really all that important to health. They have become so divorced from the fact that nutrition and what's happening in our health are closely related that most doctors don't ever make the connection between the carbohydrate-filled foods we are eating and the diseases that people develop from eating this food."

—Dr. Ken Berry

Welcome to the Dark Side of Eating Healthy HIGH-FAT

(K) iss low-fat and fat-free goodbye

(E) at a mix of mostly saturated and monounsaturated fats

(T) aste what healthy food is supposed to be like

(O) bliterate the myth that dietary fat will harm you

"We have ample scientific evidence that high-fat diets are not the primary cause of heart disease. However, overcoming the decades of misinformation can be challenging. It's understandable that people still have doubts about higher-fat diets. So what I do with my patients is explain some simple truths about how the body works and how our energy balance is regulated. Once they better understand these truths, then embracing fat makes perfect sense to them."

—Dr. Gus Vickery

The third key Keto Clarity concept is perhaps the most controversial because of public perception of it. Of all the concepts that are important when it comes to getting into ketosis, the one that trips people up the most has to be eating high-fat. With all the scaremongering about the role of saturated fat that has taken place, especially with regard to heart disease and obesity, people are quite literally scared to death to eat even a little fat—much less making it the preponderance of their daily energy intake. But think about it: When you cut down on carbohydrates and moderate your protein consumption, guess which macronutrient is left? That's right; it's dietary fat.

Keto is putting fat back on the map as it redefines what a healthy diet should look like. While fat-free and low-fat foods had their heyday in the 1980s and 1990s, people are now embracing fat as they've never embraced it before. They realize that for far too long, they've been lied to about real, whole foods like butter, coconut oil, lard, bacon, meats and full-fat cheeses, and all the other delicious and, dare we say, nutritious fats that we enjoy on a low-carb diet.

Business experts have seen this trend coming for a while. A September 2015 Credit Suisse study entitled "Fat: The New Health Paradigm" looked at more than 400 medical research papers and books written by medical professionals and industry leaders. The report noted that consumers were shifting their diets away from carbohydrates and would be looking for more high-fat options. It said investments in companies that made products for this market would be quite profitable; we've seen examples in companies like Love You Foods, LLC, and its popular FBOMB nut butter products (www.dropanfbomb.com), which are featured prominently on shelves at health food retailers. Still think eating fat is gonna harm you?

Kiss low-fat and fat-free goodbye

Remember all those times you went on a diet before and were forced to eat foods that tasted gross? We've all done it. Time after time we decided to cut the fat to lose weight and get healthy, and seeing the words *low-fat* or, better yet, *fat-free* on the front of a food package had us gobbling up those tasteless products like they were going out of style. We can't tell you how many times we forced ourselves into believing that these kind of foods were actually good for us while we held our noses so we could choke them down. Never again! You can kiss those fatless foods goodbye and embrace fat again on keto. It's encouraged, even!

That's not to say you'll gorge yourself on sticks of butter or eat whole jars of coconut oil in one sitting. But the beginning of your keto journey marks the end of the needless restriction of dietary fat. It makes sense. When you cut carbs and moderate your protein intake, fat is what's left. So consuming enough fat—upwards of 80 percent of your total calorie intake—is necessary because you have to replace the carbohydrates and extra protein you were eating.

On keto, you'll likely consume about the same number of calories in less feeding time than you did as a low-fat dieter. Here's an illustration to show you how the two approaches compare:

LOW-FAT DIET

BREAKFAST
- Oatmeal (about ¾ cup)
- Banana
- Orange juice
- Coffee

LUNCH
- ½ tuna salad sandwich (with lettuce, tomato, and light mayo)
- Cup of low-sodium vegetable soup
- Apple
- Diet soda

SNACK
- Baby carrots or low-fat microwave popcorn

DINNER
- Salmon with pineapple salsa
- Blue cheese and cherry salad
- Brown rice (about ½ cup)
- Glass of wine

DESSERT
- Homemade peach ice cream

That day's worth of low-fat meals looks like a lot of food, and it is—because you aren't eating much fat. You're gonna need every single one of those 1,800 calories to feel some semblance of satiation. We ate meals like these for many years until we found that keto offered a better way. Let's take a look at the difference between those low-fat meals and a day's worth of keto meals:

KETO DIET

BREAKFAST

• 3 eggs cooked in grass-fed butter

• 3 strips of thick-cut bacon

• ½ avocado

• Coffee with heavy cream and stevia

LUNCH

You're not hungry because you fueled yourself well enough with your breakfast meal.

SNACK

There's no need to snack because the fats you consumed for breakfast are still keeping your body happy.

DINNER

• 6-ounce rib-eye steak cooked in butter

• Broccoli and cauliflower cooked in bone broth and lard with cheddar cheese on top

DESSERT (if you even want it)

• Strawberries or blueberries with whipped heavy cream and sugar-free dark chocolate

Would it surprise you to hear that the number of calories in these luxurious keto meals is almost the same as the number of calories in the low-fat meals? Yes, you eat a greater total volume of food when you follow a low-fat diet, but that's because you have to or else you'll be hungry. Keto foods are so nourishing and delicious that you can go long periods between meals and feel just fine. A diet that keeps you content between meals is the definition of a good diet. Have you ever had that happen on a low-fat diet? Yeah, neither have we!

Eat a mix of mostly saturated and monounsaturated fats

When you see the value that dietary fat has to offer within the context of a ketogenic diet, there is no fear in embracing real food–based fats. A healthy and delicious mix of mostly saturated fats (such as butter, coconut oil, lard, and full-fat cheeses and meats) and monounsaturated fats (including avocados, avocado oil, and olive oil) along with some polyunsaturated fats (raw nuts and seeds) and omega-3 fats (fish, fish oil, and flax) will fuel your body to the max. Don't fear fat; it is your friend when you are limiting your carbohydrate consumption.

MOMENT OF CLARITY "The biggest revelation people have when they go keto is when they realize the body can use fat and ketones as its primary fuel source. Of course, this concept goes completely against what we were all taught, so most people are surprised to learn this!"

—Dr. Eric Westman

Taste what healthy food is supposed to be like

No longer do we have to put up with the notion that healthy food is supposed to taste horrible. This is something we've been conditioned to think because of the heavy promotion of low-fat diets. The reality is, food that nourishes the body and provides the nutrients it needs to thrive should taste good. Nobody should ever make you feel bad for wanting to eat tasty meals. Believe us, the recipes in this book are mouthwatering—and they just so happen to be healthy, too! This is what good eating is supposed to be like—not hunger, pain, and deprivation. Embrace the fats!

Obliterate the myth that dietary fat will harm you

Whether you realize it or not, the vilification of dietary fat as the greatest enemy to your health hasn't been in vogue since the TV show *American Idol* was last relevant (ancient history!). Health experts and medical professionals alike are increasingly embracing the fact that dietary fat is not as harmful as was once thought. For the first time in its history, in its 2018 guidelines the American Diabetes Association included a low-carb, high-fat, ketogenic diet as a therapeutic option for people with type 2 diabetes because research studies around the world are showing it to be highly effective. Yet the myth that fat will harm your body or clog your arteries persists. This is the last big hurdle that prevents so many people from experiencing the benefits of a ketogenic lifestyle change. The days of fearing fat need to end.

Now that you realize fat is the lifeblood of a ketogenic diet, let's turn our attention to the next Keto Clarity concept that can help take your keto experience to the next level. It's so simple, yet not enough people are doing it. Find out why eating mostly real, whole foods is the great unspoken secret to success on keto.

MOMENT OF CLARITY "Work was done years ago that showed the average brain burned around 120 to 130 grams of glucose daily during normal function. Somehow this finding got interpreted into the 'truism' that humans need to eat this many carbohydrates daily for proper brain function. But this does not logically follow from the finding. But because it sounds so symmetrical, most doctors easily believe this fallacy despite the fact it is based on no logic or facts whatsoever."

—Dr. Ken Berry

CHAPTER 4:

Optimize Your Diet by Choosing Mostly REAL FOOD

(K) now where your food comes from

(E) at mostly whole foods

(T) ake time to savor your meals

(O) verwhelm your body with nutrient density

MOMENT OF CLARITY "For sustainable, abundant health, you can't simply count macronutrients as the way to wellness. Just because something is low-carb, high-fat, or keto doesn't necessarily mean it's healthy or optimal for you. You are alive because of brilliant biochemistry, and real food provides you with the precise components that build and instruct a healthy biochemistry. The ketogenic diet, when paired with a real food approach, amplifies all the amazing benefits of nutritional ketosis for long-term wellness."

—Dr. Will Cole

The fourth key Keto Clarity concept is something that a segment of the keto community does not put as much value on as the previous ones. But choosing real, whole foods most of the time is an optimal ketogenic approach. In his previous book, *Real Food Keto*, which Jimmy wrote with his wife, Christine Moore, a Nutritional Therapy Practitioner, he makes the argument that a well-formulated ketogenic diet needs to be based on quality real, whole foods.

There's a disturbing trend within the keto community, known as "dirty" or "lazy" keto, in which people simply look at the macronutrient ratios of what they're eating without taking food quality or nutrient density into account. So they might opt to order a hamburger without the bun from a fast-food restaurant and consider it an acceptable ketogenic meal. While the ratios of carbs, proteins, and fats you consume certainly are important for getting into ketosis, neglecting to embrace the micronutrition that comes from real foods is a huge mistake.

MOMENT OF CLARITY "Within the mainstream of diet culture, people are still obsessed over calories being the be-all, end-all game when it comes to losing weight and gaining health. But the quality of the calories in the foods you are consuming is very rarely discussed or debated. Why do we still hold on to the archaic calorie message at the expense of getting down to the brass tacks of what is impacting people's health—too many carbs (especially refined ones) and not enough real, whole-food sources of dietary fat?"

—Dr. Tony Hampton

Know where your food comes from

If you ask kids where food comes from, most of them will tell you that it comes from the grocery store. As funny as that sounds at first blush, it's a sobering reality of where our culture is today. Adults and children alike have become completely detached from the food supply and rely heavily on big food companies to feed them. Unfortunately, those corporate conglomerates have no interest in our health and are merely seeking to squeeze every last bit of money out of consumers' pockets. Manufacturers take shortcuts and use cheap, inferior ingredients, and they hope we won't notice that these ingredients are slowly chipping away at our health until it's too late to reverse the consequences. There's got to be a better way, right?

There *is* a better way. One of the easiest and best ways to reconnect with your food is to grow your own vegetable garden. Jimmy and Christine planted a garden about five years ago, starting small with a 4-foot patch of seeds in their front yard. They had no expectations that anything would grow, but boy, did it ever! After that initial success, the garden got bigger each year until they decided to make a fenced-in 24 by 24-foot garden in which they plant every low-carb vegetable and herb you can think of. They also have two backyard gardens and a greenhouse for growing food throughout the winter months. But that's not all they did to reconnect with their food.

Three years ago they decided to get backyard chickens. What started as a humble flock of six beautiful hens has turned into more than two dozen that dig, squawk, poop, and roam all over their huge backyard. Jimmy and Christine take really good care of the birds because they provide the most delicious and nutritious eggs you've ever tasted. If you think you know what eggs taste like, then you owe it to yourself to get some free-range eggs from backyard chickens and see how they compare to supermarket versions.

Of course, not everyone has the time and space to grow gardens and raise animals, but you can visit local farmers and farmers markets to source quality real food to feed your family. When you get to know the human beings who are passionate about their food, you develop a special connection with what they are providing you for nourishment. You just don't get that when you buy cellophane-wrapped chicken breasts or ground beef at the grocery store. You appreciate your food all the more because you know where it came from. Reconnect with your food, and you'll see what a difference it makes.

(M)OMENT OF CLARITY "Eating nutrient-poor, high-calorie foods that have been engineered to be addictive is one of the major contributors to obesity and chronic disease. When my patients realize that food sourcing is far more important than specific macronutrient ratios, it makes sense to them to eat real food. They understand that it's the types of fats and not the quantity of fats that matter. They also understand how important it is to eat whole, natural foods most of the time if they want to have good health long term."

—**Dr. Gus Vickery**

Eat mostly whole foods

Some people who promote a ketogenic diet criticize us when we call for eating mostly whole foods. They say, "You don't need to eat that way to get into ketosis!" But that's not the point. Many who come to keto are highly addicted to sugar, grains, and other sources of culprit carbohydrates that have plagued their health. Something they've lacked in their diets and has gone underappreciated is micronutrients—you know, the vitamins and minerals that help sustain life and make your body work.

In *Real Food Keto,* Christine and Jimmy go into great detail about the important roles that micronutrients play. But the primary point is that people coming to keto from the Standard American Diet will undoubtedly have bodies that are extremely deficient in key nutrients. Yes, restricting carbohydrates and getting more healthy fats into your body will make you feel better when you go keto, but why not get all the way better by incorporating this additional element of real, unprocessed food?

We wish someone had told us about the added benefits we would have received had we embraced the idea of consuming mostly whole foods sooner. But better late than never! Learn from the mistakes of those of us who have gone before you.

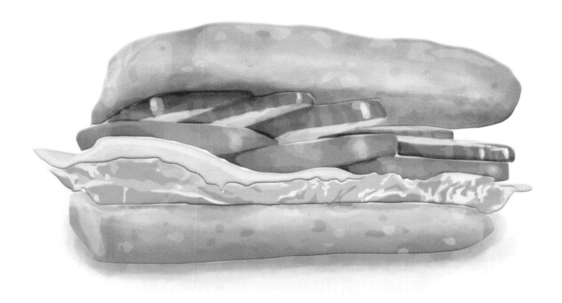

Take time to savor your meals

Jimmy was always a notorious "inhaler" when it came to food. He doesn't really know why he ate this way, but it was a bad habit that he still fights to this day. But when you consume real, delicious food that nourishes your body, how can you not slow down, savor each bite, and enjoy that food that makes your body work optimally? When you stop to think about what the good stuff is doing for you when you eat it, you appreciate it all the more, and you can linger just a little while longer at mealtimes.

MOMENT OF CLARITY "I simplify dinner for my patients—include an animal food (avoiding flour or cornmeal for breading) with two or three nonstarchy vegetable sides. This approach has led to an increase in my patients cooking at home and eating real food on a daily basis."

—Dr. Tony Hampton

Overwhelm your body with nutrient density

The goal of eating real food isn't to add more money to your food bill. That's the knee-jerk reaction some people have to the concept of adding foods like grass-fed beef, organic vegetables, and higher-quality fats. They think there is no way they can afford to shop this way, and they don't see the value in it when all it takes to be in ketosis is cutting carbs and eating more fat, regardless of the quality. But, oh, how you miss reaping so many other great health benefits if you don't choose these more nutrient-dense foods. Do what you can to get the best quality you can manage. Stock up on grass-fed meats and butter when they're on sale. Once you get a taste of higher-quality foods, you'll never go back!

We hope by now you realize that your ketogenic lifestyle needs to be dominated by whole foods. We both strongly believe in this principle, and the recipes in this book reflect the commitment to real food that we consider to be an instrumental part of your keto health journey. In the next chapter, we have one more key Keto Clarity concept to share with you that's a little off the beaten path in the discussion of diet, but it has a direct relationship to success or failure in your quest to be in nutritional ketosis.

MOMENT OF CLARITY "Honor your body's need for proper nutrition. Processed foods and refined sugars are not that different from tobacco products. They trigger inflammation and contribute to chronic diseases because they have been engineered to be addictive. They take advantage of how our brains work to promote overeating. But when you honor your body's need for nutrient-dense whole foods, you can reverse disease and potentiate your best health possible."

—Dr. Gus Vickery

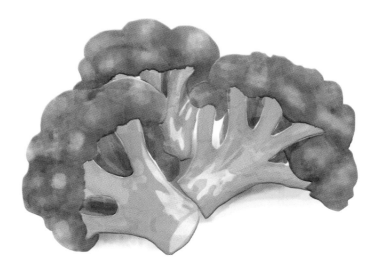

CHAPTER 5:

Major **LIFESTYLE FACTORS** That Can Impact Ketosis

(K) eep to a regular sleep schedule

(E) xercise in the right way for your body

(T) ap into strategies for complementing your diet

(O) vercome the daily stressors that hinder health

The fifth and final key Keto Clarity concept is one that most people probably don't think much about in the context of going keto, yet it could arguably be the most important one of all. While everyone likes to focus on what you're eating to help your body shift into fat-burning mode, did you realize that lifestyle factors such as sleep, exercise, and stress management can have a direct impact on your body's ability to get into and stay in ketosis? In this chapter, we explain why these things matter when your goal is being keto.

(M)OMENT OF CLARITY "Nutrition plays an integral role in many aspects of our health. However, it's important to understand that eating a diet like keto is not the only piece of the puzzle. Take someone who is on the cleanest diet ever and yet is completely sedentary, is stressed out all the time, has trouble sleeping, is filled with negativity, and has other major disruptions in life. Do you think that person is going to ever reach their maximal health potential? Absolutely not."

—**Dr. Ryan Lowery**

Keep to a regular sleep schedule

Many people give no credence to the role that sleep plays in their health. They think it's about nothing more than winding down at night, resting the body for a few hours, and then waking up to take on a new day. But getting adequate quality sleep is about more than just the length of time you spend in bed, and it plays a crucial role in your ability to recover well from the stresses of the day and even to burn fat and get into ketosis.

Getting inadequate sleep raises your cortisol (stress hormone) to unnatural levels, which in turn increases your blood sugar. Then your body has to excrete insulin to deal with the excess glucose, and that basically kills your keto progress. This is *no bueno*. That's why Jimmy tracks the four stages of sleep (awake, REM, light, and deep) using an Oura Ring (www.biohackingring.com). Testing your sleep is as important to your ketogenic lifestyle as testing your blood sugar and ketone levels. You need good sleep!

(M)OMENT OF CLARITY "Getting adequate restorative sleep is like unlocking a superpower. Our bodies and minds are designed to be outdoors in natural light to set our circadian rhythm during the day and then to get deep restorative sleep at night. If you consistently disrupt your circadian rhythm, then you can end up gaining weight and becoming sick. Maintaining proper circadian rhythm function is as essential as eating food and drinking water."

—**Dr. Gus Vickery**

Exercise in the right way for your body

Most people don't even think about exercise and ketosis, but these two things are connected in more ways than you think. The right kinds of movement and activity can boost your blood ketone levels. Don't test right after a hard workout; wait a few hours and watch what happens to your ketones. They generally go up, and that's a sign that fat-burning is taking place.

When you exercise, you want to make sure the intensity is high enough that you're getting the ketosis-inducing benefits that come from it. A leisurely walk on a treadmill at the gym is certainly better than no activity at all, but it's generally not intense enough to give you the benefits you desire. So what kind of exercise should you be doing instead? Resistance training, or lifting weights, is one option, and you don't have to start super-duper heavy. Just begin with something (even your own body weight) and work your way up. You should sweat and feel your muscles burn if you do it well.

You can also do high-intensity interval training, or HIIT, which involves short bursts of all-out effort (like running) followed by periods of rest and recovery. You repeat these intervals eight to ten times. You should be completely spent by the time you've finished the intervals, and it takes only about ten minutes a couple of times a week to achieve amazing results. When you exercise your body in the right way, it will perform for you in the way you want—and you will be a lean, mean, fat-burning machine.

Tap into strategies for complementing your diet

It's amazing how many people put the onus for weight loss and health success or failure almost exclusively on their diet. Although diet is a powerful component, it's not the only contributor. Implementing strategies such as practicing mindful meditation or prayer, using an infrared sauna or light therapy, getting a massage, soaking in a hot tub, spending time on a vibration plate, diffusing essential oils, practicing deep breathing exercises, and treating others with kindness, love, and compassion goes a long way toward helping you fulfill your healthy lifestyle goals. It's tempting to look only at your nutritional choices and predicate all of your results on food, but these other efforts matter, too.

MOMENT OF CLARITY "With a focus on nutrition, exercise, less stress, and more sleep, improved health is the natural outcome. Once I help my patients make this fundamental shift mentally, I give them simple steps to achieve this. We incorporate intermittent fasting since eating one or two times daily is easier than eating two or three times daily. I also encourage them to cook two or three times weekly with an expectation to make enough food for leftovers to simplify their meal prep."

—**Dr. Tony Hampton**

Overcome the daily stressors that hinder health

A lot of people are dealing with unresolved stress without even knowing it. Stress in and of itself isn't a bad thing, but when it's constant and your body never gets a break from it day after day after day, then that pent-up stress can be the death knell in your pursuit of nutritional ketosis. Jimmy has received so many emails from people over the years telling him how keto failed them because they didn't lose weight or see the improvements in their health. When he digs a little deeper, he learns that they went through a death in the family, got fired from a job, endured a relationship struggle, or experienced some other traumatic event. Guess what, you guys? This stuff affects your body! The daily stress from worrying about anything and everything can and will hinder your health and your pursuit of nutritional ketosis. So take a chill pill. Your body will reward you.

MOMENT OF CLARITY "You must learn to take control of your thoughts and emotions that negatively impact your stress levels so that you can make the choices that best support your health. Chronic stress leads directly to inflammation and disease and depletes our willpower, causing us to make choices that compromise our health. To put it simply, it robs us of our well-being. Starting an effective stress management program as soon as possible is an absolute must."

—Dr. Gus Vickery

That just about wraps up this section of the book that explains how keto can fit into your healthy lifestyle pursuit. In the coming pages, you will experience what this way of eating is all about—the mouthwatering foods you get to enjoy that help heal your body and give you your life back. This is the pay dirt of why you're eating low-carb, moderate-protein, and high-fat and choosing mostly real, whole foods. No other diet in the world lets you eat this well while improving your health and weight. So get in the kitchen, start cooking keto, and then reap the benefits one bite at a time!

MOMENT OF CLARITY "Throughout your ketogenic journey, you will undoubtedly face trials and tribulations. It's at these very moments when your perspective can mean the difference between staying on board for the long haul or falling off the bandwagon. Life is too short to express anything but gratitude on a daily basis. Rather than stress out that you're not able to eat your 'regular pasta' or 'full-sugar candy bar,' change your perspective and realize that you are making a conscious decision to improve your life not only for you, but for those around you. Every single morning, remind yourself of this fact—you woke up, and someone else in the world didn't. That's a gift in itself. Don't waste your life on things that won't matter fifty years from now."

—Dr. Ryan Lowery

CHAPTER 6:

Weekly
MEAL PLANS

This chapter provides eight weeks of keto meal plans, including four dairy-free plans to support those who need or want to exclude dairy. With these plans, you can create easy, filling menus that are fully keto, without the stress of having to map out every little thing you're going to eat each day. We've created these plans to take the weight off your shoulders. If weekly planning works for you, work the plan!

That being said, these meal plans are meant to serve as a jumping-off point; take what works for you and leave what doesn't. Use the meals that sound great to you and fill in with other favorite dishes or different recipes from the book. You can also swap out herbs and seasonings as you like.

The plans are designed to feed two people. If you have a big appetite, you may need to add a few extra side dishes to your weekly plan; see pages 138 to 177 for recipes. If you tend to eat smaller meals, you may end up with extra food.

Most of the recipes in this book serve four. Although we've tried to make judicious use of leftovers in the meal plans to avoid food waste, not all of the recipes used in the plans are eaten twice during the week, so you are likely to have leftovers. Most of these dishes store well when refrigerated in airtight containers; salads and drinks keep for the least amount of time. Salads are best dressed right before serving, slaw being an exception to that rule. When a plan calls for leftover salad, store the greens and dressing separately until the day you need them for the freshest and crispiest greens. For meat, it's usually best to carve only what you plan to eat right away and store the remainder as a whole piece. Most meats, soups, and roasted veggies freeze well, too.

You can freeze your leftovers or eat them instead of a dish called for later in the week. You can also halve a recipe if you don't want to end up with leftovers. Make the plan work for you and your life!

The accompanying shopping lists include all the ingredients you will need to make the meals listed for each week. (Optional ingredients are not listed.) They also serve as inspiration for how a keto pantry can look. Even if you don't intend to meal plan, just glancing over these weekly shopping lists can inspire you before you do your own grocery shopping. Make it a goal to get more adventurous in the kitchen!

The shopping lists may seem lengthy, but you are likely to accumulate keto-friendly ingredients over time, so you may not need to buy every item on the list each week. To make the shopping even easier, there are a few key pantry items that we assume you always have on hand:

- Apple cider vinegar
- Avocado oil
- Black pepper
- Coffee (decaf or regular)
- Olive oil
- Pink Himalayan salt (medium grind)
- Red wine vinegar
- Unflavored liquid stevia

WEEK 1 MEAL PLAN

	BREAKFAST	LUNCH	DINNER	SNACK
SUNDAY	Cinnamon Cream Coffee — 310	George's Soup — 162	Arugula Caesar Salad (2 servings) — 176	Chocolate Chip Cookies — 292
MONDAY	Chocolate Chip Cookies — leftover	Hot and Smoky Wedge Salad — 168	Reverse Sear Tri-Tip Roast — 236	
TUESDAY	Drinking Chocolate* — 302	Elote Chicken Wings — 118	Simple Baked Cod — 242	Chocolate Chip Cookies — leftover
WEDNESDAY	Strawberry Jam Parfaits — 278	Reverse Sear Tri-Tip Roast — leftover	French Onion Soup (2 servings) + Perfect Baked Salmon + Tartar Sauce — 174 / 230 / 77	Sparkling Green Tea Elixir — 313
THURSDAY	Elote Chicken Wings — leftover	Perfect Baked Salmon + Tartar Sauce — leftover / leftover	Everything Crusted Pork Chops + Arugula Caesar Salad (2 servings) — 228 / leftover	Strawberry Jam Parfaits — leftover
FRIDAY	Breakfast Cobb Salad — 166	French Onion Soup (2 servings) — leftover	Avocado Shrimp Salad — 140	Candied Pecans — 290
SATURDAY	Mocha Coffee — 303	Everything Crusted Pork Chops — leftover	Southwest Burgers + lettuce "buns" — 184	Chocolate-Covered Bacon Ice Cream — 282

*Reserve the extra Drinking Chocolate for use in the Mocha Coffee on Saturday.

WEEK 1 SHOPPING LIST

MEAT AND SEAFOOD

bacon, 12 strips

breakfast sausage, bulk/ground, 3 pounds

breakfast sausage links, 4

chicken wings, 15

cod fillet, 1½ pounds

ground beef, 1 pound

pork chops, boneless, 4 (about 1½ pounds)

salmon fillet, 1½ pounds

shrimp, small/250-300 size, cooked, 8 ounces

tri-tip roast, 1¾ to 2 pounds

DAIRY/EGGS

blue cheese, 1 ounce

butter, salted, 10 ounces (2½ sticks)

cheese of choice (for Breakfast Cobb Salad), 6 ounces

Cotija cheese, 1 ounce

Gruyère cheese, 3 ounces

heavy cream, 22 ounces (2¾ cups)

Parmesan cheese, 1 ounce (¼ cup grated)

Pecorino Romano or Parmesan cheese, 1¼ ounces (⅓ cup grated)

sharp cheddar cheese, 2 ounces

sour cream, ¼ cup

whole milk, 8 ounces (1 cup)

eggs, 8

FRESH PRODUCE

arugula, 9 cups (about 1½ pounds)

avocados, 3

bell peppers (any color), 3 large

butter lettuce or other lettuce of choice (for "buns"), 1 head

cherry tomatoes, 1 pint

chives, 2 tablespoons chopped

cilantro, ¼ cup plus 2 tablespoons chopped

dill, 1 tablespoon chopped

garlic, 7 cloves

iceberg lettuce, 1 head

lemon, 1

limes, 4

onions, red, 2 large

onions, yellow, 3 large and 2 medium

radishes, 8 medium

romaine lettuce or other salad greens, 2 heads

shallot, 1 small

tomatoes, 5 medium

PANTRY ITEMS

beef bone broth, 32 ounces (4 cups)

chicken bone broth, 32 ounces (4 cups)

nut milk of choice (for Drinking Chocolate), 4 ounces (½ cup)

BAKING INGREDIENTS

baking powder, 1½ tablespoons

baking soda, 1½ teaspoons

chocolate, 100% dark, 1 ounce

chocolate chips, sugar-free, 1 cup

cocoa powder, unsweetened, 2 tablespoons

erythritol, confectioner's, 1 tablespoon

erythritol, granulated, 1 cup

pecan halves, raw, 2 cups

sunflower seed flour, 300 g (about 2½ cups)

vanilla extract, 1 tablespoon plus 1⅜ teaspoons

DRIED HERBS AND SPICES

chili powder, ½ teaspoon

Chinese five-spice powder, ¼ teaspoon

chipotle powder, 1 tablespoon

cinnamon, ground, 3½ teaspoons

everything bagel seasoning, ¼ cup

garlic powder, ½ teaspoon

Italian seasoning, 3 tablespoons

nutmeg, ground, 1 pinch

onion powder, ½ teaspoon

ranch seasoning, 2 tablespoons

smoked paprika, 1 teaspoon

taco seasoning (see page 79 for ingredients if making homemade), 1 tablespoon

CONDIMENTS/SAUCES/DRESSINGS

anchovy paste, ½ teaspoon

balsamic vinegar, 2 tablespoons

blue cheese dressing (see page 83 for ingredients if making homemade), ¾ cup

Dijon mustard, 1 teaspoon

mayonnaise, 1 cup

DRINKS

green tea, 1 bag

red wine, 8 ounces (1 cup)

sparkling mineral water or club soda, 1 (8-ounce) can

WEEK 2 MEAL PLAN

	BREAKFAST	LUNCH	DINNER	SNACK
SUNDAY	224 — Pizza Baked Eggs	212 — Keto Pot Roast	194 / 114 — Asian-Style Burgers + Jalapeño Poppers with Strawberry Jam	284 — Toasted Coconut Pudding
MONDAY	310 / 270 — Cinnamon Cream Coffee + Lemon Macaroons	110 / 286 — Baked Brie + Keto Caramel Sauce*	238 / 172 / 74 — Crispy Baked Chicken + Lime Slaw + Smoky Garlic Burger Sauce**	134 — Spiced Nuts Three Ways***
TUESDAY	160 — Hot Spinach and Bacon Salad + Jalapeño Poppers with Strawberry Jam	leftover — Keto Pot Roast	232 — Salt and Pepper Chuck Steak with Blue Cheese Butter	272 — Strawberry Cream Ice Pops
WEDNESDAY	leftover / 304 — Asian-Style Burgers + Raspberry Smash	120 — Cheesy Stuffed Meatballs	174 / 164 — French Onion Soup + Grilled Romaine Salad	311 — Lemonade Slushies
THURSDAY	98 / leftover — Cinnamon Bread + Pizza Baked Eggs	148 — Instant Pot Chicken and Rice Soup	184 / 74 — Southwest Burgers + lettuce "buns"+ Smoky Garlic Burger Sauce	leftover — Lemon Macaroons
FRIDAY	166 — Breakfast Cobb Salad	leftover — French Onion Soup	204 — White Pizza	leftover — Lemon Macaroons
SATURDAY	302 / leftover — Drinking Chocolate + Breakfast Cobb Salad	leftover — White Pizza	116 / 154 — Lemon Oysters + Wasabi Broccoli Slaw	298 — Butter Pecan Pudding

*Reserve the leftover caramel sauce for use in the Butter Pecan Pudding on Saturday.

**Reserve half of the burger sauce for the Southwest Burgers on Thursday.

***Select which Spiced Nuts flavor combination you would like to make and add those ingredients to the shopping list for the week.

WEEK 2 SHOPPING LIST

MEAT AND SEAFOOD

bacon, 10 strips

breakfast sausage links, 4

chicken thighs, bone-in, skin-on, 4

chicken thighs, boneless, 1½ pounds

chuck roast, 2 to 3 pounds

chuck steak, boneless, 1½ pounds

ground beef, 3 pounds

oysters, 12

pepperoni, 2½ ounces

DAIRY/EGGS

blue cheese, 3 ounces

Brie cheese, 1 (7-ounce) round

butter, salted, 7½ ounces (about 2 sticks)

Camembert cheese, 2 ounces

cheese of choice (for Breakfast Cobb Salad), 6 ounces

cream cheese, 2 ounces (¼ cup)

Gruyère cheese, 3 ounces

heavy cream, 30 ounces (3¾ cups)

mozzarella cheese, 9 ounces

Parmesan cheese, 2¼ ounces (½ cup plus 1½ tablespoons grated)

sharp cheddar cheese, 2 ounces

sour cream, ¼ cup

egg whites, 7 (about ¾ cup plus 2 tablespoons liquid egg whites)

eggs, 12

FRESH PRODUCE

avocado, 1

basil leaves, 5 to 6

bell pepper, red, 1

broccoli, ¼ cup chopped

broccoli slaw, 2 (12-ounce) bags

butter lettuce or other lettuce of choice (for "buns"), 1 head

cabbage, 1 head

cauliflower, riced, 2 cups

cilantro, ¾ cup plus 1 tablespoon

cremini mushrooms, 8 ounces

dill, 1 tablespoon

garlic, 1 head plus 8 cloves

green onions, 9 (about 2 bunches)

jalapeño peppers, 14

lemons, 3

limes, 5

onion, white, ½ large

onions, red, 4 medium

onions, yellow, 2¼ medium

parsley, ¼ cup chopped

radishes, 11 large

raspberries, 10

romaine hearts, 4

romaine lettuce or other salad greens, 2 heads

rosemary, 2 sprigs

shallots, 2 tablespoons minced

spinach, 8 ounces

strawberries, 18 ounces

thyme, 2 sprigs

tomato, 1 medium

zucchini, 1 small

PANTRY ITEMS

beef bone broth, 48 ounces (6 cups)

chicken bone broth, 48 ounces (6 cups)

coconut milk, full-fat, 16 ounces (2 cups)

nut milk of choice (for Drinking Chocolate), 4 ounces (½ cup)

pork rinds, 1 small bag

BAKING INGREDIENTS

bacon grease, 1 teaspoon

baking powder, 2 teaspoons

chocolate, 100% dark, 1 ounce

cocoa powder, unsweetened, 1 tablespoon

coconut, unsweetened shredded, 8 ounces (about 2½ cups)

coconut flakes, unsweetened, ½ cup

erythritol, granulated, ¼ cup

gelatin, unflavored, 2 tablespoons plus 1½ teaspoons

golden flax meal, ½ cup (about 60 g)

ground psyllium husks, ½ cup

nuts, raw, whole or pieces, 1 cup

pecans, ½ cup chopped

pumpkin or sunflower seeds, ⅓ cup

rock or coarse salt

sunflower seed flour or meal, 120 g (1 cup)

vanilla extract, 2⅜ teaspoons

DRIED HERBS AND SPICES

cinnamon, ground, 1 tablespoon

garlic powder, ½ teaspoon

Italian seasoning, ¼ cup plus 1 tablespoon

nutmeg, ground, 1 pinch

oregano leaves, 1 teaspoon

parsley, ¼ cup chopped

ranch seasoning, 2 tablespoons

smoked paprika, 1 teaspoon

taco seasoning (see page 79 for ingredients if making homemade), 3 tablespoons

CONDIMENTS/SAUCES/DRESSINGS

balsamic vinegar, ¼ cup plus 2 tablespoons

kimchi, ¼ cup

mayonnaise, 1⅔ cups

mustard, Dijon, 2 tablespoons

mustard, prepared (any type), ¼ teaspoon

olive oil, garlic-infused, 1 tablespoon

Sriracha sauce, 1 teaspoon

tomato sauce, ¼ cup

wasabi paste, 2 teaspoons

DRINKS

club soda, 12 ounces (1½ cups)

sparkling mineral water, 16 ounces (2 cups)

WEEK 3 MEAL PLAN

	BREAKFAST	LUNCH	DINNER	SNACK
SUNDAY	250 — Greens and Ham Baked Eggs	168 — Hot and Smoky Wedge Salad	252 / 126 — Everyday Roasted Chicken + Caprese Skewers	282 / 286 — Chocolate-Covered Bacon Ice Cream + Keto Caramel Sauce*
MONDAY	303 — Mocha Coffee	196 — Crispy Mushroom and Blue Cheese Burgers + lettuce "buns"	262 / 70 — Flank Steak with Charred Green Onions + Smoky Chimichurri	276 — Lime Curd
TUESDAY	leftover — Flank Steak with Charred Green Onions	106 / leftover — Garlic Parmesan Chicken Wings + Smoky Chimichurri	176 / 116 / 76 — Arugula Caesar Salad + Lemon Oysters + Mignonette Sauce**	98 / leftover — Cinnamon Bread + Lime Curd
WEDNESDAY	224 — Pizza Baked Eggs	170 — Taco Soup	258 / 156 — Pork Belly + Habanero Brussels Sprouts	304 — Raspberry Smash
THURSDAY	136 — Prosciutto Meat Cups	174 — French Onion Soup	192 — Onion Horsey Burgers + lettuce "buns"	308 — Peppermint Italian Soda
FRIDAY	leftover — Taco Soup	230 — Perfect Baked Salmon	198 / 78 — Jalapeño Popper Pizza + Ranch Dressing	284 — Toasted Coconut Pudding
SATURDAY	256 — The Best Ever Grilled Cheese	234 / leftover — Marinated Fried Chicken Strips + Ranch Dressing	leftover / 150 — Crispy Mushroom and Blue Cheese Burgers + Stovetop Green Beans	298 — Butter Pecan Pudding

*Reserve the leftover caramel sauce for use in the Butter Pecan Pudding on Saturday.

**Select which Mignonette Sauce flavor you would like to make and add those ingredients to the shopping list for the week.

WEEK 3 SHOPPING LIST

MEAT AND SEAFOOD

bacon, 20 strips

chicken, whole, 3 to 5 pounds

chicken breasts or thighs, boneless, skinless, 1 pound

chicken wings, 12

flank steak, 1½ pounds

ground beef, 3¾ pounds

ground pork, 12 ounces

ham steak, 5 ounces

Italian sausage, bulk/ground, 4 ounces

oysters, 12

pepperoni, 2½ ounces

pork belly, 1 pound

prosciutto, 8 slices

salmon fillet, 1½ pounds

DAIRY/EGGS

blue cheese, 3 ounces

butter, salted, 1 pound (4 sticks)

cheddar cheese, 2 ounces

cheese of choice (for grilled cheese), 6 ounces

cream cheese, 1 to 2 tablespoons

Gruyère cheese, 3 ounces

heavy cream, 32 ounces (4 cups)

mascarpone cheese, ⅓ cup (or use mayonnaise)

mozzarella cheese, 7 ounces

mozzarella pearls, 20

Parmesan cheese, 4¼ ounces (1 cup plus 2 tablespoons grated)

Pecorino Romano (or Parmesan) cheese, 1¼ ounces (⅓ cup shredded)

sour cream, ¾ cup

whole milk, 8 ounces (1 cup)

egg whites, 6 (about ¾ cup liquid egg whites)

eggs, 19

FRESH PRODUCE

arugula, 9 cups (about 1½ pounds)

basil, 1 bunch

bell pepper, red, 1

Brussels sprouts, 1½ pounds

butter lettuce or other lettuce of choice (for "buns"), 1 head

cherry or grape tomatoes, 20

chives, 1 tablespoon chopped

cremini mushrooms, 1 pound

dill, 1 tablespoon chopped

garlic, 23 cloves (2 to 3 heads)

green beans, 1 pound

green onions, 1½ bunches

habanero peppers, 2

horseradish, 1 teaspoon grated

iceberg lettuce, 1 head

jalapeño peppers, 1 to 2

lemons, 2

limes, 4 to 5

onion, red, 1 medium

onion, white, 1 medium

onions, yellow, 3 medium and 2 large

oregano, ¼ cup

parsley, 1 cup

raspberries, 10

shallots, 4 large

zucchini, 1 small

PANTRY ITEMS

beef bone broth, 32 ounces (4 cups)

beef or chicken bone broth, 16 ounces (2 cups)

coconut milk, full-fat, 16 ounces (2 cups)

diced tomatoes, 1 (14½-ounce) can

pork rinds, 1 (3-ounce) bag

BAKING INGREDIENTS

bacon grease, ½ cup

baking powder, 2 teaspoons

chocolate, 100% dark, 1 ounce

cocoa powder, unsweetened, 2 tablespoons

coconut flakes, unsweetened, ½ cup

erythritol, confectioner's, 1 tablespoon

erythritol, granulated, ⅓ cup plus 3 tablespoons

gelatin, unflavored, 1½ tablespoons

golden flax meal, ½ cup (about 60 g)

ground psyllium husks, ½ cup

nut milk of choice (for Drinking Chocolate used in Mocha Coffee), 4 ounces (½ cup)

pecans, ½ cup

peppermint extract, ¼ teaspoon

sunflower seed flour or meal, 240 g (2 cups)

vanilla extract, 1 tablespoon plus 1⅛ teaspoons

DRIED HERBS AND SPICES

Chinese five-spice powder, ¼ teaspoon

chipotle powder, 1 tablespoon

cinnamon, ground, 1 tablespoon plus ¾ teaspoon

cumin, ground, ¼ teaspoon

garlic powder, 1½ teaspoons

Italian seasoning, ¼ cup

nutmeg, ground, 1 pinch

onion powder, ½ teaspoon

oregano leaves, 1 teaspoon

parsley, ¼ teaspoon

red pepper flakes, 1 teaspoon

rock or coarse salt

smoked paprika, ½ teaspoon

smoked salt, 1½ teaspoons

taco seasoning (see page 79 for ingredients if making homemade), 1 tablespoon

CONDIMENTS/SAUCES/DRESSINGS

anchovy paste, ½ teaspoon

balsamic vinegar, 3 tablespoons

champagne vinegar, 2 tablespoons (or use balsamic vinegar)

Dijon mustard, 1 teaspoon

dill pickle juice (from a jar of pickles), ½ cup

mayonnaise, ¾ cup

olive oil, garlic-infused, 1 tablespoon

olive oil, truffle-infused, ⅓ cup

tomato paste, 1 tablespoon

tomato sauce, ¼ cup

DRINKS

club soda, 8 ounces (1 cup)

sparkling mineral water, 16 ounces (2 cups)

WEEK 4 MEAL PLAN

	BREAKFAST	LUNCH	DINNER	SNACK
SUNDAY	310 Cinnamon Cream Coffee	200 Spicy Chicken Pizza	246 / 110 Perfect Roast Beef + Baked Brie	272 Strawberry Cream Ice Pops
MONDAY	140 Avocado Shrimp Salad	132 Salt and Vinegar Chicken Wings	212 / 130 Keto Pot Roast + Roasted Berries with Prosciutto	290 Candied Pecans
TUESDAY	122 Lime Butter Shrimp	leftover Perfect Roast Beef	118 / 160 Elote Chicken Wings + Hot Spinach and Bacon Salad	307 Orange Cranberry Spritzer
WEDNESDAY	166 Breakfast Cobb Salad	186 / 96 / leftover Fontina Burgers + Seeded Hamburger Buns* + Avocado Shrimp Salad	226 / 88 Marinated Flank Steak with Toasted Garlic + Caramelized Onions	294 Peanut Butter Tarts
THURSDAY	94 / 80 Drop Biscuits + Maple Orange Butter	188 / 96 Rosemary, Mushroom, and Swiss Burgers + Seeded Hamburger Buns	260 / 128 Chicken Cordon Bleu + Onion Rings	280 Macadamia Nut Clusters
FRIDAY	leftover Breakfast Cobb Salad	142 / leftover Mushroom Bisque + Drop Biscuits	208 Blue Cheese and Sausage Pizza	288 White Chocolate Peppermint Swirl Ice Cream
SATURDAY	leftover Keto Pot Roast	264 / 85 Buffalo Baked Chicken + Buffalo Dill Sauce	158 / 112 Steak Salad + Vanilla Bacon–Stuffed Celery	134 / leftover Spiced Nuts Three Ways** + Peanut Butter Tarts

*If you like making things ahead, make two batches of Seeded Hamburger Buns for the week, for the burgers on Wednesday and on Thursday.

**Select which Spiced Nuts flavor combination you would like to make and add those ingredients to the shopping list for the week.

WEEK 4 SHOPPING LIST

MEAT AND SEAFOOD

bacon, 14 strips

beef eye of round roast, 3 pounds

breakfast sausage links, 4

chicken breast halves, boneless, skinless, 4

chicken thighs, boneless or bone-in, skin-on, 6

chicken wings, 30

chuck roast, boneless, 2 to 3 pounds

cooked chicken, ½ cup chopped

flank steak, 1 pound

ground beef, 2 pounds

mild Italian sausage, bulk/ground, ⅓ cup cooked

prosciutto, 10 slices

shrimp, large, raw, frozen, 1 pound

shrimp, small/250-300 size, cooked, 8 ounces

steak of choice (for Steak Salad), 1½ pounds

DAIRY/EGGS

blue cheese, 2 ounces

Brie cheese, 1 (7-ounce) round

butter, salted, 14 ounces (3½ sticks)

cheese of choice (for Breakfast Cobb Salad), 6 ounces

Cotija cheese, 1 ounce

cream cheese, 1 (8-ounce) package

fontina cheese, 2 ounces

heavy cream, 24 ounces (3 cups)

mozzarella cheese, 3 ounces

Parmesan cheese, 5¼ ounces (1⅓ cups grated)

soft goat cheese or whipped cream cheese, 2 ounces

Swiss cheese, 4 ounces

egg whites, 15 (about 1¾ cups liquid egg whites)

eggs, 7

FRESH PRODUCE

arugula, 1½ cups

avocados, 4

basil, ¼ cup chopped

celery, 1 bunch

cilantro, 3 tablespoons chopped

cranberries, 10 to 15

cremini mushrooms, 1 pound

dill, 2 tablespoons

garlic, 6 cloves

green onions, 1 bunch

horseradish, 1 teaspoon grated

limes, 5

mushrooms, assorted (oyster, shiitake, cremini, and/or button), 1 pound

onions, red, 3 medium

onions, yellow, 4 medium and 2 large

orange, 1

radishes, 10 ounces

romaine lettuce or other salad greens, 12 cups chopped

rosemary, 2 sprigs plus 1 teaspoon leaves

salad greens, 12 cups

shallots, 2

spinach, 9 ounces

strawberries, 9 ounces plus 6 berries

thyme, 2 sprigs

PANTRY ITEMS

beef bone broth, 16 ounces (2 cups)

chicken or beef bone broth, 16 ounces (2 cups)

pork rinds, 1 (3-ounce) bag

red peppers, roasted, ¼ cup chopped

BAKING INGREDIENTS

almonds, raw or roasted, ½ cup

baking powder, ¼ cup

cacao butter, 3 ounces

chocolate chips, sugar-free, ¼ cup

cocoa powder, unsweetened, 2 tablespoons

coconut oil or bacon grease, 1 tablespoon

erythritol, confectioner's, ¼ cup

erythritol, granulated, ¼ cup

golden flax meal, ½ cup (about 60 g)

ground psyllium husks, ½ cup plus 1 tablespoon

macadamia nuts, roasted, salted, 2 ounces

maple syrup, sugar-free, 1 teaspoon

nut milk of choice (for ice cream), 8 ounces (1 cup)

nuts, raw, whole or pieces, 1 cup

orange extract or orange oil, ¼ teaspoon

pecan halves, raw, 2 cups

peppermint extract, 1½ teaspoons

sunflower seed flour, 470 g (about 4 cups)

vanilla extract, 3½ teaspoons

DRIED HERBS AND SPICES

chili powder, ½ teaspoon

Chinese five-spice powder, ¼ teaspoon

cinnamon, ground, 2 teaspoons

Italian seasoning, 1½ teaspoons

oregano leaves, 1 teaspoon

poultry seasoning or taco seasoning (see page 79 for ingredients if making homemade), ¼ cup

red pepper flakes, ½ teaspoon

salt and vinegar seasoning, 2 tablespoons

sesame seeds or dried onion flakes, 2 tablespoons

smoked paprika, 1 tablespoon

smoked salt, 1 teaspoon

CONDIMENTS/SAUCES/DRESSINGS

Dijon mustard, ¼ cup

hot sauce (such as Frank's RedHot), ⅓ cup plus 2 tablespoons

mayonnaise, ½ cup plus 2 tablespoons

mustard, prepared yellow, 2 tablespoons

olive oil, garlic-infused, 2 tablespoons

peanut butter or other nut butter, smooth unsweetened, ⅓ cup

tomato or marinara sauce, 1 tablespoon

DRINKS

club soda, 16 ounces (2 cups)

DAIRY-FREE WEEK 1 MEAL PLAN

	BREAKFAST	LUNCH	DINNER	SNACK
SUNDAY	Raspberry Smash — 304	Simple Baked Cod — 242	Keto Pot Roast — 212	Chocolate Chip Cookies — 292
MONDAY	Breakfast Cobb Salad — 166	Marinated Pork Loin — 220	Southwest Burgers + Seeded Hamburger Buns* + Ranch Dressing — 184, 96, 78	Ginger Lime Soda — 312
TUESDAY	Sparkling Green Tea Elixir — 313	Simple Baked Cod — leftover	Flank Steak with Charred Green Onions — 262	Vanilla Bacon–Stuffed Celery — 112
WEDNESDAY	Keto Pot Roast — leftover	Prosciutto Meat Cups + Ranch Dressing — 136, leftover	Roasted Berries with Prosciutto — 130	Strawberry Cream Ice Pops — 272
THURSDAY	Prosciutto Meat Cups — leftover	Lamb Rib Chops with Mushrooms — 240	Cheesy Stuffed Meatballs (without the cheese!) + Habanero Brussels Sprouts — 120, 156	Chocolate Chip Cookies — leftover
FRIDAY	Marinated Pork Loin — leftover	Cheesy Stuffed Meatballs + Habanero Brussels Sprouts — leftover, leftover	French Onion Soup + Drop Biscuits — 174, 94	Chocolate Chip Cookies — leftover
SATURDAY	Lamb Rib Chops with Mushrooms — leftover	French Onion Soup + Drop Biscuits — leftover, leftover	Onion Horsey Burgers + Seeded Hamburger Buns — 192, 96	Drinking Chocolate — 302

*If you like making things ahead, make two batches of Seeded Hamburger Buns for the week, for the burgers on Monday and on Saturday.

DAIRY-FREE WEEK 1 SHOPPING LIST

MEAT AND SEAFOOD

bacon, 12 strips

breakfast sausage links, 4

chuck roast, boneless, 2 to 3 pounds

cod fillet, 1½ pounds

flank steak, 1½ pounds

ground beef, 3¾ pounds

ground pork, 12 ounces

lamb rib chops, 4 (about 1 pound)

pork loin roast, boneless, 3 to 4 pounds

prosciutto, 12 slices

DAIRY SUBSTITUTES/EGGS

dairy-free cream cheese, 10 ounces (1¼ cups)

dairy-free sour cream, 1 cup

egg whites, 8 (about 1 cup liquid egg whites)

eggs, 6

FRESH PRODUCE

avocado, 1

basil leaves, 5

Brussels sprouts, 1½ pounds

celery, 1 bunch

chives, 3 tablespoons chopped

cilantro, ¼ cup

cremini mushrooms, 1 pound

dill, 2 tablespoons

garlic, 7 cloves

ginger, 1¼ teaspoons grated

green onions, 1 bunch (5 to 7 onions)

habanero peppers, 2

horseradish, 1 teaspoon grated

lemons, 3

limes, 11

onions, red, 3 medium

onions, yellow, 3 medium and 2 large

parsley leaves, 1 tablespoon

radishes, 9 medium

raspberries, 10

romaine lettuce or other salad greens, 12 cups

rosemary, 3 sprigs

shallots, 3 small

strawberries, 5 cups (about 22½ ounces)

thyme, 2 sprigs

tomato, 1 medium

zucchini, 1 large

PANTRY ITEMS

beef bone broth, 48 ounces (6 cups)

coconut milk, full-fat, 1 (14½-ounce) can

pork rinds, 1 small bag

BAKING INGREDIENTS

almond flour, ¼ cup

almonds, raw or roasted, ½ cup

baking powder, 2 teaspoons

baking soda, 1½ teaspoons

chocolate, 100% dark, 1 ounce

chocolate chips, sugar-free, 1 cup

cocoa powder, unsweetened, 1 tablespoon

coconut oil, 1 cup

erythritol, granulated, ¾ cup

gelatin, unflavored, 1 tablespoon

ground psyllium husks, ¼ cup plus 2 tablespoons

nut milk of choice, 4 ounces (½ cup)

red palm shortening or lard, 2¾ ounces

sunflower seed flour, 740 g (about 6 cups plus 2 tablespoons)

vanilla extract, ¼ cup plus ⅛ teaspoon

DRIED HERBS AND SPICES

garlic powder, ¼ teaspoon

Italian seasoning, ¼ cup

nutmeg, ground, 1 pinch

parsley, ¼ teaspoon

ranch seasoning, 2 tablespoons

red pepper flakes, ¼ teaspoon

sesame seeds or dried onion flakes, 2 tablespoons

smoked salt, 1 teaspoon

taco seasoning (see page 79 for ingredients if making homemade), 1 tablespoon

thyme, ground, ¼ teaspoon

CONDIMENTS/SAUCES/DRESSINGS

balsamic vinegar, 1 tablespoon

mayonnaise, ⅔ cup

mustard, prepared (any type), 1 teaspoon

tomato paste, 1 tablespoon

DRINKS

green tea, 1 bag

sparkling mineral water, 48 ounces (6 cups)

DAIRY-FREE WEEK 2 MEAL PLAN

	BREAKFAST	LUNCH	DINNER	SNACK
SUNDAY	310 — Cinnamon Cream Coffee	126, 136, 78 — Caprese Skewers + Prosciutto Meat Cups + Ranch Dressing*	124, 244 — Bruschetta Mushrooms + Cabbage, Sausage, and Pepper Sheet Pan Dinner	294 — Peanut Butter Tarts
MONDAY	leftover — Prosciutto Meat Cups	130 — Roasted Berries with Prosciutto	182, 96 — Balsamic Onion, Truffle, and Arugula Burgers + Seeded Hamburger Buns**	284 — Toasted Coconut Pudding
TUESDAY	leftover — Cabbage, Sausage, and Pepper Sheet Pan Dinner	148 — Instant Pot Chicken and Rice Soup	266, 81 — Steak Tacos + Lime-Marinated Red Onions***	307 — Orange Cranberry Spritzer
WEDNESDAY	303 — Mocha Coffee	leftover — Steak Tacos	264, 78, 172 — Buffalo Baked Chicken + Ranch Dressing + Lime Slaw	102 — Spiced Seeds
THURSDAY	140 — Avocado Shrimp Salad	leftover — Instant Pot Chicken and Rice Soup	132, 164 — Salt and Vinegar Wings + Grilled Romaine Salad	leftover — Peanut Butter Tarts
FRIDAY	313 — Sparkling Green Tea Elixir	146, 78, leftover — Southwest Chicken Salad + Ranch Dressing + Spiced Seeds	162 — George's Soup	288 — White Chocolate Peppermint Swirl Ice Cream
SATURDAY	leftover — George's Soup	180, 96 — Triple Onion Burgers + Seeded Hamburger Buns	258, 160 — Pork Belly + Hot Spinach and Bacon Salad	311 — Lemonade Slushies

*If you like making things ahead, make two batches of ranch dressing for the week, for the Prosciutto Meat Cups, Buffalo Baked Chicken, and Southwest Chicken Salad.

**If you like making things ahead, make two batches of Seeded Hamburger Buns for the week, for the burgers on Monday and on Saturday.

***Reserve one-third of the Lime-Marinated Red Onions for use in the Grilled Romaine Salad for Thursday dinner.

DAIRY-FREE WEEK 2 SHOPPING LIST

MEAT AND SEAFOOD

bacon, 10 strips

bacon, center-cut, 8 strips

breakfast sausage, bulk/ground, 3 pounds

chicken thighs, boneless or bone-in, skin-on, 6

chicken thighs, boneless, skinless, 3 pounds

chicken wings, 15

ground beef, 2¾ pounds

ground pork, 12 ounces

hanger or flank steak, 1½ pounds

Italian sausage links, mild, 1½ pounds

pork belly, 1 pound

prosciutto, 12 slices

shrimp, small/250-300 size, cooked, 8 ounces

DAIRY SUBSTITUTES/EGGS

dairy-free cream cheese, 2 ounces (¼ cup)

dairy-free shredded cheese, 1 cup (4 ounces)

dairy-free sour cream, ½ cup

egg whites, 4 (about ½ cup liquid egg whites)

eggs, 2

FRESH PRODUCE

arugula, 1½ cups

avocados, 3

basil, 1 bunch

bell peppers, 4 green and 3 any color

button mushrooms, 10 large

cabbage, 1½ heads

cauliflower, riced, 2 cups

cherry tomatoes, about 30

chives, 2 tablespoons chopped

cilantro, ¼ cup plus 2 tablespoons

cranberries, 10 to 15

dill, 2 tablespoons

garlic, 12 cloves

green onions, 6 to 7

lemons, 3

limes, 4

onion, white, 1

onions, red, 2 medium

onions, yellow or white, 6

orange, 1

parsley leaves, 2 tablespoons

radishes, 4 medium

romaine hearts, 4

romaine lettuce leaves (for taco "shells")

salad greens, 12 cups

spinach, 8 ounces

strawberries, 6

tomatoes, 4 large

tomatoes, Roma, 3

zucchini, 1 small

PANTRY ITEMS

chicken bone broth, 80 ounces (10 cups)

coconut milk, full-fat, 4 (14½-ounce) cans

nut milk of choice, 5 ounces (½ cup plus 2 tablespoons)

pork rinds, 1 (3-ounce) bag

BAKING INGREDIENTS

almond flour, ¼ cup

baking powder, 1½ tablespoons

cacao butter, 3 ounces

chocolate, 100% dark, 1 ounce

cocoa powder, unsweetened, 3 tablespoons

coconut flakes, unsweetened, ½ cup

coconut oil, 2 tablespoons

erythritol, confectioner's, ¼ cup

gelatin, unflavored, 1 tablespoon

ground psyllium husks, ¼ cup plus 2 tablespoons

peppermint extract, 1½ teaspoons

sunflower or pumpkin seeds, 1 cup

sunflower seed flour, 230 g (about 2 cups)

vanilla extract, 2⅛ teaspoons

DRIED HERBS AND SPICES

Chinese five-spice powder, ¼ teaspoon

cinnamon, ground, 1¼ teaspoons

coriander, ground, 1 teaspoon

cumin, ground, ¼ teaspoon

garlic powder, ½ teaspoon

garlic salt, 1 teaspoon

Italian seasoning, ¼ cup plus 2 tablespoons

mustard seeds, brown, ½ teaspoon

mustard seeds, yellow, ½ teaspoon

nutmeg, ground, 1 pinch

onion powder, ½ teaspoon

parsley, ¼ teaspoon

salt and vinegar seasoning, 2 tablespoons

sesame seeds or dried onion flakes, 2 tablespoons

smoked salt, ½ teaspoon

taco seasoning (see page 79 for ingredients if making homemade), 1 teaspoon

CONDIMENTS/SAUCES/DRESSINGS

balsamic vinegar, ¾ cup

hot sauce (such as Frank's RedHot), ⅓ cup

mayonnaise, 1¼ cups

mustard (any type), ¼ teaspoon

olive oil, truffle-infused, 2 teaspoons

peanut butter or other nut butter of choice, smooth unsweetened, ⅓ cup

tomato paste, 1 tablespoon

DRINKS

club soda, 28 ounces (3½ cups)

green tea, 1 bag

red wine (or additional bone broth or stock), 8 ounces (1 cup)

DAIRY-FREE WEEK 3 MEAL PLAN

	BREAKFAST	LUNCH	DINNER	SNACK
SUNDAY	166 Breakfast Cobb Salad	156 · 102 Habanero Brussels Sprouts + Spiced Seeds	108 · 220 Smoky Chicken Pâté + Marinated Pork Loin	296 Dairy-Free Spiced Chocolate Coconut Ice Cream
MONDAY	310 Cinnamon Cream Coffee	238 Crispy Baked Chicken	116 · 142 Lemon Oysters + Mushroom Bisque	306 Blackberry Lime Slushies
TUESDAY	leftover Marinated Pork Loin	158 · 78 Steak Salad + Ranch Dressing	190 · 96 · 74 Garlic Tomato Burgers + Seeded Hamburger Buns + Smoky Garlic Burger Sauce	292 Chocolate Chip Cookies
WEDNESDAY	leftover Mushroom Bisque	leftover Crispy Baked Chicken	218 Tri-Tip and Broccoli Bowls	290 Candied Pecans
THURSDAY	303 Mocha Coffee	244 Cabbage, Sausage, and Pepper Sheet Pan Dinner	230 · 150 Perfect Baked Salmon + Stovetop Green Beans	304 Raspberry Smash
FRIDAY	leftover Tri-Tip and Broccoli Bowls	146 Southwest Chicken Salad	118 · 154 Elote Chicken Wings + Wasabi Broccoli Slaw	leftover Chocolate Chip Cookies
SATURDAY	leftover Cabbage, Sausage, and Pepper Sheet Pan Dinner	136 Prosciutto Meat Cups	254 · 70 · 164 Butter-Basted New York Strip Steak + Smoky Chimichurri + Grilled Romaine Salad	312 Ginger Lime Soda

DAIRY-FREE WEEK 3 SHOPPING LIST

MEAT AND SEAFOOD

bacon, 8 ounces plus 12 strips

breakfast sausage links, 4

chicken breasts or thighs, boneless, skinless, 1½ pounds

chicken livers, 1 pound

chicken thighs, bone-in, skin-on, 4

chicken wings, 15

ground beef, 1¾ pounds

ground pork, 12 ounces

Italian sausage links, mild, 1½ pounds

oysters, 12

pork loin roast, boneless, 3 to 4 pounds

prosciutto, 12 slices

salmon fillet, 1½ pounds

steak, New York strip, 1 large or 2 small

steak of choice (for Steak Salad), 1½ pounds

tri-tip roast, 1½ pounds

DAIRY SUBSTITUTES/EGGS

dairy-free sour cream, ¼ cup

eggs, 9

FRESH PRODUCE

avocados, 3

basil, ¼ cup

bell peppers, green, 3

blackberries, 14

broccoli florets, 12 ounces

broccoli slaw, 2 (12-ounce) bags

Brussels sprouts, 1½ pounds

cabbage, ½ head

chives, 3 tablespoons chopped

cilantro, ¼ cup

dill, ¼ cup

garlic, 3 heads

ginger, 1¾ teaspoons grated

green beans, 1 pound

green onions, 1 cup chopped

habanero peppers, 2

lemons, 2

limes, 10

mushrooms, assorted (oyster, shiitake, cremini, and/or button), 1 pound

onions, red, 2 medium

onions, yellow, 3 medium

oregano, ¼ cup

parsley leaves, ¾ cup

radishes, 4 medium

raspberries, 10

romaine hearts, 4

romaine lettuce or other salad greens, 12 cups

rosemary, ½ teaspoon

salad greens, 24 cups

shallots, 3 medium and 2 large

tomatoes, Roma, 2

zucchini, 1 small

PANTRY ITEMS

chicken or beef bone broth, 16 ounces (2 cups)

coconut milk, full-fat, 3 (14½-ounce) cans plus 8 ounces (1 cup)

nut milk of choice, 8 ounces (1 cup)

pork rinds, 1 small bag

BAKING INGREDIENTS

almond flour, ¼ cup

bacon grease, 1 cup

baking powder, 1½ tablespoons

baking soda, 1½ teaspoons

chocolate, 100% dark, 1 ounce

chocolate chips, sugar-free, 1 cup

cocoa powder, unsweetened, 3 tablespoons

coconut oil, ⅔ cup

erythritol, granulated, 1 cup

ground psyllium husks, 3 tablespoons

pecan halves, raw, 2 cups

pumpkin or sunflower seeds, 1⅓ cups

sunflower seed flour, 400 g (about 3⅓ cups)

toasted sesame oil, 2 tablespoons

vanilla extract, 1 tablespoon plus ⅜ teaspoon

DRIED HERBS AND SPICES

chili powder, ½ teaspoon

cinnamon, ground, 1 tablespoon

cloves, ground, ½ teaspoon

coriander, ground, 1 teaspoon

garlic powder, 1¾ teaspoons

garlic salt, 1 teaspoon

Italian seasoning, 3 tablespoons

nutmeg, ground, ½ teaspoon

onion powder, ½ teaspoon

parsley, ¼ teaspoon

red pepper flakes, 1 teaspoon

rock or coarse salt

sesame seeds, 2 tablespoons

smoked paprika, 2 teaspoons

spice mix of choice (for Crispy Baked Chicken), 2 tablespoons

taco seasoning (see page 79 for ingredients if making homemade), 1 teaspoon

CONDIMENTS/SAUCES/DRESSINGS

balsamic vinegar, ¼ cup

Dijon mustard, 2 tablespoons

mayonnaise, 1⅓ cups

mustard, prepared yellow, 1¼ teaspoons

tomato paste, 1 tablespoon

wasabi paste, 2 teaspoons

DRINKS

club soda, 28 ounces (3½ cups)

sparkling mineral water, 16 ounces (2 cups)

DAIRY-FREE WEEK 4 MEAL PLAN

	BREAKFAST	LUNCH	DINNER	SNACK
SUNDAY	216 — Slow Cooker Rich Beef Shanks	180 / 96 — Triple Onion Burgers + Seeded Hamburger Buns*	246 — Perfect Roast Beef	282 — Chocolate-Covered Bacon Ice Cream
MONDAY	313 / leftover — Sparkling Green Tea Elixir + Slow Cooker Rich Beef Shanks	240 — Lamb Rib Chops with Mushrooms	234 / 78 — Marinated Fried Chicken Strips + Ranch Dressing	98 — Cinnamon Bread
TUESDAY	leftover — Perfect Roast Beef	146 — Southwest Chicken Salad	226 / 152 — Marinated Flank Steak with Toasted Garlic + Diner Roasted Radishes	leftover — Chocolate-Covered Bacon Ice Cream
WEDNESDAY	303 — Mocha Coffee	leftover — Marinated Fried Chicken Strips	242 / 150 / 77 — Simple Baked Cod + Stovetop Green Beans + Tartar Sauce	leftover — Cinnamon Bread
THURSDAY	leftover — Southwest Chicken Salad	158 — Steak Salad + dressing of choice	194 / 96 — Asian-Style Burgers + Seeded Hamburger Buns	134 — Spiced Nuts Three Ways**
FRIDAY	166 — Breakfast Cobb Salad	118 / leftover — Elote Chicken Wings + Breakfast Cobb Salad	leftover — Lamb Rib Chops with Mushrooms	294 — Peanut Butter Tarts
SATURDAY	310 — Cinnamon Cream Coffee	170 — Taco Soup	leftover / 140 — Elote Chicken Wings + Avocado Shrimp Salad	312 — Ginger Lime Soda

*If you like making things ahead, make two batches of buns for the week, for the burgers on Sunday and on Thursday.

**Select which Spiced Nuts flavor combination you would like to make and add those ingredients to the shopping list for the week.

DAIRY-FREE WEEK 4 SHOPPING LIST

MEAT AND SEAFOOD

bacon, 10 strips

beef eye of round roast, 3 pounds

beef shanks, 4

breakfast sausage links, 4

chicken breasts or thighs, boneless, skinless, 2½ pounds

chicken wings, 15

cod fillet, 1½ pounds

flank steak, 1 pound

ground beef, 3 pounds

lamb rib chops, 4 (about 1 pound)

prosciutto, 2 slices

shrimp, small/250-300 size, cooked, 8 ounces

steak of choice (for Steak Salad), 1½ pounds

DAIRY SUBSTITUTES/EGGS

dairy-free sour cream, ¼ cup

egg whites, 7 (about ¾ cup plus 2 tablespoons liquid egg whites)

eggs, 8

FRESH PRODUCE

arugula, 1 cup

avocados, 5

chives, 3 tablespoons

cilantro, ½ cup plus 2 tablespoons

cremini mushrooms, 8 ounces

dill, 3 tablespoons

garlic, 1 head

ginger, ¼ teaspoon grated

green beans, 1 pound

green onions, 1 cup

jalapeño peppers, 1 to 2

lemon, 1

limes, 5

onion, white, 1 medium

onion, yellow, 1 medium

onions, red, 2 medium

onions, yellow or white, 5

parsley leaves, 1½ tablespoons

radishes, 16 medium (about 2 pounds)

romaine lettuce or other salad greens, 12 cups

rosemary, 1 sprig

salad greens of choice, 24 cups

shallots, 2 medium and 2 small

PANTRY ITEMS

beef or chicken bone broth, 16 ounces (2 cups)

coconut cream or nut milk of choice, 2 ounces (¼ cup)

coconut milk, full-fat, 4 (14½-ounce) cans

nut milk of choice, 5 ounces (½ cup plus 2 tablespoons)

pork rinds, 1 small bag

tomatoes, diced, 2 (14½-ounce) cans

BAKING INGREDIENTS

baking powder, 1½ tablespoons plus 2 teaspoons

chocolate, 100% dark, 1 ounce

cocoa powder, unsweetened, ¼ cup

coconut oil, 2 tablespoons

erythritol, confectioner's, 1 tablespoon

erythritol, granulated, 3 tablespoons

golden flax meal, ¼ cup (about 30 g)

ground psyllium husks, ½ cup plus 2 tablespoons

nuts, raw, whole or pieces, 1 cup

sunflower seed flour, 340 g (about 2¾ cups plus 2 tablespoons)

vanilla extract, 2⅝ teaspoons

DRIED HERBS AND SPICES

chili powder, ½ teaspoon

Chinese five-spice powder, ¼ teaspoon

cinnamon, ground, 1½ tablespoons

garlic powder, 1½ tablespoons plus ¾ teaspoon

Italian seasoning, 2 teaspoons

mustard seeds, brown, ½ teaspoon

mustard seeds, yellow, ½ teaspoon

nutmeg, ground, 1 pinch

sesame seeds or dried onion flakes, 2 tablespoons

smoked paprika, 1 tablespoon plus ½ teaspoon

smoked salt, ½ teaspoon

taco seasoning (see page 79 for ingredients if making homemade), 1 tablespoon plus 1 teaspoon

thyme, ground, ¼ teaspoon

turmeric powder, 1½ teaspoons

CONDIMENTS/SAUCES/DRESSINGS

dill pickle juice (from a jar of pickles), ½ cup

dill pickles, 2 tablespoons chopped

kimchi, ¼ cup

mayonnaise, 1½ cups

mustard, prepared yellow, 2 tablespoons

olive oil, butter-flavored, ¼ cup

peanut butter or other nut butter, smooth unsweetened, ⅓ cup

salad dressing of choice, homemade or store-bought (for Steak Salad)

Sriracha sauce, 1 teaspoon

DRINKS

club soda or sparkling mineral water, 32 ounces (4 cups)

green tea, 1 bag

CHAPTER 7

RECIPES

Before you get started cooking Heather's delicious recipes, she would like to address a few important topics.

Allergen icons

For those of you who are allergic or sensitive to dairy, eggs, and/or nuts, the recipes that are free of these ingredients are marked with icons. The word *OPTION* under an icon means that the recipe can be made free of that allergen, depending on the ingredient(s) you choose.

Why no macros?

If you're a regular consumer of keto cookbooks, then you might notice something rather inauspicious about this one—there are no macronutrients or other nutrition info included with the recipes. While so many people who eat a low-carb, moderate-protein, high-fat, ketogenic diet hang their hats on meticulously counting macronutrient ratios and getting just the right amounts of fat, protein, and carbohydrates into their meals, the primary reason we do it is because that's what we've always done when we go on a diet. The thinking that nutrition should be a math game of counting and dividing, of getting that perfect equation for what you eat, is quite frankly born out of the miserable diet mentality that so many of us have been fighting to get out of. Let *Keto Clarity Cookbook* be your first step in overcoming what has kept you in bondage for far too long.

We all love eating great-tasting food, and being keto is no different. That's the joy of this way of eating—it nourishes our bodies with real, whole foods that help manage blood sugar and insulin levels naturally. To that end, we don't eat macronutrients. We eat food. That's why counting macros is pretty irrelevant.

We have all gone down the rabbit hole of feeling like we need to track every single morsel we put in our mouths as a means of determining how good or bad we have been on our diets. When you stop and think about it, we allow this process of tracking to wield great power over who we are. How you measure up can affect your sense of self-worth, making you judge yourself based on what your dieting record happens to be. Has this process ever made you feel good? Do you think it made you more successful in your efforts to be healthy? Yeah, me neither. Honestly, it didn't make me feel good at all; in fact, it stressed me out to no end (which made things like weight loss and getting healthy that much harder). I became so obsessed with counting everything that it made me go completely batty. Most days it turned into deep sadness because I always felt like a failure. I internalized it as something that was my problem, without ever giving a single thought to how this act of tabulating all the numbers in my food was the root cause of these feelings.

Break the cycle by learning to be more intuitive in your eating. Jimmy and I are fully committed to helping you learn to listen to your body, become more intuitive with your food choices, and reap the benefits that come from freeing yourself from the constraints of diet mode. It's time to live—or, as Jimmy calls it, start livin' la vida low-carb!

When you do this, you turn the volume in your head way down, quieting those messages that are constantly assessing you for the dietary choices you are making. You start to hear what's truly important, getting back in touch with your hunger signals and allowing those signals to determine when it's time to eat. Be patient with yourself as you shift your thinking; it may take months for you to get in tune with your body's natural rhythms, perhaps for the first time in your life. But when you let go of the tracking and are freed from the bondage, you'll discover a whole new appreciation for living in a world without macros, calories, and dieting. Let it go!

There's joy that comes from sharing a meal with a friend, being in the moment together, and not worrying about the food you are eating. When you eat keto, you know to eat smaller amounts of foods like fruit, nuts, and seeds; to find the amount of protein that is right for you, bearing in mind not to eat too little or too much; and to eat healthy fats to satiety, realizing that fat is not a free-for-all macronutrient that you gorge yourself on, but rather something to be enjoyed until you are satisfied. That's it. Don't make it harder than it needs to be, and you'll do just fine.

Yes, this shift in thinking will take some time to develop along with your experiments with increasing or decreasing fat, protein, and carbohydrates to find just the right balance. But finding your sweet spot on a ketogenic lifestyle is a part of this lifelong journey to better health. The time you invest now will reap great dividends in the years to come. When you get to the end of your long and healthy life, you'll look back with gratitude on this decision to release yourself from the burden that had plagued you for far too long. Let today be day one of that newfound commitment to the new you.

If you're still not completely convinced to let go of counting macronutrients, here's a final sobering thought to ponder: most of the numbers you see in cookbooks for fat, protein, carbohydrates, and calories are so grossly inaccurate that you're really just guessing about what you're eating. Why keep putting yourself through the dieting game? Break the cycle and embrace intuitive keto eating once and for all.

Kitchen tools and equipment

Let's talk for a minute about the tools and equipment you'll need to make the recipes in this book. You really don't need much to have an effective kitchen. This section lists the basic tools and equipment that I use on a regular basis— the items I reached for over and over while creating these recipes. If you've been cooking for a while, there's a chance that you already have all of these items, but you might find a gem in this list that makes your life in the kitchen easier, which is the whole point of any tool!

Cast-iron skillet A nice cast-iron skillet cooks steaks better than any other vessel. Since it's thick, it takes a little longer to heat up, so I usually preheat mine. The thickness also means that the skillet heats evenly and is less likely to develop hot spots than thinner pans. In addition to steaks, I cook bacon and burgers and sear roasts and other larger cuts of meat in my cast-iron skillet. My first choice is a 12-inch skillet; if you have room for a second size, I would go for an 8- or 10-inch for smaller jobs.

There is a minimal amount of care involved in keeping cast iron nonstick, called seasoning. This involves starting with a clean skillet, wiping it down with a thin layer of saturated fat, like coconut oil or bacon grease, and then baking it in a low oven until the fat has fully soaked in.

Cheese grater The best cheese grater is a box grater. It is stable, has four different grating options, and has a larger grating capacity, meaning that you can grate a lot of cheese really fast.

Dutch oven A Dutch oven can go from stovetop to oven—which means fewer dishes to clean!—and can cook soups and braise meats to perfection. You can brown beef on the stovetop and then finish it in the oven low and slow for deliciously tender meat. Dutch ovens don't have to be expensive, either; mine is from Target! You don't need a Dutch oven if you have an electric pressure cooker like the Instant Pot (opposite) and are tight on space, but it is really nice to have.

Glass measuring cups   I love my old Pyrex liquid measuring cups—in 2-, 4-, and 8-cup sizes—and use them all the time in cooking. They are dishwasher safe, and you can use a stick blender in them. Look for deals in a secondhand store.

Glass storage containers and jars   I use glass jars for just about everything! I make most of my sauces right in a jar with my stick blender. After it's blended, I pop the lid on, and into the fridge it goes—almost zero dishes to clean! I much prefer glass storage containers to plastic. Plastic holds odors and eventually gets that gross cloudy look and ends up in the trash. We have asked for glass containers as gifts over time and have purchased one small set as well. If you are making the switch from plastic to glass, check out big sales days like Black Friday and Cyber Monday. We also reuse a lot of jars from store-bought products, which is like free glass storage. I never store liquids in glass in the freezer—well, I did once, and it broke, so lesson learned.

Handheld electric mixer   I use my electric mixer exclusively for making cookies and whisking egg whites. If you are looking to buy one, they are not pricey. I upgraded mine recently and got one with rubber-coated beaters so that I can get right up to side of the bowl with the mixer running and not hear that terrible scraping noise.

Ice cream maker   If you plan to make a lot of ice cream at home (or make any of the four ice cream recipes in this book), you can't beat an electric ice cream maker. This small appliance makes ice cream in under a half-hour and is pretty inexpensive. You want one with an opening on the top to add mix-ins. I prefer a 2-quart capacity because ice cream increases in volume as air is churned into it, so I was constantly overflowing my smaller old one.

Instant Pot or electric pressure cooker   I highly recommend getting one of these if you have the space to store it. For my family of two, a 6-quart Instant Pot has been perfect, but if you have a family of four or you like to make meals in big batches, you may want a larger one. I also have a silicone steamer basket insert, which is the only accessory I've needed. I use it to steam vegetables, hard-boil eggs, and cook wings that turn out perfectly every time!

Kitchen scale   The few baking recipes included in this book call for certain ingredients in grams rather than cups or tablespoons. If you love to bake and you don't have a small kitchen scale, your life will become so much easier when you get one. Make sure to choose one that can switch between grams and ounces and has a tare button. When you're baking, you just place the mixing bowl on the scale and press the tare button to zero out the scale. Then you add the first ingredient, press the tare button again, add the second ingredient, and so on. Think of all the dishes you won't have to do!

Kitchen shears/poultry scissors   I recently lost my good kitchen shears and replaced them with a set of poultry scissors. I have not regretted it once. The poultry scissors can do everything regular scissors do but are spring-assisted, which really helps when cutting raw chicken. I have the OXO Good Grips Spring-Loaded Poultry Shears, which cost around $25. They make spatchcocking (butterflying) a whole chicken or turkey a dream!

Knives   If you are looking at knives, my best advice is to not buy a set. Instead, buy good-quality knives one at a time as you need them. The most used knives in my kitchen are a chef's knife and a paring knife for smaller jobs.

Kraut smasher   I use this tool for making sauerkraut, obviously, but also for a lot of the drink recipes in this book that call for smashing berries. It makes quick work of anything! Mine is made of wood and berries do stain it, but the discoloration doesn't hurt a thing. If you don't have a kraut smasher, a potato masher would work in most instances—or any household object, really. You can cover whatever you decide to use with plastic wrap to keep your food clean.

Loaf pan   A 9 by 5-inch loaf pan is necessary only if you plan on making keto breads. I have just one bread recipe in this book, my Cinnamon Bread on page 98, and it could be baked in a muffin tin if you don't have a loaf pan. If you don't plan on making breads often, most grocery stores sell single-use foil loaf pans that you can use for one-offs.

Nonstick skillets   A cast-iron skillet (see page 64) just doesn't work for certain jobs, including foods that are high in acid and anything tomato based. I also prefer to cook eggs in a nonstick skillet. I have two lightweight nontoxic, nonstick skillets that I use all the time, a 12-inch and a 10-inch. If you make a lot of meals for one, a smaller skillet is nice to have as well, but it's not a must-have.

These pans work great for eggs; anything with acidic ingredients, like tomatoes; pan sauces; and quick jobs like dry-toasting nuts and seeds. The nonstick surface is super easy to clean, too—most debris just slides right out!

Parchment paper   I use parchment paper constantly in my kitchen. I suggest looking for a jumbo-sized box either at a warehouse club like Costco or from an online retailer. Just trust me, you will want to use it to roll out pizza dough and to keep baking sheets and your oven clean. I like that parchment paper is recyclable, too!

Pizza stone   Even if you don't make a lot of pizza, you will love having a pizza stone in your oven. Did you know that when you open a preheated oven to put your dish inside, the oven temperature drops rapidly? When you preheat the oven, the gauge measures the temperature of the air inside the oven, but you really need the walls of the oven to heat up to maintain the temperature if the oven door is opened. A pizza stone helps even out the heat in your oven and retains more heat. I leave mine in the oven at all times, and of course I cook pizza on it, too! (You can find my pizza recipes on pages 198 to 209.)

Rimmed baking sheet and wire rack   Everyone needs a rimmed baking sheet or two for cookies and all the savory roasted foods, too. The combination of a rimmed baking sheet and an oven-safe wire cooling rack is the best setup for roasting veggies, wings, and even larger cuts of meat. Take things to the next level by lining that baking sheet with parchment paper, aluminum foil, or a silicone baking mat (see below), and cleaning the pan will be a breeze. I call for this setup in many of the recipes in this book.

Saucepans and stockpot   Most sets of cookware come with two sizes of saucepans. I love a medium-sized saucepan in the 4-quart range. If you are cooking for a larger family, you may want a stockpot as well; we use a Dutch oven instead to keep cookware to a minimum in our small kitchen.

Silicone baking mat   If you want to waste less, invest in a nonstick baking mat that fits inside your rimmed baking sheet. Some brands can be cut to fit, and others come sized to fit standard baking sheets. I still use parchment paper for certain jobs, like rolling out dough, but for rimmed baking sheets, a silicone baking mat can reduce the amount of parchment paper you go through.

Silicone spatulas/wooden spoons   I use silicone spatulas or wooden spoons exclusively in my nonstick pans to keep from scratching their surfaces. Another pro tip: when making any mayo-, sour cream–, or cream cheese–based recipe, use a silicone spatula for easy cleanup. A spatula also enables you to get the last bit of mayo out of the jar with ease.

Splatter screen   This mesh screen comes in various sizes and keeps the splatter down when you cook foods in fat, which we do a lot on a keto diet. Get one or two that cover the pans you use most often. Bottom line: fewer bacon splatters to the face!

Stick blender   A combination of a stick (aka immersion) blender and a wide-mouth jar can do almost any job that a high-powered blender can do. The end result may not be as smooth as you can get with one of those fancy countertop blenders, but those blenders cost hundreds of dollars that a lot of us do not have room in the budget for! My husband blends his daily coffee with a stick blender; I make slushies and smoothies, blended soups, and even nut butter. It does not work as quickly as a high-powered blender, so it may take a little extra patience, but a stick blender is a kitchen workhorse and inexpensive to boot.

Thin spatula   I like to have one super thin spatula to lift delicate foods like cookies, crepes, and pancakes. I prefer the brand OXO.

Whisk   Sauces created over heat come together much easier with a whisk. I consider this tool a basic need for every kitchen! Buy a silicone whisk, if possible, because it is easier to clean than a metal whisk.

SAUCES and BASICS

Smoky Chimichurri | *70*

Roasted Garlic Two Ways | *72*

Smoky Garlic Burger Sauce | *74*

Beyond Basic Blue Cheese Butter | *75*

Mignonette Sauce Three Ways | *76*

Tartar Sauce | *77*

Ranch Dressing | *78*

Smoky Taco Seasoning | *79*

Maple Orange Butter | *80*

Lime-Marinated Red Onions | *81*

Roasted Strawberry Jam | *82*

Blue Cheese Dressing | *83*

Mustard Seed Aioli | *84*

Buffalo Dill Sauce | *85*

Nut-Free Pesto | *86*

Berry Vinaigrette | *87*

Caramelized Onions Three Ways | *88*

Crispy Mushrooms | *90*

Psyllium Husk Pizza Crust | *92*

Drop Biscuits | *94*

Seeded Hamburger Buns | *96*

Cinnamon Bread | *98*

SMOKY CHIMICHURRI

YIELD: 1½ cups (2 tablespoons per serving)

PREP TIME: 10 minutes

The best part of keto is the sauces! Sauces make everything a little more fun; just a drizzle can turn a plate of leftovers or a boring dish around.

Chimichurri is an Argentinian sauce that is usually served with grilled meats, especially beef. It contains raw garlic and red pepper flakes, so it packs a flavor punch, but it's not too spicy or acidic. The secret ingredient in this version is the shallots, which give this velvety sauce a subtle "certain something" that takes it to a new level. To give it a slightly smoky and savory element, I have replaced half of the olive oil with bacon grease and added a bit of smoked paprika. When blending, you can leave the sauce a little chunky or blend until it is completely smooth.

I serve this chimichurri the traditional way, over grilled meats or eggs, but it's delicious on just about anything!

½ cup roughly chopped fresh parsley (about ½ ounce)

¼ cup loosely packed fresh oregano leaves

⅓ cup roughly chopped shallots (about 2 large shallots)

6 cloves garlic, peeled

1 teaspoon red pepper flakes

1 teaspoon pink Himalayan salt (see Ingredient Spotlight)

½ teaspoon smoked paprika

½ cup bacon grease, room temperature

½ cup olive oil

¼ cup plus 2 tablespoons red wine vinegar

1. Put all the ingredients in a blender and blend until smooth and creamy, about 1 minute. Alternatively, you can use a stick blender and a mason jar. Even if the chimichurri isn't 100 percent smooth, it will still be delicious.

2. Store in the refrigerator for up to 1 week.

INGREDIENT SPOTLIGHT:

I use a medium grind of pink Himalayan salt for all my recipes unless another type is specified. If you use a different type or grind, you may need to adjust the amount of salt.

ROASTED GARLIC TWO WAYS

YIELD: 1 head

PREP TIME: 1 minute

COOK TIME: 10 minutes or 45 minutes, depending on method

Roasted garlic is incredibly versatile. You can use it on sandwiches, on a cheese plate, in eggs, or even mixed into dressings or dips, such as my Smoky Garlic Burger Sauce (page 74). I love it on pizza, too!

Roasting garlic in an Instant Pot is easier, faster, and cleaner than the regular oven method, but I have included both options in case you don't have an electric pressure cooker. You can roast as many heads at a time as you like.

1 head garlic

1 teaspoon olive oil or ghee

Pinch of pink Himalayan salt

OVEN METHOD:

1. Preheat the oven to 400°F.

2. Chop the top off the head of garlic to expose the tops of the cloves. Drizzle with the olive oil and sprinkle with a pinch of salt. Wrap the entire head in a 9-inch square piece of aluminum foil.

3. Roast in the oven for 45 minutes, or until the garlic is slightly browned and tender. Remove from the oven and let cool.

4. Once the garlic is cool to the touch, remove the cloves from the head by pinching the root area; most of the cloves will pop right out.

5. Store the roasted garlic in the fridge for up to 2 weeks.

INSTANT POT/ELECTRIC PRESSURE COOKER METHOD:

1. Pour 1 cup of water into the Instant Pot and place a steamer basket in the pot.

2. Chop the top off the head of garlic to expose the tops of the cloves. Place the garlic in the steamer basket and drizzle the olive oil over the garlic.

3. Place the lid on the pot and lock it. Cook on high pressure for 10 minutes.

4. After 10 minutes of cooking, let the pressure release naturally, then open the pot. Carefully remove the garlic to a clean work surface.

5. Sprinkle the hot garlic with a pinch of salt and let cool.

6. Once the garlic is cool to the touch, remove the cloves from the head by pinching the root area; most of the cloves will pop right out.

7. Store the roasted garlic in the fridge for up to 2 weeks.

SMOKY GARLIC BURGER SAUCE

YIELD: about ½ cup
(2 tablespoons per serving)

PREP TIME: 5 minutes,
plus 30 minutes to chill (not
including time to roast garlic)

This sauce is simple but delicious. It just goes to show how easy it can be to make yummy food. This recipe was born before a big day of grilling burgers for a crowd. It's best to make this sauce the night before so that the flavors have time to really combine. Top every burger, lettuce wrap, and hot dog in sight with this stuff! It's a super easy way to get fat into the mix when you are grilling meats.

1 head roasted garlic (page 72)

⅓ cup mayonnaise

1 teaspoon smoked paprika, plus more for garnish

1 teaspoon bacon grease

INGREDIENT SPOTLIGHT:

If you need this or any other of the recipes in this book that call for mayonnaise to be egg-free, purchase or make an egg-free mayonnaise.

1. Squeeze the roasted garlic cloves into a small jar or other container with a lid. Add the rest of the ingredients and stir to combine. The roasted garlic should be soft enough that you can smash it with a spoon and mix it into the sauce.

2. Cover with the lid and place in the refrigerator for at least 30 minutes, or ideally overnight, to allow the flavors to come together. Garnish with more smoked paprika before serving. Store in the refrigerator for up to 1 week.

BEYOND BASIC BLUE CHEESE BUTTER

YIELD: about ½ cup
(1 tablespoon per serving)

PREP TIME: 10 minutes,
plus 20 minutes to chill

  Compound butter is a great way to get creative in the kitchen. I have included a couple of flavor combinations in this book to get your juices flowing, but I encourage you to play around! Flavored butter makes a nice topping for meats, fish, and even a keto burger. Before you begin, make sure that the butter is truly at room temperature, nice and soft for easy mixing.

¼ cup (½ stick) salted butter, softened

¼ cup blue cheese crumbles (about 1 ounce)

1 clove garlic, minced

¼ cup chopped fresh parsley

INGREDIENT SPOTLIGHT:

Don't waste your money on prepackaged blue cheese crumbles. They cost extra and are far less flavorful. Get the stuff from the fancier cheese area of the grocery store; blue cheese is usually sold in wedges priced by the pound.

1. In a small bowl, mix all the ingredients together with a silicone spatula until thoroughly combined.

2. If not serving immediately, scoop the compound butter onto a square of plastic wrap. Cover the butter with both sides of the wrap and shape into a log. Wrap tightly and roll on the counter until you have a perfectly shaped cylinder. Store in the refrigerator for up to 2 weeks or in the freezer for up to 1 month.

MIGNONETTE SAUCE THREE WAYS

YIELD: about ¼ cup
(1 tablespoon per serving)

PREP TIME: 5 minutes

  Mignonette sauce is how I learned to love raw oysters. You just spoon a little bit right into the shell and knock it back. Here I have a classic version and two fun variations.

CLASSIC:

¼ cup red wine vinegar

1 tablespoon minced shallots

¼ teaspoon lemon juice

¼ teaspoon ground black pepper

Pinch of pink Himalayan salt

CUCUMBER:

¼ cup red wine vinegar

1 tablespoon lime juice

1 tablespoon minced cucumbers

1 tablespoon minced shallots

Pinch of pink Himalayan salt

HOT:

¼ cup red wine vinegar

1 tablespoon minced shallots

1 clove garlic, minced

1 teaspoon hot sauce

In a small dish, combine all the ingredients. Serve with raw oysters. Store in the refrigerator for up to 2 weeks.

TARTAR SAUCE

YIELD: about ½ cup
(2 tablespoons per serving)

PREP TIME: 5 minutes

Tartar sauce is one of my favorite dipping sauces. Before I truly liked seafood, I would dunk every bite into the tartar sauce that my mom so generously would make. The yummiest way to use tartar sauce? As a dip for onion rings (page 128)!

½ cup mayonnaise

2 tablespoons chopped dill pickles

1½ teaspoons chopped fresh parsley

1 teaspoon lemon juice

Pink Himalayan salt and ground black pepper

In a small bowl, mix together the mayonnaise, pickles, parsley, and lemon juice. Season with salt and pepper to taste. For the best flavor, allow to sit for at least 30 minutes before serving. Store in the refrigerator for up to 5 days.

RANCH DRESSING

  Ranch dressing is simple to make; you can even grow most of the herbs on your kitchen windowsill! Fresh herbs are preferred over dried for a much more flavorful and fresh-tasting dressing. If you prefer a thicker consistency, omit the heavy cream. For a thinner consistency, add more heavy cream or water a little bit at a time.

¼ cup mayonnaise

¼ cup full-fat sour cream
(or dairy-free sour cream or
additional mayonnaise for
dairy-free)

2 tablespoons heavy cream
(or water or nut milk of choice
for dairy-free)

1 tablespoon apple cider vinegar

1 tablespoon lemon juice

1 tablespoon chopped fresh
chives

1 tablespoon chopped fresh dill

1 tablespoon chopped fresh
parsley

1 teaspoon pink Himalayan salt

1 clove garlic, minced

In a small bowl, mix all the ingredients together until thoroughly combined. Pour into a container to serve. Store in the refrigerator for up to 1 week.

SMOKY TACO SEASONING

YIELD: about ½ cup
(1 tablespoon per serving)

PREP TIME: 5 minutes

I use taco seasoning on just about everything. I love it on chicken, on pork, and especially mixed into ranch dressing for topping burgers and salads! I usually make my own—it's way cheaper, and the premade mixes at the store contain undesirable fillers.

You can make a salt-free version if you prefer and/or increase the heat by adding more chili powder or other hot spices, such as chipotle powder or cayenne pepper. Another fun variation is to add ½ to 1 teaspoon of turmeric powder to the mix! You can easily cut this recipe in half or even in quarters if you need less. Two tablespoons is enough to season a pound of meat.

¼ cup chili powder

1 tablespoon smoked paprika

2 teaspoons ground cumin

2 teaspoons pink Himalayan salt (optional)

1½ teaspoons dried oregano leaves

1 teaspoon garlic powder

1 teaspoon onion powder

1. In a small bowl, mix all the ingredients together until thoroughly combined.

2. Store in the refrigerator for up to 1 month or in the freezer for up to 3 months.

MAPLE ORANGE BUTTER

YIELD: ¼ cup (1 tablespoon per serving)

PREP TIME: 5 minutes

  Compound butters are a fun way to add fat and flavor to a keto diet. This version is good on anything breadlike, such as waffles, pancakes, and my Cinnamon Bread (page 98). You can easily make extra and freeze some for later! The best way to store the butter is to roll it into a log in plastic wrap.

¼ cup (½ stick) salted butter, softened

1 teaspoon grated orange zest

1 teaspoon sugar-free maple syrup

¼ teaspoon orange extract or orange oil

1. In a small bowl, mix all the ingredients together with a silicone spatula until thoroughly combined.

2. If not serving immediately, scoop the compound butter onto a square of plastic wrap. Cover the butter with both sides of the wrap and shape into a log. Wrap tightly and roll on the counter until you have a perfectly shaped cylinder. Store in the refrigerator for up to 2 weeks or in the freezer for up to 1 month.

LIME-MARINATED RED ONIONS

YIELD: about ½ cup
(2 tablespoons per serving)

PREP TIME: 5 minutes,
plus 1 hour to marinate

 I've found that stocking what I call "flavor boosters" at home makes eating keto a whole lot more fun. These red onions are a go-to for salads, tacos, burgers, and more. A little marinating goes a long way to give red onions less bite and a delicious tang with a hint of lime. You won't want to run out! You can easily double or triple this recipe once you're hooked.

1 medium-sized red onion

2 tablespoons lime juice (about 1 lime; see Tip)

1 teaspoon pink Himalayan salt

TIP: Roll the lime on the counter, pressing down hard, to release more juice before slicing and juicing.

1. Slice the onion in half vertically. Set the halves cut side down on a cutting board and slice the onion as thinly as you can.

2. In a bowl, toss the onion slices with the lime juice and salt until evenly coated.

3. Let marinate at room temperature for 1 hour before serving; if you won't be using the onions in an hour, place the bowl in the refrigerator to marinate. Store the onions in the lime juice brine in the refrigerator for up to 1 week. The flavor will continue to develop the longer they marinate.

ROASTED STRAWBERRY JAM

YIELD: 1 cup (2 tablespoons per serving)

PREP TIME: 10 minutes

COOK TIME: 15 minutes

I was inspired to make this jam after visiting a restaurant in Astoria, Oregon, that serves jalapeño poppers with strawberry jam! Ever since, we always enjoy our poppers with strawberry jam (see my recipe on page 114). This version has no added sweetener and is extra flavorful due to the fact that the berries are roasted beforehand.

2 cups halved fresh strawberries (about 9 ounces)

¼ teaspoon pink Himalayan salt

5 to 6 fresh basil leaves

1 tablespoon unflavored gelatin

1. Preheat the oven to 400°F and line a rimmed baking sheet with parchment paper.

2. Spread the strawberries on the lined baking sheet and sprinkle with the salt.

3. Roast for 15 minutes, or until the berries are deep red and releasing juice.

4. Place the roasted strawberries, basil leaves, and gelatin in a blender and blend until smooth. Alternatively, place the basil and gelatin in a pan with the roasted berries and use a stick blender to blend the jam.

5. Store in the refrigerator for up to 10 days.

BLUE CHEESE DRESSING

YIELD: ¾ cup (2 tablespoons per serving)

PREP TIME: 10 minutes, plus 1 hour to chill

After trying a classic homemade blue cheese dressing like this one, you won't want to go back to store-bought dressing.

¼ cup mayonnaise

¼ cup full-fat sour cream

¼ cup blue cheese crumbles (about 1 ounce)

1 tablespoon diced yellow onions

1 tablespoon lemon juice

¼ teaspoon pink Himalayan salt

In a mixing bowl, combine all the ingredients. Cover and place in the refrigerator for at least 1 hour to allow the flavors to combine before serving. Store in the refrigerator for up to 2 weeks.

MUSTARD SEED AIOLI

YIELD: about ½ cup
(2 tablespoons per serving)

PREP TIME: 10 minutes

A tasty sauce can take a dish from good to great and from low-fat to high-fat. We are lucky on the keto diet because of all the great sauces we get to eat. This sauce is a star in my Triple Onion Burgers (page 180), but the slightly hot pop of mustard seeds would make it great on pork sausage or even a juicy grilled pork chop. You can give it a little more punch by using white instead of yellow onions and increasing the amount of brown mustard seeds.

¼ cup mayonnaise

2 tablespoons olive oil or avocado oil

2 tablespoons finely chopped yellow or white onions

½ teaspoon brown mustard seeds

½ teaspoon yellow mustard seeds

½ teaspoon smoked salt

TIP: If the aioli starts to separate, stir well or shake if stored in a sealed jar.

In a mixing bowl, combine all the ingredients. Cover and let sit on the counter for at least 5 minutes to allow the flavors to combine; if not using the aioli within 20 minutes, place the bowl in the refrigerator rather than on the counter. Store in the refrigerator for up to 2 weeks.

BUFFALO DILL SAUCE

YIELD: about ½ cup
(2 tablespoons per serving)

PREP TIME: 5 minutes, plus
10 minutes to rest

COOK TIME: 30 minutes

This sauce is perfect for people who like a little heat. It goes great with Onion Rings (page 128), Marinated Fried Chicken Strips (page 234), or burgers. As with most sauces, the flavor of this one gets better the longer the ingredients marinate.

¼ cup mayonnaise

3 tablespoons finely chopped yellow onions

2 tablespoons hot sauce, such as Frank's RedHot

1½ teaspoons chopped fresh dill

In a small bowl, mix all the ingredients together. Cover and let sit on the counter for at least 10 minutes to allow the flavors to combine; if not using the sauce within 20 minutes, place the bowl in the refrigerator rather than on the counter. Store in the refrigerator for up to 2 weeks.

NUT-FREE PESTO

YIELD: about ¾ cup
(3 tablespoons per serving)

PREP TIME: 10 minutes

  Everyone loves pesto! Not only is this version nut-free, but sunflower seeds are lower in carbohydrates than most nuts—perfect for a keto diet! Add additional raw or roasted garlic (page 72) for more garlic flavor, or add roasted red peppers or sun-dried tomatoes to mix things up.

1 cup loosely packed fresh basil leaves

¼ cup olive oil

¼ cup grated Parmesan cheese (about 1 ounce)

2 tablespoons hulled sunflower seeds

2 cloves garlic, raw or roasted

Place all the ingredients in a blender and blend well. Store in the refrigerator for up to 1 week.

BERRY VINAIGRETTE

YIELD: about ¾ cup
(2 tablespoons per serving)

PREP TIME: 5 minutes (not
including time to make jam)

A light and fruity salad dressing is perfect for summer! Enjoy this vinaigrette over light and crunchy greens like butter lettuce, your favorite crumbled cheese, and a sprinkle of nuts and seeds.

½ cup avocado oil

2 tablespoons apple cider vinegar

2 tablespoons champagne vinegar

1 tablespoon Roasted Strawberry Jam (page 82)

1 teaspoon pink Himalayan salt

¼ teaspoon prepared yellow mustard

Place all the ingredients in a mason jar and blend with a stick blender, or whisk vigorously in a medium-sized bowl. Store in the refrigerator for up to 2 weeks.

CARAMELIZED ONIONS THREE WAYS

OPTION

Caramelized onions add flavor wherever they go. If you have just one recipe that calls for them, make sure to start the onions first, as they take about 45 minutes to caramelize on the stovetop. If you are an onion lover like me, you can make a big batch in a slow cooker or an electric pressure cooker to have on hand. Add them to burgers and other meat dishes, casseroles, eggs—the sky's the limit! I call for yellow onions here because they are already slightly sweet, but you can caramelize any color of onion you'd like.

STOVETOP METHOD

YIELD: 4 servings

PREP TIME: 5 minutes

COOK TIME: 45 minutes

1 tablespoon salted butter
(or avocado oil for dairy-free)

2 large yellow or white onions, sliced

1 teaspoon pink Himalayan salt

1. In a medium-sized pan over low heat, melt the butter slightly. Add the onions and sprinkle with the salt. Toss the onions to distribute the salt and butter.

2. Cook over low heat, stirring occasionally, for 45 minutes, or until golden brown.

SLOW COOKER METHOD

YIELD: 6 to 8 servings

PREP TIME: 10 minutes

COOK TIME: 9 hours

4 to 6 large yellow or white onions, sliced

2 tablespoons salted butter
(or avocado oil for dairy-free)

1 tablespoon pink Himalayan salt

Place the onions, butter, and salt in a 6-quart slow cooker. Cover and cook on low for about 9 hours. Stir once every hour or so, especially in the first few hours of cooking; after that, it's okay to stop stirring. The onions are done when they have significantly reduced in size and are soft and caramel colored.

INSTANT POT METHOD

YIELD: 6 servings

PREP TIME: 10 minutes

COOK TIME: 40 minutes

4 large yellow or white onions, sliced

2 tablespoons salted butter
(or avocado oil for dairy-free)

1 tablespoon pink Himalayan salt

1. Place the onions, butter, and salt in a 6-quart Instant Pot. Press Sauté to melt the butter, stirring to coat the onions in the butter. Press Cancel to stop the Sauté.

2. Seal the lid, press Manual or Pressure Cook, and set the timer for 25 minutes. After 25 minutes, let the pressure release naturally, or wait 5 minutes and then manually release the remaining pressure. The onions will be caramelized but may not be golden. If you want them to be brown, press Sauté again and cook until browned.

3. Store in the refrigerator for up to 10 days.

CRISPY MUSHROOMS

YIELD: 4 servings

PREP TIME: 10 minutes

COOK TIME: 40 minutes

   Crispy mushrooms will change your life! They give an amazing savory flavor and crunch to anything you add them to. I missed croutons terribly when I switched to a keto diet, and these mushrooms work nicely as a replacement. If you can track down some truffle-infused olive oil, it is worth the extra effort: think truffle fries but less carbs! If not, regular olive oil is fine. Make sure to slice the mushrooms yourself; presliced mushrooms won't get crispy.

1 pound cremini mushrooms, thinly sliced

⅓ cup truffle-infused olive oil

1 tablespoon Italian seasoning

1 teaspoon pink Himalayan salt

1. Preheat the oven to 400°F and line two rimmed baking sheets with parchment paper.

2. In a large bowl, toss the mushrooms with the oil, Italian seasoning, and salt. Spread the mushrooms in a single layer on the lined baking sheets. They will shrink significantly while baking.

3. Let the mushrooms sit on the baking sheets until the oven reaches temperature.

4. Bake until the mushrooms are very dark brown and crisp, 30 to 40 minutes, depending on the thickness of the sliced mushrooms. Stir halfway through cooking for even browning.

5. Store in the refrigerator for up to 1 week.

PSYLLIUM HUSK PIZZA CRUST

YIELD: one 8- to 9-inch crust

PREP TIME: 5 minutes

COOK TIME: 6 minutes

This is my go-to recipe for pizza crust. It comes together in a flash and bakes just as quickly. You can add any toppings you like and finish the pizza under the oven broiler or use a toaster oven instead. I usually make a few crusts at once to have some in the fridge for later use.

When par-baking the crust, keep the top sheet of parchment on, as the dough has a tendency to stick to it. The paper comes off easily after the par-baking is complete. Watch the crust carefully; if it is overcooked, it can burn when you bake the pizza after adding the toppings. The edges tend to get dark and very crispy after the second trip to the oven.

¼ cup (30 g) golden flax meal

2 tablespoons grated Parmesan cheese (omit for dairy-free; see Note)

1½ tablespoons ground psyllium husks

½ teaspoon dried oregano leaves

Pinch of pink Himalayan salt

3 large egg whites (about 6 tablespoons liquid egg whites)

1 tablespoon garlic-infused olive oil

NOTE: The crust will be slightly smaller in diameter if you omit the Parmesan cheese.

1. Place a pizza stone or baking sheet in the oven and preheat the oven to 400°F.

2. In a medium-sized bowl, whisk together all the dry ingredients. Add the egg whites and olive oil and stir with a spoon or silicone spatula. Let the dough sit for 2 minutes so that the dry ingredients fully absorb the liquids.

3. Turn the dough out onto a sheet of parchment paper. If the dough is a bit crumbly, use the parchment to fold it over on itself a few times. Form the dough into a ball and top with a second large sheet of parchment. Flatten the dough slightly with your palm, then use a rolling pin to roll it out into a thin circle, 8 to 9 inches in diameter.

4. Carefully slide the crust, still between the sheets of parchment paper, onto the hot pizza stone in the oven. Par-bake for 5 to 6 minutes, until the crust is slightly browned. (It will get crispier when it is baked again with toppings.)

5. Remove the top piece of parchment paper and use immediately (see pages 198 to 209 for ideas), or store for later use.

6. Store the par-baked crust wrapped in plastic wrap in the refrigerator for up to 5 days. To freeze, wrap the crust in wax paper or plastic wrap and then in foil, or place in a resealable plastic freezer bag, and store in the freezer for up to 1 month. To use a frozen crust, top as desired and place under the oven broiler or in a toaster oven on the broil setting until the toppings are melted.

TIP: If you prefer a cracker-crisp crust, you can finish the pizza in a dry cast-iron skillet over medium heat for about 2 minutes for that extra crunch.

DROP BISCUITS

YIELD: 8 biscuits (1 per serving)

PREP TIME: 10 minutes

COOK TIME: 20 minutes

A drop biscuit is the perfect base for a warm sandwich or even a slider. These keto biscuits are fairly simple to make, and the sunflower seed flour gives them a delicious nutty taste.

240 g (2 cups) sunflower seed flour

2 teaspoons baking powder

½ teaspoon pink Himalayan salt

2¾ ounces salted butter, frozen (or very cold cubed red palm shortening or lard for dairy-free)

4 large egg whites (about ½ cup liquid egg whites)

INGREDIENT SPOTLIGHT:

For best results, I always weigh my sunflower seed flour rather than measure it by volume.

1. Preheat the oven to 350°F. Line a rimmed baking sheet with parchment paper.

2. In a large bowl, whisk together the sunflower seed flour, baking powder, and salt. Grate the frozen butter over the top. Mix with a fork to form a crumbly mixture.

3. Fold the egg whites into the mixture, then form the dough into 8 balls. Place the balls of dough on the lined baking sheet and lightly flatten.

4. Bake for 15 to 20 minutes, until golden brown.

5. Let cool on the pan for at least 20 minutes before serving; the biscuits will be very crumbly while still warm.

6. To store, wrap carefully in plastic wrap and refrigerate for up to 1 week or freeze for up to 1 month. Split them open while cold and reheat in a 300°F oven.

SEEDED HAMBURGER BUNS

YIELD: 4 buns (1 per serving)

PREP TIME: 15 minutes

COOK TIME: 1 hour

  Every burger lover needs a bun once in a while! These buns come together very simply—you just mix and go. The trick is to keep them nice and tall when you form them. They will spread slightly and get thinner as they bake.

100 g (about ¾ cup plus 1 tablespoon) sunflower seed flour

3 tablespoons ground psyllium husks

½ teaspoon pink Himalayan salt

2 large egg whites (about ¼ cup liquid egg whites)

1½ teaspoons apple cider vinegar

1 cup boiling water, slightly cooled

1 tablespoon sesame seeds or dried onion flakes, for topping

1. Preheat the oven to 350°F. Line a rimmed baking sheet with parchment paper.

2. In a large bowl, whisk together the sunflower seed flour, ground psyllium husks, and salt.

3. Add the egg whites and vinegar and mix well with a spoon. Then add the hot water and mix well.

4. Divide the dough into 4 even portions and shape into discs. The dough will spread slightly when baked, so make the discs on the tall side so they don't become too thin after baking. Place the discs on the lined baking sheet and sprinkle with the sesame seeds.

5. Bake for 1 hour or until golden brown. Let cool before slicing horizontally.

6. Store in the refrigerator for up to 1 week.

INGREDIENT SPOTLIGHT:

For best results, I always weigh my sunflower seed flour rather than measure it by volume.

CINNAMON BREAD

YIELD: one 9 by 5-inch loaf (16 slices)

PREP TIME: 10 minutes

COOK TIME: 1 hour 20 minutes

  Unlike a lot of other keto breads, this one is light and has no hint of egg taste—Scout's honor! It toasts up beautifully and makes the best grilled cheese on Earth (see page 256). This bread is very easy to throw together. The hardest part is adding the egg whites; after mixing in the boiling water, you need to allow the dough to cool a bit before adding the whites (to avoid scrambled eggs!), and then you need to really work the dough to get the whites incorporated. It's a messy task, but your hands are the best tool for the job.

120 g (1 cup) sunflower seed flour or meal

¼ cup (30 g) golden flax meal

¼ cup ground psyllium husks

3 tablespoons granulated erythritol, divided

2 teaspoons baking powder

2 teaspoons ground cinnamon, divided

½ teaspoon pink Himalayan salt

1¼ cups boiling water

2 teaspoons apple cider vinegar

3 large egg whites (about 6 tablespoons liquid egg whites)

INGREDIENT SPOTLIGHT:

For best results, I always weigh my sunflower seed flour rather than measure it by volume.

1. Preheat the oven to 350°F. Line a 9 by 5-inch loaf pan with parchment paper.

2. In a large mixing bowl, whisk together the sunflower seed flour, flax meal, ground psyllium husks, 1 tablespoon of the erythritol, the baking powder, 1 teaspoon of the cinnamon, and the salt.

3. Add the boiling water and mix with a silicone spatula. The dough will come together easily. Add the vinegar and mix again.

4. Let the dough cool for about 1 minute, then add the egg whites. Using your hands, work the whites into the dough. It will take a full minute or two of constant mixing, but the egg whites will eventually incorporate. The dough will be slightly sticky and clumpy at this point.

5. In a small bowl, mix the remaining 2 tablespoons of erythritol with the remaining 1 teaspoon of cinnamon. Sprinkle about a quarter of the mixture into the loaf pan.

6. Sprinkle about one-third of the remaining cinnamon mixture onto the dough. Fold the dough in on itself once, then add another one-third of the cinnamon mixture. Fold once more and add the final third of the cinnamon mixture. The dough will be only slightly clumpy now.

7. Drop the dough into the prepared loaf pan. Spread the dough evenly and smooth the top with the spatula.

8. Bake for 1 hour 20 minutes, or until the top is dark brown and a toothpick inserted in the center of the loaf comes out clean.

9. Place the pan upside down on a wire rack to cool. Once the bread has cooled significantly, run a butter knife around the edges of the pan. Turn the pan upside down again and give it a few good taps until the bread releases from the pan.

10. Wrap the loaf in plastic wrap or aluminum foil and store in the refrigerator for up to 1 week. To freeze, wrap the loaf in wax paper or plastic wrap and then in foil (otherwise, the foil will stick to the bread) and store in the freezer for up to 1 month. Consider preslicing the loaf before freezing.

APPETIZERS and SNACKS

Spiced Seeds | *102*

Caramelized Onion Dip | *104*

Garlic Parmesan Chicken Wings | *106*

Smoky Chicken Pâté | *108*

Baked Brie | *110*

Vanilla Bacon–Stuffed Celery | *112*

Jalapeño Poppers with Strawberry Jam | *114*

Lemon Oysters | *116*

Elote Chicken Wings | *118*

Cheesy Stuffed Meatballs | *120*

Lime Butter Shrimp | *122*

Bruschetta Mushrooms | *124*

Caprese Skewers | *126*

Onion Rings | *128*

Roasted Berries with Prosciutto | *130*

Salt and Vinegar Chicken Wings | *132*

Spiced Nuts Three Ways | *134*

Prosciutto Meat Cups | *136*

SPICED SEEDS

YIELD: 1 cup (¼ cup per serving)

PREP TIME: 5 minutes

COOK TIME: 10 minutes

   Spiced seeds are a delicious after-dinner treat! If you are craving a little nibble while watching TV and unwinding for the night, these will hit the spot. They also make a great travel snack. You can easily double or triple this recipe and bring these on vacation.

1 cup hulled sunflower or pumpkin seeds

1 tablespoon melted bacon grease or avocado oil

1 teaspoon garlic salt (see Ingredient Spotlight)

INGREDIENT SPOTLIGHT:

Regular garlic salt will work here, but the black garlic salt from Jacobson Salt Co. is my favorite for this recipe and for all of my everyday garlic salt needs. It truly makes these seeds addicting!

1. Preheat the oven to 400°F and line a rimmed baking sheet with parchment paper.

2. In a medium-sized bowl, mix the seeds, bacon grease, and garlic salt with a silicone spatula. Spread the seeds in a single layer on the lined baking sheet.

3. Bake for 10 minutes, then let cool. Store in the refrigerator for up to 2 weeks.

CARAMELIZED ONION DIP

YIELD: 1 cup (2 tablespoons per serving)

PREP TIME: 5 minutes, plus time to rest overnight (not including time to caramelize onions)

This dip is good on just about everything. My husband especially likes it with leftover sliced Marinated Pork Loin (page 220). You can easily make this recipe dairy-free by using any combination of mayonnaise, dairy-free cream cheese, or similar ingredients. It all tastes great, I promise!

⅓ cup full-fat sour cream (or dairy-free sour cream for dairy-free), room temperature

⅓ cup mascarpone cheese or mayonnaise, room temperature

⅓ cup Caramelized Onions (page 88), drained

1 teaspoon smoked salt or pink Himalayan salt, plus more for garnish

In a medium-sized bowl, mix all the ingredients together. For the best flavor, cover and place in the refrigerator overnight to let the flavors come together before serving, then garnish with a sprinkle of smoked salt.

GARLIC PARMESAN CHICKEN WINGS

YIELD: 12 wings (2 per serving)

PREP TIME: 5 minutes

COOK TIME: 30 minutes

The best of all worlds: perfectly tender and crispy wings! Steaming chicken wings in an electric pressure cooker gives you tender meat—so tender that all the meat comes off the bone. No more half-eaten wing bones in the trash! A quick trip under the broiler gives you perfectly crispy skin, too.

This recipe is easily doubled or tripled. In fact, if you have a rack and a steamer basket, you can cook layers of wings in an Instant Pot. If you are making a big batch, grab a large mixing bowl and toss the wings with the seasonings, butter, and Parmesan cheese before placing them under the broiler. It will be much faster this way!

12 chicken wings

1 teaspoon garlic powder

½ teaspoon onion powder

½ teaspoon pink Himalayan salt

1½ tablespoons salted butter

4 cloves garlic, minced

1 tablespoon grated Parmesan cheese

Dipping sauce of choice and/or reserved garlic butter, for serving

SPECIAL EQUIPMENT:
6-quart Instant Pot or electric pressure cooker

TIP: An electric pressure cooker like the Instant Pot is a dream for cooking tender meats. I use mine for wings all the time. There is a trade-off, though: pressure cooking and then broiling chicken wings gives you very tender, fall-off-the-bone meat, but the skin does not get as crispy as it does with my baked wings recipes. But pressure cooking them takes half the time!

1. Line a rimmed baking sheet with parchment paper. Pat the chicken wings dry with a paper towel.

2. Place the wings in a medium-sized bowl and add the garlic powder, onion powder, and salt. Toss to coat the wings with the seasonings.

3. Pour 1 cup of water into a 6-quart Instant Pot. Place the rack that came with the Instant Pot or a steamer basket inside the pot. Place the wings on the rack or in the steamer basket. Seal the lid, press Manual or Pressure Cook, and set the timer for 10 minutes.

4. While the wings are cooking, melt the butter in a small saucepan over very low heat, then add the minced garlic. Turn off the heat and let the butter be infused with the garlic until the wings are ready.

5. After 10 minutes of cooking, let the pressure release naturally, or wait 5 minutes and then manually release the remaining pressure.

6. Transfer the wings to the lined baking sheet. Place an oven rack in the middle position and turn on the oven broiler.

7. Spoon the garlic butter over the wings, reserving a little for serving, if desired. Sprinkle the wings with the Parmesan cheese.

8. Place the baking sheet on the middle rack of the oven and broil the wings until the skin is crispy, about 10 minutes.

9. Serve hot with your favorite dipping sauces and perhaps a little extra garlic butter!

SMOKY CHICKEN PÂTÉ

YIELD: 8 servings

PREP TIME: 10 minutes

COOK TIME: 20 minutes

Chicken pâté is something your grandparents probably ate and has since fallen out of favor. Now we know how nutrient-dense liver is, but many people are afraid to try it. This is a perfect recipe if you are interested in trying liver, even if it sounds a little gross. Mixing bacon with the chicken livers will make you love this dish! The amazing energy and vitality you get from eating liver will keep you making it again and again. My favorite way to eat this pâté is on flax crackers with a little butter on top!

8 ounces bacon

1 pound chicken livers

½ large yellow onion, roughly chopped (about 1½ cups)

2 cloves garlic, roughly chopped

1 tablespoon Italian seasoning

Melted salted butter or avocado oil, if needed

SERVING OPTIONS:

Flax crackers

Bell pepper strips

Celery sticks

Cucumber slices

Cured meat slices

Hard cheese slices

1. Place the bacon in a large skillet over medium-low heat. Cook it low and slow for about 10 minutes to render as much of the fat as possible. Remove the cooked bacon to a plate, leaving the grease in the skillet.

2. Add the chicken livers, onion, and garlic to the skillet with the bacon grease and sprinkle the Italian seasoning over the top. Cook, still over medium-low heat, until the livers are just done and no longer bright pink inside, about 5 minutes on each side.

3. Transfer the liver mixture and bacon to a blender. Pour the grease from the skillet into a measuring cup. If there is less than ⅓ cup, add enough melted butter to reach ⅓ cup. Add the grease to the blender and blend on high until the pâté is smooth.

4. Transfer the pâté to a serving dish and serve with the dippers of your choice. Store in the refrigerator for up to 1 week.

VANILLA BACON–STUFFED CELERY

YIELD: 8 servings

PREP TIME: 10 minutes (not including time to cook bacon)

OPTION

These celery sticks stuffed with a delicious flavored cream cheese are not only quick to make but also very high in fat. You can easily serve them to kids or keep them all to yourself for a high-fat snack. Try making the cream cheese mixture ahead of time and storing it in the refrigerator, then scoop it into celery sticks right before devouring!

4 strips bacon, cooked and crumbled

½ cup raw or roasted almonds

1 tablespoon coconut oil or bacon grease

1 teaspoon vanilla extract

1 (8-ounce) package full-fat cream cheese (1 cup) (or nut-based nondairy cream cheese for dairy-free), room temperature

1 bunch celery, for serving

SPECIAL EQUIPMENT:
high-powered blender

1. Place the bacon, almonds, coconut oil, and vanilla extract in a high-powered blender. Blend on high until a thick paste forms.

2. Place the cream cheese in a medium-sized bowl and fold in the almond butter mixture from the blender.

3. Cut the celery into 3-inch sticks and fill the sticks evenly with the cream cheese mixture just before serving. Store in the refrigerator for up to 3 days.

JALAPEÑO POPPERS WITH STRAWBERRY JAM

YIELD: 28 poppers (4 per serving)

PREP TIME: 10 minutes (not including time to make jam)

COOK TIME: 10 minutes

  You will never want to eat a popper another way after you've tried one with a dab of strawberry jam. The sweetness of the fruit mixed with the heat of the peppers and the cool creaminess of the cream cheese is an absolute flavor explosion! I have to thank the restaurant that served them this way so many years ago; I have literally never served poppers without jam since.

14 jalapeño peppers

2 ounces full-fat cream cheese (¼ cup), room temperature

2 green onions, finely chopped

1 tablespoon chopped fresh cilantro

¼ cup shredded mozzarella cheese (about 1 ounce)

Roasted Strawberry Jam (page 82), for dipping

1. Preheat the oven to 400°F and line a rimmed baking sheet with parchment paper.

2. Slice each jalapeño pepper in half lengthwise, remove the seeds and veins, and place the peppers cut side up on the lined baking sheet.

3. In a medium-sized bowl, mix together the cream cheese, green onions, and cilantro. Scoop the cream cheese mixture into the pepper halves and sprinkle with the shredded mozzarella.

4. Bake for 5 to 10 minutes, until the cheese is melted and bubbly.

5. Serve with strawberry jam for dipping.

LEMON OYSTERS

YIELD: 4 servings

PREP TIME: 5 minutes

COOK TIME: 4 minutes

OPTION

If you love oysters, this recipe will knock your socks off! The pork rind crumbs mixed with Parmesan cheese and lemon zest add a citrusy crunch that makes for a delicious and fancy appetizer. If you have never prepared oysters before, ask the fishmonger to shuck them for you. Make sure to pick up some very large-grain coarse salt; you will use it to create a little "sandbox" on the baking sheet to hold the half shells and keep them from tipping over.

Rock salt or coarse pink Himalayan salt

3 tablespoons crushed pork rinds

1½ tablespoons shredded Parmesan cheese (omit for dairy-free)

½ teaspoon grated lemon zest

12 oysters, scrubbed, shucked, and left on the half shell

Ground black pepper

Lemon juice, for serving

1. Turn on the oven broiler.

2. Prepare a rimmed baking sheet with a half-inch layer of salt.

3. In a small bowl, combine the crushed pork rinds, Parmesan cheese (if using), and lemon zest. Mix well.

4. Place each oyster on the half shell on the layer of salt on the baking sheet. Top each oyster with an equal amount of the pork rind mixture.

5. Broil for 2 to 4 minutes, until the oysters are sizzling and the cheese is melted.

6. Sprinkle the oysters with additional salt, pepper, and lemon juice to taste. Let cool slightly before serving.

ELOTE CHICKEN WINGS

YIELD: 15 wings (3 per serving)

PREP TIME: 5 minutes

COOK TIME: 1 hour 15 minutes

   Elote is a spicy roasted type of street corn that is absolutely delicious but 100% not keto-friendly. The same flavors work perfectly on these crispy oven-baked wings. Double or triple this recipe for a killer potluck dish!

15 chicken wings

¼ cup shredded or finely crumbled Cotija cheese (about 1 ounce), plus more for garnish (omit for dairy-free)

1½ tablespoons baking powder

½ teaspoon pink Himalayan salt

½ teaspoon chili powder

½ teaspoon smoked paprika

1. Preheat the oven to 250°F. Line a rimmed baking sheet with parchment paper and set a wire rack on top.

2. Pat the chicken wings dry with a paper towel.

3. Place all the ingredients, except the wings, in a large bowl and mix together. Add the wings one by one and roll them in the mixture to coat. Then set the wings on the wire rack so that they dry out further as the oven comes to temperature.

4. Bake for 35 minutes, then increase the oven temperature to 400°F and bake for another 35 to 40 minutes, until the skin is very crispy. Garnish with more cheese and serve immediately.

CHEESY STUFFED MEATBALLS

YIELD: 20 meatballs
(4 per serving)

PREP TIME: 10 minutes

COOK TIME: 35 minutes

  Take your meatball game to the next level! Camembert cheese is similar to Brie in texture, but the flavor is slightly bolder. It pairs perfectly with beef. When shaping these meatballs, make sure to fully cover the cheese so it doesn't ooze out as it melts during cooking.

1 pound ground beef

⅓ cup finely shredded zucchini

¼ cup finely chopped yellow onions (about ¼ medium onion)

2 tablespoons Italian seasoning

1½ teaspoons pink Himalayan salt

2 ounces Camembert cheese, cut into 20 cubes

TIP: These meatballs are delicious without the cheese, too, if you need a dairy-free version.

1. Preheat the oven to 375°F and line a rimmed baking sheet with parchment paper.

2. Place all the ingredients, except the cheese, in a large bowl and mix with your hands to combine.

3. Take a heaping tablespoon of the meat mixture and form it into a ball. Insert a chunk of cheese into the middle of the meatball, making sure it's covered on all sides. Repeat with the remaining meat mixture and cheese, making a total of 20 stuffed meatballs.

4. Place the meatballs on the lined baking sheet with the sides just barely touching. Bake for 30 to 35 minutes, until cooked through.

LIME BUTTER SHRIMP

YIELD: 4 servings

PREP TIME: 5 minutes

COOK TIME: 15 minutes

  This is an easy and tasty way to get some extra seafood into your life. The sauce is creamy and perfectly lime flavored. These shrimp are great to serve as an appetizer, or you can use them to top a salad for a complete meal.

¼ cup (½ stick) salted butter

1 pound frozen large raw shrimp

2 tablespoons heavy cream

1 tablespoon chopped fresh cilantro

¼ teaspoon chopped fresh dill

¼ teaspoon grated lime zest

2 tablespoons lime juice

Arugula, for serving (optional)

1. Melt the butter in a large skillet over medium heat. Once melted, add the shrimp and cook until it has just turned pink, about 10 minutes. Remove the shrimp from the pan and set aside; leave the melted butter in the skillet.

2. Reduce the heat to medium-low and slowly pour in the cream, whisking to combine it with the butter. Add the cilantro and dill while still whisking.

3. Once the sauce starts to reduce, slowly add the lime zest and juice, whisking continuously as the sauce thickens. When the sauce is thick enough to coat the back of a spoon, about 5 minutes, remove the pan from the heat.

4. If desired, place a bed of arugula on a small serving plate. Top with the shrimp and spoon the sauce over the shrimp.

BRUSCHETTA MUSHROOMS

YIELD: 10 mushrooms
(2 per serving)

PREP TIME: 10 minutes

COOK TIME: 10 minutes

OPTION

Enjoy your favorite bruschetta flavors without the bread and carbs! Tomatoes are a bit watery, so make sure to give them a little time to drain before you proceed with the recipe.

3 Roma tomatoes, diced

½ teaspoon pink Himalayan salt

20 mozzarella pearls (omit for dairy-free)

2 tablespoons olive oil

¼ teaspoon ground black pepper

10 large button mushrooms, stems removed (see Tip)

Balsamic vinegar, for drizzling

TIP: Use a damp paper towel to gently wipe the mushrooms clean. Do not submerge them in water, or the cooked mushrooms will be soggy.

1. Place the tomatoes in a colander set over a bowl to catch the juices. Toss with the salt and set aside to drain for 1 to 2 minutes.

2. Preheat a grill pan, skillet, or outdoor grill to medium heat.

3. In a small bowl, gently mix together the mozzarella pearls, olive oil, pepper, and drained tomatoes.

4. Scoop a heaping tablespoon of the tomato mixture into each mushroom cap. Place the mushrooms in the pan or on the grill and cook for 10 minutes, or until the cheese is melty.

5. Remove the mushrooms to a serving dish and drizzle with balsamic before serving.

CAPRESE SKEWERS

OPTION

This is a great appetizer to serve to non-keto friends and family. Everyone loves caprese salad, and putting the salad on skewers is simple but looks slightly fancy. It's a handy recipe for using up summer fresh tomatoes and eating outdoors!

FOR THE DRESSING:

¼ cup olive oil

2 tablespoons champagne vinegar or balsamic vinegar

1 tablespoon Italian seasoning

1 tablespoon coarsely chopped red onions

¼ teaspoon pink Himalayan salt

20 cherry or grape tomatoes

20 mozzarella pearls (omit for dairy-free)

1 bunch fresh basil leaves

SPECIAL EQUIPMENT:
10 wooden skewers

1. To make the dressing, place the oil, vinegar, Italian seasoning, onions, and salt in a blender and blend well. Set the dressing aside.

2. Cut the tomatoes in half or, if they are on the larger side, into bite-sized chunks.

3. Thread each skewer with alternating tomato pieces, mozzarella pearls, and basil leaves. Place the skewers in a shallow dish and drizzle with the dressing.

4. For the best flavor, let the skewers sit at room temperature for at least 15 minutes before serving; the dish gets more flavorful as it sits.

ONION RINGS

YIELD: 4 servings

PREP TIME: 10 minutes

COOK TIME: 15 minutes

 Onion rings are one of the best foods on the planet. This recipe uses my favorite breading: a combination of crushed pork rinds, Parmesan cheese, and spices. The spices are totally customizable to your tastes, so play around with what sounds good to you! Some ideas to try: ranch seasoning, taco seasoning, or chili powder for a little kick. Serve the onion rings with your favorite dipping sauce, like Blue Cheese Dressing (page 83), Ranch Dressing (page 78), or, my favorite, Tartar Sauce (page 77).

1 large egg

2 tablespoons heavy cream

²/₃ cup grated Parmesan cheese (about 2½ ounces)

²/₃ cup crushed pork rinds (any flavor)

1½ teaspoons smoked paprika

1½ teaspoons Italian seasoning

½ teaspoon pink Himalayan salt

1 medium onion, sliced into 30 to 40 rings

1. Preheat the oven to 400°F. Line a rimmed baking sheet with parchment paper and set a wire rack on top.

2. In a shallow dish, whisk together the egg and heavy cream until well combined.

3. Place the Parmesan cheese, crushed pork rinds, paprika, Italian seasoning, and salt in another shallow dish and stir to combine.

4. Dip each onion slice into the egg mixture and gently shake off the excess liquid. Then dip the onion into the dry mixture to fully coat.

5. Place the breaded onion rings on the wire rack and bake for 15 minutes, or until golden brown. They are best when eaten immediately.

ROASTED BERRIES WITH PROSCIUTTO

YIELD: 12 bites (1 per serving)

PREP TIME: 10 minutes

COOK TIME: 10 minutes

OPTION

A simple but flavorful appetizer. Roasting the berries heightens their flavor and juiciness. Make sure to soak the toothpicks in water beforehand so they don't burn in the oven.

6 slices prosciutto, cut in half lengthwise

2 ounces soft goat cheese, whipped cream cheese, or dairy-free cream cheese (¼ cup), room temperature

6 fresh strawberries or other berries of choice, destemmed and halved

SPECIAL EQUIPMENT:

12 toothpicks, soaked in water

1. Preheat the oven to 400°F and line a rimmed baking sheet with parchment paper.

2. Take a half slice of prosciutto and spread a small scoop of the cheese down the middle. Wrap the prosciutto around a berry and secure with a toothpick. Place on the lined baking sheet. Repeat with the remaining prosciutto, cheese, and berries.

3. Roast until the berries are soft and the prosciutto is crispy, about 15 minutes. Serve immediately.

SALT AND VINEGAR CHICKEN WINGS

YIELD: 15 wings (3 per serving)

PREP TIME: 5 minutes

COOK TIME: 1 hour 15 minutes

OPTION   OPTION

This simple recipe will leave you wanting more. Salt and vinegar wings are highly addictive and are extra delicious when served with a creamy ranch or blue cheese dip or, my favorite, Caramelized Onion Dip (page 104).

15 chicken wings

1½ tablespoons baking powder

2 tablespoons salt and vinegar seasoning

Dipping sauce of choice, for serving

1. Preheat the oven to 250°F. Line a rimmed baking sheet with parchment paper and set a wire rack on top.

2. Pat the chicken wings dry with a paper towel.

3. In a large bowl, mix together the baking powder and salt and vinegar seasoning. Add the wings one by one and roll them in the mixture to coat. Then set the wings on the wire rack so that they dry out further as the oven comes to temperature.

4. Bake for 35 minutes, then increase the oven temperature to 400°F and bake for another 35 to 40 minutes, until the skin is very crispy. Serve immediately with the dipping sauce of your choice.

SPICED NUTS THREE WAYS

YIELD: 1 cup (¼ cup per serving)

PREP TIME: 10 minutes

COOK TIME: 12 minutes

  Warm nuts are such a fancy snack. They are filling and keep your mouth busy in the event of an evening snack attack. My husband makes this recipe every single night with cashews and some pumpkin seeds. You can use any nuts and spices you'd like; here are three flavor combinations to get you started!

1 batch seasoning mix of choice (ingredients below)

1 cup raw whole nuts or nut pieces of choice

1 teaspoon avocado oil or bacon grease

ANTI-INFLAMMATION MIX:

1½ teaspoons turmeric powder

½ teaspoon pink Himalayan salt

½ teaspoon ground black pepper

WINTRY MIX:

½ teaspoon ground cinnamon

½ teaspoon ground nutmeg

½ teaspoon pink Himalayan salt

SPICY MIX:

2 teaspoons taco seasoning, store-bought or homemade (page 79), or chili powder

½ teaspoon pink Himalayan salt

1. Preheat the oven to 400°F and line a rimmed baking sheet with parchment paper.

2. In a small bowl, combine the seasonings for the flavor mix of your choice and set aside.

3. In another small bowl, toss the nuts in the oil, then spread them on the lined baking sheet. Bake for 6 minutes.

4. Remove the baking sheet from the oven and toss the nuts around a bit so that they bake evenly. Sprinkle the seasoning mix over the nuts.

5. Bake for another 6 minutes, or until lightly browned. Serve hot!

PROSCIUTTO MEAT CUPS

OPTION

This is a great meal-prep recipe. You can make more than one batch and store the extra meat cups for dinners or lunches to go. The cups can be eaten cold or popped back into the oven or microwaved for a delicious warm meal!

12 ounces ground beef

12 ounces ground pork

1 teaspoon pink Himalayan salt

¼ cup finely shredded zucchini

¼ cup grated Parmesan cheese (about 1 ounce) (or almond flour for dairy-free)

¼ teaspoon dried parsley

1 tablespoon Italian seasoning

1 tablespoon tomato paste

6 slices prosciutto

1. Preheat the oven to 350°F.

2. In a large mixing bowl, combine all the ingredients except the prosciutto with your hands.

3. Cut the prosciutto slices in half lengthwise. Place a half slice in each well of a standard-sized muffin tin. If there are little breaks or tears in the meat, just push it together a bit. Divide the ground meat mixture evenly among the wells, then pat it down into the meat cups.

4. Bake for 35 to 40 minutes, until the internal temperature is 160°F.

5. Remove to a paper towel–lined plate to drain. Serve warm.

6. Store in the refrigerator for up to 5 days. To reheat, place the meat cups in an oven-safe dish and lightly cover. Bake in a preheated 350°F oven for about 5 minutes, until warmed through.

SOUPS, SALADS, and SIDES

Avocado Shrimp Salad | *140*

Mushroom Bisque | *142*

Truffle Garlic–Roasted Broccoli | *144*

Southwest Chicken Salad | *146*

Instant Pot Chicken and Rice Soup | *148*

Stovetop Green Beans | *150*

Diner Roasted Radishes | *152*

Wasabi Broccoli Slaw | *154*

Habanero Brussels Sprouts | *156*

Steak Salad | *158*

Hot Spinach and Bacon Salad | *160*

George's Soup | *162*

Grilled Romaine Salad | *164*

Breakfast Cobb Salad | *166*

Hot and Smoky Wedge Salad | *168*

Taco Soup | *170*

Lime Slaw | *172*

French Onion Soup | *174*

Arugula Caesar Salad | *176*

AVOCADO SHRIMP SALAD

YIELD: 4 servings

PREP TIME: 15 minutes

OPTION

This is perhaps the best salad in this entire book! Shrimp feels a little fancy, and the dressing is the perfect flavor complement to peppery arugula. While a dressed salad doesn't keep long in the refrigerator, you can eat this one over a couple of days.

2 avocados, peeled and pitted, divided

¼ cup mayonnaise

2 tablespoons lime juice (about 1 lime)

8 ounces small cooked shrimp (250/300 size)

1 cup roughly chopped arugula

1 cup chopped red onions (about 1 medium red onion)

4 medium radishes, chopped

2 tablespoons chopped fresh cilantro

1 teaspoon pink Himalayan salt

1. Make the dressing: Place one of the avocados, the mayonnaise, and lime juice in a large bowl. Mash with a fork until fairly smooth.

2. Add the shrimp, arugula, red onions, radishes, cilantro, and salt to the bowl with the dressing.

3. Cut the remaining avocado into chunks and add to the salad. Serve!

MUSHROOM BISQUE

If you are looking for a hearty soup during the winter and love mushrooms, this recipe is for you. It's filling, creamy, and warming from the inside out! Use whatever mushrooms you like. Oyster, shiitake, cremini, and button are good options.

2 tablespoons salted butter or avocado oil

2 tablespoons olive oil

1 pound assorted mushrooms, roughly chopped

2 medium-sized yellow onions, roughly chopped

2 cloves garlic, roughly chopped

½ teaspoon chopped fresh rosemary leaves

1 teaspoon smoked salt or pink Himalayan salt

¼ teaspoon ground black pepper

2 cups chicken or beef bone broth

½ cup heavy cream (see Note)

Chopped fresh chives, for garnish (optional)

1. In a Dutch oven or other heavy-bottomed pot over medium-low heat, melt the butter with the olive oil. Once melted, add the mushrooms, onions, garlic, rosemary, salt, and pepper. Cook, stirring occasionally, until the mushrooms and onions are soft, about 10 minutes.

2. Add the broth to the pot and simmer with the lid ajar for 20 minutes.

3. Ladle the soup into a large blender and blend until super smooth (see Tip). Alternatively, use a stick blender and blend the soup right in the pot.

4. Return the blended soup to the pot over very low heat. Slowly stir in the heavy cream.

5. Serve with a sprinkle of pepper and garnish with chopped chives, if desired.

TIP: When blending hot liquids, you need to vent the blender so that the steam can escape. Most blenders have a little plug in the middle of the lid. Hold a kitchen towel near the vent hole in case the soup tries to escape.

NOTE: To make this soup dairy-free, use avocado oil instead of butter and coconut milk instead of heavy cream. The coconut milk needs to be cooked so that the soup does not taste like coconut. Before adding the broth, pour in the coconut milk and cook, stirring well, for 5 minutes. Then add the broth and continue with the recipe as written, omitting the cream in Step 4.

TRUFFLE GARLIC– ROASTED BROCCOLI

YIELD: 6 servings

PREP TIME: 5 minutes

COOK TIME: 20 minutes

Find yourself some truffle-infused olive oil to make this dish. My mom loved it so much that she asked me to bring it to Christmas dinner!

12 cups fresh broccoli florets (from 2 to 3 large heads)

½ cup truffle-infused olive oil

1 tablespoon garlic powder

½ teaspoon pink Himalayan salt

¼ cup grated Parmesan cheese (about 1 ounce) (or nutritional yeast for dairy-free) (optional)

1. Preheat the oven to 400°F and line a rimmed baking sheet with parchment paper.

2. In a large bowl, toss the broccoli with the olive oil, garlic powder, and salt. Spread the broccoli in a single layer on the lined baking sheet and sprinkle with the Parmesan cheese, if using.

3. Roast for 20 minutes, or until tender. Serve hot.

SOUTHWEST CHICKEN SALAD

YIELD: 4 servings

PREP TIME: 20 minutes
(not including time to make
dressing)

COOK TIME: 10 minutes

  (N)

OPTION   OPTION

Sometimes the salad game gets a little boring. The same greens and dressing combination can get tired fast. Use this salad as inspiration for adding flavor back into your everyday meals! Simply cooking the chicken with some taco seasoning and adding fresh herbs like cilantro can take a salad from ho-hum to wow!

1½ pounds boneless, skinless chicken breasts or thighs

1 teaspoon taco seasoning, store-bought or homemade (page 79)

1 teaspoon pink Himalayan salt

¼ cup avocado oil

12 cups salad greens of choice

½ cup chopped green onions

¼ cup chopped fresh cilantro

½ cup Ranch Dressing (page 78)

1 avocado, peeled, pitted, and sliced

1. Sprinkle the chicken with the taco seasoning and salt.

2. Heat the oil in a large skillet over medium heat. Add the chicken and cook until the internal temperature is 160°F, about 5 minutes per side, depending on the thickness of the chicken.

3. In a large bowl, toss the salad greens with the green onions, cilantro, and dressing.

4. Remove the chicken from the pan and cut it into cubes. Top the salad with the cubed chicken and sliced avocado.

INSTANT POT CHICKEN AND RICE SOUP

YIELD: 4 servings

PREP TIME: 20 minutes

COOK TIME: 15 minutes

  Chicken and rice soup was a staple in my house growing up. It turns out that one simple swap of riced cauliflower for the carb-heavy regular rice works beautifully! Make sure you take the time to sauté the riced cauliflower before adding it to the soup; that is what gives it a flavor and texture similar to traditional rice.

¼ cup avocado oil

2 cups riced cauliflower

½ cup diced white onions

6 cloves garlic, minced

1 tablespoon Italian seasoning

1½ teaspoons pink Himalayan salt

1½ pounds boneless, skinless chicken thighs, cut into bite-sized pieces

6 cups chicken bone broth

1 tablespoon apple cider vinegar

½ teaspoon ground black pepper

SPECIAL EQUIPMENT (OPTIONAL):

6-quart Instant Pot or electric pressure cooker

1. Place the oil in the Instant Pot and press Sauté. Once hot, add the riced cauliflower, onions, garlic, Italian seasoning, and salt. Sauté for 3 minutes, then add the chicken and sauté for 6 more minutes. Press Cancel to stop the Sauté.

2. Add the broth, vinegar, and pepper. Seal the lid, press Manual or Pressure Cook, and set the timer for 15 minutes. After 15 minutes, let the pressure release naturally.

3. Season the soup with additional salt and pepper to taste before serving.

VARIATION: STOVETOP METHOD

If you don't have an electric pressure cooker, start this soup in a heavy-bottomed pot, like a Dutch oven. Warm the oil over medium heat for 2 minutes, then add the riced cauliflower, onions, garlic, Italian seasoning, and salt and sauté for 3 minutes. Add the chicken and sauté for 6 more minutes. Add the broth, vinegar, and pepper, reduce the heat to low, and simmer for 25 minutes. Season the soup with additional salt and pepper to taste before serving.

STOVETOP GREEN BEANS

YIELD: 4 servings

PREP TIME: 10 minutes

COOK TIME: 15 minutes

   This recipe checks all the boxes for a weeknight meal: the whole family will love it, it's quick to cook right on the stovetop, and it gets extra veggies into your day!

1 tablespoon salted butter (or more olive oil for dairy-free)

1 tablespoon olive oil

½ teaspoon pink Himalayan salt

½ teaspoon garlic powder

1 pound green beans, trimmed

2 shallots, chopped

2 slices prosciutto, chopped small

2 teaspoons lemon juice

¼ teaspoon grated lemon zest

1. In a large skillet, heat the butter and olive oil over medium heat. Once the butter is melted, add the salt and garlic powder, then stir.

2. Add the green beans, shallots, and prosciutto. Cook, stirring occasionally, for 15 minutes, or until the beans are tender.

3. Increase the heat to medium-high and add the lemon juice. Cook for 1 minute, tossing the beans in the juice.

4. Remove the green beans to a serving dish, then drizzle the pan drippings over the beans and serve.

DINER ROASTED RADISHES

YIELD: 4 servings

PREP TIME: 15 minutes

COOK TIME: 30 minutes

  Did you know that the radish is the new potato? Yes! It is a delicious keto vegetable that is just waiting to be roasted and to take on any flavor you like. This recipe gives you mini diner-style jojos with a traditional garlic and onion seasoning.

1 pound radishes, trimmed

¼ cup avocado oil

1½ tablespoons garlic powder

2 teaspoons Italian seasoning

2 teaspoons smoked paprika

2 teaspoons ground black pepper

2 teaspoons pink Himalayan salt

1. Preheat the oven to 400°F and line a rimmed baking sheet with parchment paper.

2. Slice the radishes in half, then cut each half into 3 wedges.

3. In a large bowl, place the radish wedges, oil, spices, and salt. Toss to coat all the wedges evenly. Lay the wedges in a single layer on the lined baking sheet, being careful not to crowd them. They need space to become crispy.

4. Roast for 30 minutes, or until the radishes are fork-tender and crispy on the outside. If you like them extra crispy, you can cook them longer.

WASABI BROCCOLI SLAW

Coleslaw is my absolute favorite side dish. Not only is it flavorful, but it's one of the few salads that gets better the longer it sits. This spicy take on coleslaw uses broccoli instead of cabbage. You can absolutely substitute cabbage if you prefer!

¾ cup mayonnaise

2 tablespoons Dijon mustard

2 tablespoons apple cider vinegar

2 teaspoons wasabi paste

1 teaspoon pink Himalayan salt

1 teaspoon ground black pepper

½ teaspoon garlic powder

¼ teaspoon grated lemon zest

2 (12-ounce) bags broccoli slaw, divided

¼ cup chopped green onions

⅓ cup hulled pumpkin or sunflower seeds, toasted, for garnish (see Tip)

1. In a large bowl, whisk together the mayonnaise, mustard, vinegar, wasabi paste, salt, pepper, garlic powder, and lemon zest.

2. Add the broccoli slaw, one-third at a time, stirring well to combine it with the dressing after each addition.

3. Top the slaw with the green onions. Cover and place in the refrigerator to chill for at least 30 minutes.

4. Garnish with the toasted seeds before serving.

TIP: To toast the pumpkin or sunflower seeds, place the seeds in a dry nonstick skillet over medium heat for about 5 minutes, stirring continually to keep them from burning. I like to toss the warm seeds in a tiny bit of oil and salt after they come out of the pan.

HABANERO BRUSSELS SPROUTS

YIELD: 4 servings

PREP TIME: 15 minutes

COOK TIME: 25 minutes

  (N) This recipe is very simple, but it packs a flavorful punch. If you like things a little spicy and are tired of the same old roasted Brussels sprouts, this version will light you up! Try making it with two habaneros the first time. If you need even more heat, add more peppers next time!

¼ cup olive oil

2 habanero peppers, seeded and quartered

2 cloves garlic, peeled

1½ pounds whole Brussels sprouts

4 strips bacon, cut crosswise into ½-inch strips

½ teaspoon pink Himalayan salt

¼ teaspoon ground black pepper

1. Preheat the oven to 400°F and line a rimmed baking sheet with parchment paper.

2. Place the olive oil, habaneros, and garlic in a small blender and blend until smooth (a few little chunks are fine). Alternatively, place these ingredients in a jar and blend with a stick blender. Set aside.

3. Cut the stems off the Brussels sprouts and then slice the sprouts in half. Make sure to use any leaves that get dislodged. They will get extra crispy when roasted.

4. Arrange the Brussels sprouts and bacon in an even layer on the lined baking sheet and sprinkle with the salt and pepper. Drizzle the olive oil mixture over the top. Stir the sprouts and bacon around to fully distribute the oil.

5. Bake for 20 to 25 minutes, until the sprouts are crispy. For extra crispy bits, turn on the oven broiler and broil for 1 to 2 minutes.

TIP: If you want to speed up this recipe, you can buy two packages of shaved Brussels sprouts instead of chopping up whole ones. Reduce the baking time to 15 minutes, or until the sprouts are as crispy as you like them.

STEAK SALAD

   To me, the pairing of warm steak and crunchy, cool greens makes steak salad the perfect meal. Extra points if you top your salad with blue cheese dressing—a classic flavor combination!

1½ pounds steak of choice

Pink Himalayan salt and ground black pepper

1 to 2 tablespoons salted butter or avocado oil

12 cups salad greens of choice

¼ cup blue cheese crumbles (about 1 ounce) (omit for dairy-free)

¼ cup chopped green onions

¼ cup sliced red onions or Lime-Marinated Red Onions (page 81)

1 avocado, peeled, pitted, and sliced (optional)

Dressing of choice, for serving

1. Generously season the steak on both sides with salt and pepper. Let the steak sit in the seasoning for 15 minutes, then pat dry with a paper towel.

2. Melt the butter in a skillet over medium-high heat. Once melted, add the steak and cook for 5 to 6 minutes per side for medium-rare, or until cooked to your liking. Cut the steak into slices.

3. Place 3 cups of the salad greens in each of four bowls. Top the greens with the sliced steak, blue cheese crumbles, green and red onions, and avocado slices, if using. Drizzle the dressing over the salad and serve.

HOT SPINACH AND BACON SALAD

YIELD: 4 servings

PREP TIME: 5 minutes

COOK TIME: 15 minutes

   This is one of my favorite summertime salads. My mom always used to make it, and just the smell reminds me of home. The dressing is warm, so it lightly wilts the spinach after you add it. The traditional version of this dressing has sugar in it, but I don't miss the sweetness at all.

6 strips bacon

8 ounces fresh spinach

3 to 4 green onions

¼ cup red wine vinegar

1. In a large skillet over medium-low heat, fry the bacon until crispy, about 10 minutes.

2. While the bacon cooks, place half of the spinach in a large serving bowl. Chop the green onions and add them to the spinach.

3. Remove the bacon to a paper towel–lined plate to drain, leaving the bacon grease in the skillet.

4. Reduce the heat to the lowest possible setting and carefully pour in the vinegar. Whisk to combine the vinegar with the bacon grease.

5. Top the salad with the warm dressing. Toss, then add the rest of the spinach to the bowl and toss again. Crumble the bacon, then top the dressed salad with the crumbled bacon and serve.

GEORGE'S SOUP

YIELD: 6 servings

PREP TIME: 25 minutes

COOK TIME: 8 hours 20 minutes

  This is my husband's favorite soup. He loves breakfast sausage and would have it at every meal if he could, so naturally it had to go into this soup!

2 tablespoons salted butter or avocado oil

3 large bell peppers (any color), chopped

3 large yellow or white onions, chopped

4 cloves garlic, chopped

2 tablespoons pink Himalayan salt

2 tablespoons Italian seasoning

3 pounds bulk breakfast sausage

1 cup red wine or chicken bone broth, for deglazing (see Tip)

4 large tomatoes, sliced

½ cup halved cherry tomatoes

4 cups chicken bone broth

SPECIAL EQUIPMENT:

6-quart slow cooker

1. In a Dutch oven or other heavy-bottomed pot, melt the butter. Add the peppers, onions, garlic, salt, and Italian seasoning and sauté until the vegetables are soft, about 7 minutes. Transfer the vegetable mixture to a 6-quart slow cooker.

2. In the same pot, brown the sausage over medium heat, about 10 minutes. Use a wooden spoon or spatula to crumble the sausage as it cooks.

3. When the sausage is fully cooked, drain the excess fat and transfer the meat to the slow cooker with the vegetables.

4. Deglaze the pot with the red wine, scraping the bottom of the pot to lift up all the browned bits. Pour the wine into the slow cooker.

5. Add the tomatoes and broth, cover, and cook on low for 8 hours. Serve!

TIP: Deglazing is the process of adding liquid to a pan and scraping up the stuck-on bits from the bottom of the pan. I do it with a wooden spoon. Those stuck-on bits melt back into the liquid and add tons of flavor!

GRILLED ROMAINE SALAD

YIELD: 4 servings

PREP TIME: 10 minutes
(not including time to make
marinated onions)

COOK TIME: 3 minutes

  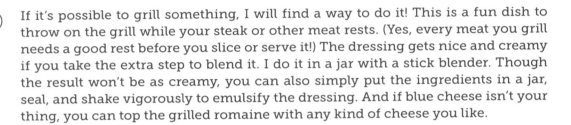

OPTION

If it's possible to grill something, I will find a way to do it! This is a fun dish to throw on the grill while your steak or other meat rests. (Yes, every meat you grill needs a good rest before you slice or serve it!) The dressing gets nice and creamy if you take the extra step to blend it. I do it in a jar with a stick blender. Though the result won't be as creamy, you can also simply put the ingredients in a jar, seal, and shake vigorously to emulsify the dressing. And if blue cheese isn't your thing, you can top the grilled romaine with any kind of cheese you like.

FOR THE DRESSING:

½ cup olive oil

¼ cup balsamic vinegar

1 tablespoon Italian seasoning

½ teaspoon pink Himalayan salt

¼ teaspoon prepared mustard
(any type)

FOR THE SALAD:

4 romaine hearts

2 tablespoons olive oil

½ cup blue cheese crumbles
(2 ounces) (omit for dairy-free)

⅓ cup Lime-Marinated Red
Onions (page 81) or sliced red
onions

1. Preheat an outdoor grill or grill pan to medium heat.

2. Meanwhile, make the dressing and prepare the romaine. To make the dressing, place the olive oil, balsamic vinegar, Italian seasoning, salt, and mustard in a blender or blender cup and blend until creamy. Set aside.

3. Cut the romaine hearts in half lengthwise to make eight long pieces. Brush the cut sides lightly with the oil.

4. Place the romaine cut side down on the hot grill or grill pan and cook for about 3 minutes, until lightly browned and slightly wilted. (If you're using a grill pan, you will likely need to work in two batches.)

5. Remove the romaine to a large plate or serving platter and top with the dressing, blue cheese crumbles, and red onions. Store any extra dressing in the refrigerator for up to 4 days.

BREAKFAST COBB SALAD

YIELD: 4 servings

PREP TIME: 15 minutes
(not including time to cook
sausage, bacon, or eggs)

A salad is a great way to switch up your breakfast routine! The beauty of this salad is that it uses up some of your favorite leftover keto foods. You can batch-cook all the ingredients and serve them in different ways. The creamy dressing can be made with just a spoon and a bowl, but if you want to whip it up really fast, break out the stick blender. Bonus: The dressing is dairy-free!

FOR THE DRESSING:

½ avocado, pitted and peeled

3 tablespoons olive oil

2 tablespoons red wine vinegar

2 tablespoons water

1 tablespoon chopped fresh dill, or 1 teaspoon dried dill

1 tablespoon lime juice

1 teaspoon pink Himalayan salt

FOR THE SALAD:

12 cups finely chopped romaine lettuce or other salad greens of choice

4 breakfast sausage links, cooked and sliced

4 strips bacon, cooked and crumbled

4 hard-boiled eggs, peeled and sliced

6 ounces cheese of choice, cubed (omit for dairy-free)

4 medium radishes, sliced

½ avocado, peeled, pitted, and sliced

1. Put all the dressing ingredients in a blender or blender cup and blend well. Set aside.

2. Divide the lettuce evenly among four bowls. Top the lettuce in each bowl with one-fourth of the sausage, bacon, eggs, cheese, radishes, and avocado slices.

3. Just before serving, drizzle the dressing over the salad.

HOT AND SMOKY WEDGE SALAD

YIELD: 4 servings

PREP TIME: 15 minutes (not including time to make marinated onions or cook bacon)

As a blue cheese lover, this is my favorite salad ever, and I would always order it at restaurants before I went keto. Now I make my dressings at home with healthy keto ingredients, so I make this recipe often. If you want to serve this salad for a dinner party, you can make everything ahead of time and even plate it, then add the dressing and bacon right before serving.

1 head iceberg lettuce

¾ cup blue cheese dressing, store-bought or homemade (page 83)

1 tablespoon chipotle powder

4 strips bacon, cooked and crumbled

¼ cup blue cheese crumbles (about 1 ounce)

¼ cup Lime-Marinated Red Onions (page 81)

1. Slice the head of lettuce into quarters and place on four plates.

2. In a small bowl, mix together the blue cheese dressing and chipotle powder. Drizzle the dressing over the lettuce wedges.

3. Top each salad with one-fourth of the bacon, blue cheese crumbles, and marinated onions. Serve immediately.

TACO SOUP

YIELD: 6 servings

PREP TIME: 15 minutes

COOK TIME: 55 minutes

OPTION

Every day should be taco Tuesday! When you want delicious tacos but are also feeling like soup, this is the perfect dish. It's a little less labor-intensive than preparing tacos from scratch, and it makes amazing leftovers.

When you are shopping for items like diced tomatoes and taco seasoning, take an extra second to survey the options your grocery store offers. I found some great flavor combinations in the diced tomatoes, including a fire-roasted variety. It can add another level of flavor to your soup with no extra effort. As for taco seasoning, check the ingredients, as some products contain corn or rice flour—*no bueno!*

1 pound ground beef

1 tablespoon taco seasoning, store-bought or homemade (page 79)

2 strips bacon, chopped

1 medium white onion, diced

1 medium yellow onion, diced

1 to 2 jalapeño peppers, seeded and diced

1 teaspoon pink Himalayan salt

1 (14½-ounce) can diced tomatoes

2 cups beef or chicken bone broth

TOPPINGS (OPTIONAL):

Full-fat sour cream (or dairy-free sour cream for dairy-free)

Shredded cheese of choice (omit for dairy-free)

Chopped fresh cilantro

Red onion slices

Avocado slices

Jalapeño slices

Lime slices

1. Put the ground beef and taco seasoning in a large skillet over medium heat. Cook, crumbling the meat with a wooden spoon or spatula as it cooks, for about 15 minutes, until browned. Drain the excess fat and set aside.

2. Place the chopped bacon, white and yellow onions, jalapeños, and salt in a Dutch oven or other heavy-bottomed pot. Cook over medium heat for 10 minutes, or until the bacon is fully cooked and the onions are soft.

3. Add the seasoned ground beef, tomatoes, and broth to the pot. Simmer with the lid ajar for 20 minutes.

4. Serve with your favorite taco toppings.

LIME SLAW

   This slaw serves as the base for every taco bowl I make. The lime flavor adds the perfect taco pizazz to any fixin's you can dream up. Cabbage retains its crunch, too, so you won't miss the taco shell! This slaw just gets better over time as the lime juice and salt really seep into the cabbage.

½ teaspoon grated lime zest

½ cup lime juice (2 to 3 large limes)

2 tablespoons avocado oil

2 teaspoons pink Himalayan salt

1 head cabbage, thinly sliced

¼ cup chopped fresh cilantro

1. Place the lime zest, lime juice, avocado oil, and salt in a small bowl and whisk to combine.

2. Place the cabbage and cilantro in a large bowl, top with the dressing, and toss to coat. Cover and place in the refrigerator for at least 30 minutes to give the flavors time to meld. Serve!

FRENCH ONION SOUP

OPTION

I love a good French onion soup! To get my cheese to "float" on top, I ladle some soup into a small oven-safe bowl or mug and lay the cheese over the top. Then under the broiler it goes!

2 cups sliced yellow onions (about 2 medium onions)

2 cloves garlic, minced

2 tablespoons salted butter or ghee (or avocado oil for dairy-free)

1 tablespoon balsamic vinegar

1 teaspoon pink Himalayan salt

4 cups beef bone broth

1 tablespoon Italian seasoning or dried thyme leaves

¾ cup shredded Gruyère cheese (about 3 ounces) (omit for dairy-free)

SPECIAL EQUIPMENT:

6-quart Instant Pot or electric pressure cooker

1. Place the onions, garlic, butter, balsamic vinegar, and salt in a 6-quart Instant Pot. Seal the lid, press Manual or Pressure Cook, and set the timer for 10 minutes. After 10 minutes, let the pressure release naturally.

2. Remove the lid, add the broth and Italian seasoning, and stir.

3. Reseal the lid, press Manual or Pressure Cook, and set the timer for 12 minutes. After 12 minutes, let the pressure release naturally.

4. Remove the lid and ladle the soup into four oven-safe soup bowls or mugs.

5. If adding the cheese, turn on the oven broiler. Top the soup with the cheese. Place the bowls on a rimmed baking sheet and broil for 5 minutes to melt the cheese. Serve immediately.

ARUGULA CAESAR SALAD

YIELD: 4 servings

PREP TIME: 5 minutes, plus 30 minutes for dressing to sit (not including time to make Crispy Mushrooms)

This recipe is a little twist on the classic Caesar salad. You can use any salad greens you like, but arugula adds a peppery flavor that pairs well with the Caesar dressing. You can use all arugula or mix in some romaine lettuce for extra crunch. Instead of the crispy croutons you're used to, try Crispy Mushrooms.

FOR THE DRESSING:

½ cup mayonnaise

½ teaspoon anchovy paste

1 clove garlic, minced

1 tablespoon lemon juice

¼ teaspoon apple cider vinegar

1 teaspoon Dijon mustard

⅓ cup grated Pecorino Romano or Parmesan cheese (about 1¼ ounces), plus more for topping

Pinch of pink Himalayan salt and ground black pepper

8 to 10 loosely packed cups arugula and/or romaine lettuce

Crispy Mushrooms (page 90), for topping (optional)

Lemon slices, for garnish (optional)

1. In a large salad bowl, whisk all the dressing ingredients together. Set aside for at least 30 minutes to allow the flavors to combine, or make the dressing in a smaller bowl the day before and refrigerate overnight.

2. Add the arugula to the bowl with the dressing and toss to coat. The salad tastes best if you let it sit for a few minutes, then toss it again.

3. Divide the dressed salad evenly among four plates. Top with additional cheese and the crispy mushrooms, if using, then garnish each salad with a lemon slice, if desired. Serve!

BURGERS and PIZZA

Triple Onion Burgers | *180*

Balsamic Onion, Truffle, and Arugula Burgers | *182*

Southwest Burgers | *184*

Fontina Burgers | *186*

Rosemary, Mushroom, and Swiss Burgers | *188*

Garlic Tomato Burgers | *190*

Onion Horsey Burgers | *192*

Asian-Style Burgers | *194*

Crispy Mushroom and Blue Cheese Burgers | *196*

Jalapeño Popper Pizza | *198*

Spicy Chicken Pizza | *200*

Prosciutto Arugula Pizza | *202*

White Pizza | *204*

Sausage and Provolone Pizza | *206*

Blue Cheese and Sausage Pizza | *208*

TRIPLE ONION BURGERS

YIELD: 4 servings

PREP TIME: 10 minutes
(not including time to make
caramelized onions or aioli)

COOK TIME: 14 minutes

The perfect burger for onion lovers! This recipe uses both fresh and caramelized onions for extra oomph. Adding the onions while the burgers are cooking takes just a bit of the edge off the flavor while leaving some of the sharpness that raw onions have. The Mustard Seed Aioli adds extra fat along with its own delicious flavor!

1 pound ground beef

Pink Himalayan salt and ground black pepper

¼ cup diced white or yellow onions

2 ounces cheddar cheese, sliced (omit for dairy-free)

8 lettuce leaves, for buns, or 4 Seeded Hamburger Buns (page 96)

1 batch Mustard Seed Aioli (page 84)

1 cup Caramelized Onions (page 88)

1. Preheat a cast-iron skillet or outdoor grill for 5 minutes over medium heat. While the pan or grill heats up, divide the ground beef into 4 equal portions and shape each portion into a patty about ½ inch thick. Sprinkle both sides of the patties generously with salt and pepper.

2. Place the patties in the skillet or on the grill and cook to your liking. Depending on the thickness of the patties, 5 to 7 minutes on each side should give you medium-done burgers. After flipping, top the burgers with equal portions of the raw onions and cheese.

3. Once the burgers are cooked to your liking and the cheese has melted, place each burger on a lettuce "bun." Top with the aioli and caramelized onions and serve!

INGREDIENT SPOTLIGHT:

There are tons of ways to serve your burgers instead of using typical buns! You can wrap them in large lettuce leaves; butter lettuce is a great choice. You can also use cabbage leaves, which are little sturdier but can add an unwanted flavor in some situations. You can also take a head of iceberg lettuce and cut "steaks" right off the top to make large lettuce buns. You can even use portabella mushrooms! Or, if you're like me, you can just go plain fork and knife.

TIP: When forming the patties, I make them on the thin side—about ½ inch thick. This does a couple of things: A wider patty will shrink down to the perfect size when cooked, and the cooking time is reduced, so you can eat sooner. Try to flip the patties only once, then add the cheese right after flipping so it gets very melted!

BALSAMIC ONION, TRUFFLE, AND ARUGULA BURGERS

YIELD: 4 servings

PREP TIME: 10 minutes (not including time to make buns or cook bacon)

COOK TIME: 24 minutes

For a special night in, take a little extra care with dinner. While this meal takes a few minutes longer to put together than a plain old cheeseburger, the flavor bomb you get from the balsamic onions is worth the extra five minutes it takes to cook them!

1 pound ground beef

Pink Himalayan salt and ground black pepper

½ medium white onion, thinly sliced

¼ cup balsamic vinegar

1 teaspoon avocado oil or olive oil

¼ cup mayonnaise

2 teaspoons truffle-infused olive oil

2 ounces cheddar cheese, sliced (omit for dairy-free)

FOR SERVING:

4 Seeded Hamburger Buns (page 96), or 8 lettuce leaves, for buns

8 strips center-cut bacon, cooked

½ cup arugula

1. Preheat a cast-iron skillet or outdoor grill for 5 minutes over medium heat. While the pan or grill heats up, divide the ground beef into 4 equal portions and shape each portion into a patty about ½ inch thick. Sprinkle both sides of the patties generously with salt and pepper and set aside.

2. Make the balsamic onions: Place the onion, balsamic vinegar, and oil in a small skillet over medium-low heat and toss. Cook the onion until soft, 5 to 10 minutes.

3. Make the truffle mayo: In a small bowl, mix together the mayonnaise and truffle oil. Set aside.

4. Place the patties in the cast-iron skillet or on the grill and cook to your liking. Depending on the thickness of the patties, 5 to 7 minutes on each side should give you medium-done burgers. After flipping, top the burgers with equal portions of the cheese.

5. Once the burgers are cooked to your liking and the cheese has melted, place each burger on a bun. Top with some balsamic onions, 2 strips of bacon, 2 tablespoons of arugula, and 1 tablespoon of truffle mayo. Serve!

SOUTHWEST BURGERS

If you love tacos but want to change things up, this is your burger. If you have salsa on hand, you can sub it in instead of chopping the red onions, tomatoes, and cilantro. I always add lime juice for that extra fresh taco taste, though!

1 pound ground beef

Pink Himalayan salt and ground black pepper

1 tablespoon taco seasoning, store-bought or homemade (page 79)

½ cup chopped red onions

½ cup chopped fresh tomatoes

¼ cup chopped fresh cilantro leaves

2 tablespoons lime juice

¼ cup full-fat sour cream (or dairy-free sour cream or mayonnaise for dairy-free)

2 tablespoons ranch seasoning

2 ounces sharp cheddar cheese, sliced (omit for dairy-free)

8 lettuce leaves, for buns, or 4 Seeded Hamburger Buns (page 96)

1. Preheat a cast-iron skillet or outdoor grill for 5 minutes over medium heat. While the pan or grill heats up, divide the ground beef into 4 equal portions and shape each portion into a patty about ½ inch thick. Sprinkle both sides of the patties generously with salt and pepper, season both sides with the taco seasoning, and set aside.

2. In a small bowl, combine the onions, tomatoes, cilantro, and lime juice. Set aside.

3. In another small bowl, mix the sour cream with the ranch seasoning and set aside.

4. Place the patties in the skillet or on the grill and cook to your liking. Depending on the thickness of the patties, 5 to 7 minutes on each side should give you medium-done burgers. After flipping, top the burgers with equal portions of the cheese.

5. Once the burgers are cooked to your liking and the cheese has melted, place each burger on a lettuce "bun." Top with the ranch sour cream and the onion mixture. Serve!

FONTINA BURGERS

YIELD: 4 servings

PREP TIME: 10 minutes (not including time to make buns)

COOK TIME: 19 minutes

  You may not have fontina cheese sitting in your fridge right now, but you should! It melts amazingly well and has a fondue-like texture.

1 pound ground beef

Pink Himalayan salt and ground black pepper

¼ cup Dijon mustard

1 teaspoon freshly grated horseradish (see Ingredient Spotlight)

1 tablespoon salted butter

2 shallots, thinly sliced

2 ounces fontina cheese, sliced

FOR SERVING:

4 Seeded Hamburger Buns (page 96), or 8 lettuce leaves, for buns

½ cup baby arugula

INGREDIENT SPOTLIGHT:

Buy horseradish root whole if possible. It is a large funky-looking root that can be found in most grocery stores, but you may have to ask for help to find it. Peel it with a vegetable peeler and then grate a little at a time. A little goes a looooooong way! Wrap it well and store the root in the freezer for next time.

1. Preheat a cast-iron skillet or outdoor grill for 5 minutes over medium heat. While the pan or grill heats up, divide the ground beef into 4 equal portions and shape each portion into a patty about ½ inch thick. Sprinkle both sides of the patties generously with salt and pepper and set aside.

2. Make the mustard horseradish sauce: In a small bowl, mix together the mustard and horseradish. Set aside.

3. Melt the butter in a small skillet over medium heat. Once melted, add the sliced shallots and fry until golden brown, about 4 minutes. Remove the shallots from the pan and set aside.

4. Place the patties in the cast-iron skillet or on the grill and cook to your liking. Depending on the thickness of the patties, 5 to 7 minutes on each side should give you medium-done burgers. After flipping, top the burgers with equal portions of the cheese.

5. Once the burgers are cooked to your liking and the cheese has melted, place each burger on a bun. Top with fried shallots, mustard horseradish sauce, and 2 tablespoons of arugula. Serve!

ROSEMARY, MUSHROOM, AND SWISS BURGERS

YIELD: 4 burgers

PREP TIME: 5 minutes

COOK TIME: 24 minutes

OPTION

A classic flavor combination for a burger. Mushrooms and Swiss go together like PB&J.

1 pound ground beef

Pink Himalayan salt and ground black pepper

2 tablespoons salted butter

½ teaspoon chopped fresh rosemary leaves

8 ounces cremini mushrooms, sliced

½ teaspoon pink Himalayan salt

2 ounces Swiss cheese, sliced

8 lettuce leaves, for buns, or 4 Seeded Hamburger Buns (page 96)

1. Preheat a cast-iron skillet or outdoor grill for 5 minutes over medium heat. While the pan or grill heats up, divide the ground beef into 4 equal portions and shape each portion into a patty about ½ inch thick. Sprinkle both sides of the patties generously with salt and pepper.

2. Place the patties in the skillet or on the grill and cook to your liking. Depending on the thickness of the patties, 5 to 7 minutes on each side should give you medium-done burgers. After flipping, top the burgers with equal portions of the cheese.

3. Once the burgers are cooked to your liking and the cheese has melted, remove the burgers to a plate.

4. In another skillet over medium-low heat, melt the butter with the rosemary. Add the sliced mushrooms and sprinkle with the salt. Cook for 8 to 10 minutes, until the mushrooms are soft.

5. Place each burger on a lettuce "bun" and top with some of the mushrooms. Serve!

GARLIC TOMATO BURGERS

YIELD: 4 servings

PREP TIME: 10 minutes (not including time to make buns)

COOK TIME: 19 minutes

OPTION OPTION

Warmed fresh tomatoes on a burger are literally the taste of summer. This delicious burger will become your new favorite summer griller!

1 pound ground beef

Pink Himalayan salt and ground black pepper

2 Roma or other medium-sized tomatoes, sliced

¼ teaspoon garlic powder

¼ teaspoon pink Himalayan salt

¼ cup chopped fresh basil

2 ounces mozzarella cheese, sliced (omit for dairy-free)

4 slices prosciutto

1 cup chopped lettuce of choice, for topping the burgers (optional)

4 Seeded Hamburger Buns (page 96), or 8 lettuce leaves, for buns

1. Preheat a cast-iron skillet or outdoor grill for 5 minutes over medium heat. While the pan or grill heats up, divide the ground beef into 4 equal portions and shape each portion into a patty about ½ inch thick. Sprinkle both sides of the patties generously with salt and pepper.

2. Place the patties in the skillet or on the grill and cook to your liking. Depending on the thickness of the patties, 5 to 7 minutes on each side should give you medium-done burgers. After flipping, top the burgers with equal portions of the basil and then the cheese.

3. While the burgers are cooking, lay the sliced tomatoes on a plate and season with the garlic powder and salt. Set aside.

4. Once the burgers are cooked to your liking and the cheese has melted, remove the burgers to a plate. Add the prosciutto to the skillet (or, if you used an outdoor grill, place the prosciutto in a skillet) and cook over medium heat for 5 minutes, or until crisp.

5. Place each burger on a bun and top with the garlic tomatoes, crisp prosciutto, and lettuce (if using). Serve!

ONION HORSEY BURGERS

YIELD: 4 servings

PREP TIME: 10 minutes (not including time to make dip)

COOK TIME: 14 minutes

OPTION OPTION

If you once loved a beef and cheddar sandwich with horseradish, this burger is for you. Adding a little freshly grated horseradish to my onion dip takes no extra time, but the flavor is just a bit hot, balanced with a little sweet onion! If you like things extra horsey, add more horseradish to taste.

1 pound ground beef

Pink Himalayan salt and ground black pepper

½ cup Caramelized Onion Dip (page 104)

1 teaspoon freshly grated horseradish (see Ingredient Spotlight, page 186)

2 ounces white cheddar cheese, sliced (omit for dairy-free)

8 lettuce leaves, for buns, or 4 Seeded Hamburger Buns (page 96)

1. Preheat a cast-iron skillet or outdoor grill for 5 minutes over medium heat. While the pan or grill heats up, divide the ground beef into 4 equal portions and shape each portion into a patty about ½ inch thick. Sprinkle both sides of the patties generously with salt and pepper and set aside.

2. In a small bowl, combine the onion dip and horseradish.

3. Place the patties in the skillet or on the grill and cook to your liking. Depending on thickness of the patties, 5 to 7 minutes on each side should give you medium-done burgers. After flipping, top the burgers with equal portions of the cheese.

4. Once the burgers are cooked to your liking and the cheese has melted, place each burger on a lettuce "bun." Top with the onion horseradish sauce and serve!

NOTE: In addition to omitting the cheese for dairy-free burgers, be sure to make the caramelized onions for the dip dairy-free as well.

ASIAN-STYLE BURGERS

YIELD: 4 servings

PREP TIME: 10 minutes (not including time to make buns)

COOK TIME: 14 minutes

OPTION OPTION

If you've never had kimchi on a burger, you are missing out! It adds a little heat and gives your gut a nice dose of healthy probiotics. If you don't usually like fermented foods, this is a great way to give kimchi a try.

1 pound ground beef

Pink Himalayan salt and ground black pepper

¼ cup mayonnaise

1 teaspoon Sriracha sauce

2 ounces sharp cheddar cheese, sliced (omit for dairy-free)

4 Seeded Hamburger Buns (page 96), or 8 lettuce leaves, for buns

¼ cup kimchi

¼ cup matchstick-chopped radishes

¼ cup chopped fresh cilantro

1. Preheat a cast-iron skillet or outdoor grill for 5 minutes over medium heat. While the pan or grill heats up, divide the ground beef into 4 equal portions and shape each portion into a patty about ½ inch thick. Sprinkle both sides of the patties generously with salt and pepper and set aside.

2. In a small bowl, mix together the mayonnaise and Sriracha. Set aside.

3. Place the patties in the skillet or on the grill and cook to your liking. Depending on the thickness of the patties, 5 to 7 minutes on each side should give you medium-done burgers. After flipping, top the burgers with equal portions of the cheese.

4. Once the burgers are cooked to your liking and the cheese has melted, place each burger on a bun and top with some Sriracha mayo, kimchi, radishes, and cilantro. Serve!

CRISPY MUSHROOM AND BLUE CHEESE BURGERS

YIELD: 4 servings

PREP TIME: 10 minutes (not including time to make blue cheese butter or Crispy Mushrooms)

COOK TIME: 14 minutes

OPTION

This burger combines a few recipes from the book. It's a perfect way to use up the leftovers from those recipes.

1 pound ground beef

Pink Himalayan salt and ground black pepper

¼ cup Beyond Basic Blue Cheese Butter (page 75)

8 lettuce leaves, for buns, or 4 Seeded Hamburger Buns (page 96)

1 cup Crispy Mushrooms (page 90)

1. Preheat a cast-iron skillet or outdoor grill for 5 minutes over medium heat. While the pan or grill heats up, divide the ground beef into 4 equal portions and shape each portion into a patty about ½ inch thick. Sprinkle both sides of the patties generously with salt and pepper.

2. Place the patties in the skillet or on the grill and cook to your liking. Depending on the thickness of the patties, 5 to 7 minutes on each side should give you medium-done burgers. After flipping, top the burgers with equal portions of the blue cheese butter.

3. Once the burgers are cooked to your liking, place each burger on a lettuce "bun." Top with the crispy mushrooms and serve!

JALAPEÑO POPPER PIZZA

YIELD: one 8- to 9-inch pizza (1 to 2 servings)

PREP TIME: 10 minutes (not including time to make crust)

COOK TIME: 15 minutes

 My husband loves spicy food, especially jalapeño poppers! Whenever we go out to a restaurant that serves something popper related, he has to try it. That's where I got the idea for this pizza. For the best results, make sure to preheat a pizza stone or baking sheet on the middle rack of your oven.

2 strips bacon

4 ounces bulk Italian sausage

1 Psyllium Husk Pizza Crust (page 92), par-baked

1 to 2 tablespoons full-fat cream cheese, room temperature

½ jalapeño pepper, seeded and sliced (see Tips)

¼ cup shredded mozzarella cheese (about 1 ounce)

1. In a large skillet over medium heat, fry the bacon until crispy, about 6 minutes. Then crumble the bacon.

2. Pour out the excess fat from the skillet, leaving about 1 tablespoon in the pan.

3. Add the sausage to the skillet and cook for 10 minutes, or until cooked through. Use a wooden spoon or spatula to crumble the sausage as it cooks.

4. Place a pizza stone or baking sheet on the middle rack of the oven and turn on the oven broiler (see Tips).

5. Spread the cream cheese on the pizza crust; a small spatula works perfectly for this task. The warmer the cream cheese, the easier it is to spread.

6. Top the cream cheese with the jalapeño slices, crumbled bacon, and cooked sausage. Then sprinkle the cheese on top.

7. Place the pizza on the pizza stone and broil for about 5 minutes, until the cheese is melted. Watch carefully to prevent burning.

8. Remove the pizza from the oven, cut into slices, and serve!

TIPS: I keep a box of disposable latex gloves in my kitchen for chopping hot peppers. Otherwise, the oils get on your fingers, and if you rub your eye, nose, or mouth, you could be in for an evening of pain!

When using the oven broiler to make pizza, you will get better results if you turn on the oven a few minutes before the pizza goes in. This is essentially preheating the oven, so when you broil the pizza, the cheese melts quickly and the toppings warm up evenly.

SPICY CHICKEN PIZZA

YIELD: one 8- to 9-inch pizza
(1 to 2 servings)

PREP TIME: 10 minutes (not
including time to make crust
or cook chicken)

COOK TIME: 5 minutes

 Pizza is a perfect way to use up leftovers. Here, you take leftover chicken and turn it into the star of a new dish!

1½ teaspoons olive oil

1 Psyllium Husk Pizza Crust (page 92), par-baked

½ teaspoon red pepper flakes

½ cup chopped cooked chicken

¼ cup finely diced cremini mushrooms

½ cup shredded mozzarella cheese (about 2 ounces)

2 tablespoons grated Parmesan cheese

¼ cup chopped fresh spinach

1. Place a pizza stone or baking sheet on the middle rack of the oven and turn on the oven broiler.

2. Spread the olive oil on the pizza crust with a silicone basting brush. Sprinkle the red pepper flakes on the oiled crust and top with the chicken, mushrooms, and cheeses.

3. Place the pizza on the pizza stone and broil for about 5 minutes, until the cheese is melted. Watch carefully to prevent burning.

4. Open the oven door. Before removing the pizza from the oven, top with the chopped spinach. The heat of the pizza will wilt the spinach slightly.

5. Remove the pizza from the oven, cut into slices, and serve!

PROSCIUTTO ARUGULA PIZZA

YIELD: one 8- to 9-inch pizza
(1 to 2 servings)

PREP TIME: 10 minutes (not
including time to make crust)

COOK TIME: 15 minutes

 Savory prosciutto paired with the peppery punch of arugula is a beloved pizza topping combination!

1 tablespoon garlic-infused olive oil

1 Psyllium Husk Pizza Crust (page 92), par-baked

2 slices prosciutto

⅓ cup shredded mozzarella cheese (about 1⅓ ounces)

¼ cup arugula

1 teaspoon balsamic vinegar, for drizzling

1. Place a pizza stone or baking sheet on the middle rack of the oven and turn on the oven broiler.

2. Using a silicone basting brush, spread the olive oil on the pizza crust.

3. Cut the prosciutto into bite-sized pieces; the smaller the pieces, the crispier they will get when cooked. Top the oiled crust with the cheese and prosciutto.

4. Place the pizza on the pizza stone and broil for about 5 minutes, until the cheese is melted. Watch carefully to prevent burning.

5. Open the oven door. Before removing the pizza from the oven, top with the arugula and drizzle with the balsamic vinegar. The heat of the pizza will wilt the arugula slightly.

6. Remove the pizza from the oven, cut into slices, and serve!

WHITE PIZZA

YIELD: one 8- to 9-inch pizza
(1 to 2 servings)

PREP TIME: 15 minutes (not including time to make crust)

COOK TIME: 15 minutes

 I don't really care for tomatoes, so I seldom ate pizza growing up. Everything changed when I discovered white pizza. Now I can't live without it!

1 tablespoon salted butter

2 tablespoons minced shallots or yellow onions

1 clove garlic, minced

¼ cup heavy cream

1 Psyllium Husk Pizza Crust (page 92), par-baked

½ cup shredded mozzarella cheese (about 2 ounces)

2 tablespoons grated Parmesan cheese

¼ cup chopped fresh broccoli

2 teaspoons balsamic vinegar, for drizzling (optional)

1. In a medium-sized skillet, melt the butter over medium heat. Add the shallots and garlic and sauté for 5 minutes, until the shallots are soft.

2. Reduce the heat to medium-low and slowly pour in the heavy cream. Whisk continuously until the sauce is thick, 2 to 3 minutes.

3. Place a pizza stone or baking sheet on the middle rack of the oven and turn on the oven broiler.

4. Spread the sauce on the pizza crust. Top with the cheeses and broccoli.

5. Place the pizza on the pizza stone and broil for about 5 minutes, until the cheese is melted. Watch carefully to prevent burning.

6. Remove the pizza from the oven and drizzle with the balsamic vinegar, if using. Cut into slices and enjoy!

SAUSAGE AND PROVOLONE PIZZA

YIELD: one 8- to 9-inch pizza
(1 to 2 servings)

PREP TIME: 10 minutes (not
including time to make crust
or cook sausage)

COOK TIME: 8 minutes

 My mouth waters just thinking about this pizza! Leeks and shallots are absolutely delicious on pizza. They have all that oniony taste, but not the spicy zing that a white onion has. Their more delicate flavor is the perfect pairing for provolone cheese, which has the most delicious flavor and melts beautifully!

1 tablespoon salted butter

¼ cup thinly sliced leeks

1 tablespoon thinly sliced shallots

1 tablespoon tomato sauce or marinara sauce

1 Psyllium Husk Pizza Crust (page 92), par-baked

¼ cup cooked and crumbled hot Italian sausage

¼ green bell pepper, chopped

2 ounces provolone cheese, sliced or shredded

¼ cup shredded mozzarella cheese (about 1 ounce)

1. Place a pizza stone or baking sheet on the middle rack of the oven and turn on the oven broiler.

2. In a medium-sized skillet, melt the butter over medium heat. Add the leeks and shallots and cook for 3 minutes, until softened.

3. Spread the tomato sauce on the pizza crust with a silicone basting brush, then layer the sausage, green pepper, cheeses, and finally the cooked leek and shallot mixture on top of the sauce.

4. Place the pizza on the pizza stone and broil for about 5 minutes, until the cheese is melted. Watch carefully to prevent burning.

5. Remove the pizza from the oven, cut into slices, and serve!

BLUE CHEESE AND SAUSAGE PIZZA

YIELD: one 8- to 9-inch pizza
(1 to 2 servings)

PREP TIME: 10 minutes (not
including time to make crust
or cook sausage)

COOK TIME: 5 minutes

 A pizza for the blue cheese lover! If you adore blue cheese but have never had it on pizza, you're really missing out. It packs a powerful punch of flavor and melts into the meaty umami taste of the sausage so well. Try it; you will love it!

1 tablespoon tomato sauce or marinara sauce

1 Psyllium Husk Pizza Crust (page 92), par-baked

⅓ cup cooked and crumbled mild Italian sausage

¼ cup chopped roasted red peppers

¼ cup blue cheese crumbles (about 1 ounce)

¼ cup shredded mozzarella cheese (about 1 ounce)

¼ cup chopped fresh basil

1. Place a pizza stone or baking sheet on the middle rack of the oven and turn on the oven broiler.

2. Spread the tomato sauce on the pizza crust with a silicone basting brush, then layer the sausage, red peppers, and cheeses on top of the sauce.

3. Place the pizza on the pizza stone and broil for about 5 minutes, until the cheese is melted. Watch carefully to prevent burning.

4. Open the oven door. Before removing the pizza from the oven, top with the chopped basil. The heat of the pizza will wilt the basil slightly.

5. Remove the pizza from the oven, cut into slices, and serve!

MAIN DISHES

Keto Pot Roast | *212*

Roast Leg of Lamb | *214*

Slow Cooker Rich Beef Shanks | *216*

Tri-Tip and Broccoli Bowls | *218*

Marinated Pork Loin | *220*

Chicken, Bacon, and Ranch–Stuffed Peppers | *222*

Pizza Baked Eggs | *224*

Marinated Flank Steak with Toasted Garlic | *226*

Everything Crusted Pork Chops | *228*

Perfect Baked Salmon | *230*

Salt and Pepper Chuck Steak with Blue Cheese Butter | *232*

Marinated Fried Chicken Strips | *234*

Reverse Sear Tri-Tip Roast | *236*

Crispy Baked Chicken | *238*

Lamb Rib Chops with Mushrooms | *240*

Simple Baked Cod | *242*

Cabbage, Sausage, and Pepper Sheet Pan Dinner | *244*

Perfect Roast Beef | *246*

Rib-Eye Steak with Shallots and Garlic | *248*

Greens and Ham Baked Eggs | *250*

Everyday Roasted Chicken | *252*

Butter-Basted New York Strip Steak | *254*

The Best Ever Grilled Cheese | *256*

Pork Belly | *258*

Chicken Cordon Bleu | *260*

Flank Steak with Charred Green Onions | *262*

Buffalo Baked Chicken | *264*

Steak Tacos | *266*

KETO POT ROAST

YIELD: 6 to 8 servings

PREP TIME: 45 minutes

COOK TIME: 3 hours 15 minutes

   Most pot roast recipes require a lot of work—cooking and removing the veggies first, then searing the roast, and finally adding everything back to the pot to cook in the oven. This keto recipe is another take on pot roast, cutting the number of steps way down and using delicious low-carb, nutrient-dense vegetables instead the usual high-carb ones.

1 (2- to 3-pound) boneless chuck roast

1 teaspoon pink Himalayan salt

½ teaspoon ground black pepper

3 tablespoons avocado oil

2 cups beef bone broth, plus more if needed

2 medium-sized red onions, peeled and quartered

2 cups halved radishes

1 cup sliced cremini mushrooms (about 8 ounces)

2 sprigs fresh rosemary

2 sprigs fresh thyme

Chopped fresh parsley, for garnish (optional)

SPECIAL EQUIPMENT:

Dutch oven

1. Take the chuck roast out of the refrigerator and let sit for 45 minutes to come to room temperature.

2. Preheat the oven to 275°F. Season the roast on all sides with the salt and pepper.

3. Heat the avocado oil in a Dutch oven over medium-high heat. Carefully place the roast in the hot oil and sear on all sides, 5 to 7 minutes per side.

4. Turn off the burner and pour in the broth. Use a wooden spoon to deglaze the pot, scraping any bits off the bottom.

5. Add the vegetables and herbs to the pot. The liquid should cover about half of the roast. Add more broth, if needed, and cover with the lid.

6. Place the pot in the oven and cook for 2 to 3 hours (1 hour per pound). The roast is done when a fork can be inserted without resistance.

7. Remove the roast and vegetables to a serving platter and tent with foil to keep warm. Discard the herb sprigs. Leave the cooking liquid in the pot.

8. To make a truly delicious au jus, place the pot back on the stovetop over medium-high heat. Boil the liquid, uncovered, for 20 to 30 minutes, until reduced and quite thick. Serve the au jus over the roast and vegetables. Garnish with parsley, if desired.

TIP: When I sear a large cut of meat, I use large barbecue tongs to turn the meat. They are stronger than normal tongs and keep me farther away from any splattering grease.

ROAST LEG OF LAMB

YIELD: 4 to 6 servings

PREP TIME: 45 minutes, plus 20 minutes to rest

COOK TIME: 45 minutes

 A simple rub takes a leg of lamb from bland and boring to flavorful and tender. The longer prep time here is really just for bringing the meat to room temperature before cooking; the rub comes together in just a minute!

1 (3-pound) bone-in leg of lamb

⅓ cup avocado oil

10 cloves garlic, peeled

2 tablespoons lemon juice

2 tablespoons pink Himalayan salt

2 teaspoons dried oregano leaves

1 teaspoon fresh mint leaves

1. Take the leg of lamb out of the refrigerator and let sit for 45 minutes to come to room temperature (see Tip).

2. Preheat the oven to 375°F.

3. Place the avocado oil, garlic, lemon juice, salt, oregano, and mint in a blender and blend until a paste forms. Spread the paste evenly all over the leg of lamb.

4. Place the lamb on a rimmed baking sheet or roasting pan. Roast until the internal temperature in the thickest part is 130°F for medium-rare, about 45 minutes.

5. Remove the pan from the oven and tent the lamb with aluminum foil. Allow to rest for at least 20 minutes before carving.

6. Slice the roast and serve!

TIP: For large roasts like this leg of lamb, you want give the meat a good amount of time to come to room temperature before cooking it. This ensures that the roast cooks evenly.

SLOW COOKER RICH BEEF SHANKS

YIELD: 4 to 6 servings

PREP TIME: 5 minutes, plus 20 minutes to rest

COOK TIME: 6 hours 40 minutes

OPTION

Beef shanks make the richest and most delicious broth you can imagine. Cooking this bone-in cut in a slow cooker gives you a tender and flavorful dinner that's hot and ready to eat when you get home.

4 beef shanks

Pink Himalayan salt and ground black pepper

2 tablespoons salted butter or avocado oil

2 cups diced yellow or white onions

4 cloves garlic, chopped

1 (14½-ounce) can diced tomatoes

SPECIAL EQUIPMENT:
6-quart slow cooker

1. Season the beef shanks generously on both sides with salt and pepper and set aside.

2. In a large skillet, heat the butter over medium-high heat. Working in batches, brown the shanks, 3 to 5 minutes on each side.

3. Place the shanks in a 6-quart slow cooker and top with the onions, garlic, and tomatoes.

4. Cook on low for 6 hours, or until the shanks are tender.

5. Serve the shanks and vegetables with some of the cooking liquid spooned over the top.

TRI-TIP AND BROCCOLI BOWLS

YIELD: 4 servings

PREP TIME: 15 minutes

COOK TIME: 23 minutes

  This is a great recipe to make over the weekend and eat for lunch all week. It reheats beautifully in the microwave or in a skillet on the stovetop.

Many tri-tip roasts come in one piece. To speed up the cooking, this recipe directs you to cut the roast in half. Make sure to include the toasted sesame oil; it really makes the flavor of this dish!

1 (1½-pound) tri-tip roast

2 tablespoons avocado oil

½ teaspoon pink Himalayan salt

½ teaspoon ground black pepper

2 tablespoons toasted sesame oil

1 clove garlic, minced

½ teaspoon freshly grated ginger

8 cups broccoli florets (about 12 ounces)

1 tablespoon sesame seeds, for garnish

Sliced green onions, for garnish (optional)

1. Preheat the oven to 300°F. Line a rimmed baking sheet with parchment paper.

2. Cut the tri-tip roast in half and place on the lined baking sheet. Brush the meat with the avocado oil and season on all sides with the salt and pepper.

3. Bake until the internal temperature is 110°F, about 20 minutes, depending on the thickness of the roast. (The meat will not be fully cooked at this point.) Set aside.

4. In a large bowl, combine the sesame oil, garlic, and ginger. Add the broccoli and toss to coat.

5. In a large skillet, sauté the broccoli over medium heat for 10 minutes, or until tender. Divide the broccoli evenly among four bowls.

6. Using the same skillet, sear the tri-tip roast halves over medium heat until browned, about 4 minutes per side. The internal temperature should be between 120°F and 130°F for medium-rare.

7. Slice the meat against the grain and add to the bowls with the broccoli. Before serving, top each bowl with sesame seeds and sliced green onions, if desired.

MARINATED PORK LOIN

YIELD: 4 servings

PREP TIME: 10 minutes, plus time to marinate overnight and 15 minutes to rest

COOK TIME: 30 minutes

Pork loin dries out very easily, so take the time to marinate it before cooking. I also cook mine with an oven-safe thermometer to prevent overcooking—140°F is about perfect to keep the meat tender. After cooking, as usual, tent the meat with foil before slicing so that all the juices don't run out.

FOR THE MARINADE:

½ cup lime juice

¼ cup avocado oil

1 teaspoon pink Himalayan salt

1 teaspoon prepared mustard (any type)

1 teaspoon freshly grated ginger

1 (3- to 4-pound) boneless pork loin roast

Chopped fresh parsley, for garnish (optional)

1. Place the marinade ingredients in a small bowl and whisk together.

2. Pour the marinade into a resealable plastic bag and add the pork loin. Seal and set in the refrigerator to marinate overnight.

3. When ready to cook the pork, preheat the oven to 400°F. Line a rimmed baking sheet with parchment paper.

4. Remove the pork from the marinade and place the roast on the lined baking sheet. Discard the marinade.

5. Bake the pork, uncovered, for 25 minutes, or until the internal temperature is 140°F. Turn on the oven broiler.

6. Broil the pork for about 5 minutes, until the outside of the roast develops a nice golden brown color.

7. Remove the roast from the oven, tent with aluminum foil, and let rest for at least 15 minutes before slicing and serving. Garnish with parsley, if desired.

TIP: Although pork loin dries out easily, you can reheat the leftovers. I like to use the Steam setting on my Instant Pot, placing the meat in a steamer basket over water. Then I set the timer for 10 minutes to warm the meat through.

CHICKEN, BACON, AND RANCH–STUFFED PEPPERS

YIELD: 4 servings

PREP TIME: 10 minutes (not including time to cook chicken or make dressing)

COOK TIME: 15 minutes

Back in my pre-keto days, my favorite sandwich was a toasted chicken bacon ranch with melted cheese. Heaven! I still enjoy these flavors, but I bake them right into a bell pepper instead. I get way more of the yummy stuff—the chicken, bacon, and cheese—and less of the stuff that doesn't add any flavor—the bread!

1 tablespoon olive oil

2 cups riced cauliflower

½ teaspoon pink Himalayan salt

¼ teaspoon ground black pepper

12 ounces chopped cooked chicken

1 cup cooked chopped bacon

½ cup Ranch Dressing (page 78)

4 red bell peppers

¾ cup shredded cheddar cheese (3 ounces)

1. Preheat the oven to 375°F. Line a rimmed baking sheet with parchment paper.

2. Heat the oil in a large skillet over medium heat. Add the riced cauliflower, salt, and black pepper and sauté for 2 minutes.

3. Remove the sautéed cauliflower to a large bowl and add the chicken, bacon, and ranch dressing. Mix to combine.

4. Cut each bell pepper in half vertically, removing the ribs and seeds. Place the bell pepper halves on the lined baking sheet and add a generous scoop of the chicken filling to each half.

5. Sprinkle the stuffed peppers with the shredded cheese and bake for 10 minutes.

6. Turn on the oven broiler and finish the peppers under the broiler for about 3 minutes to melt the cheese.

PIZZA BAKED EGGS

YIELD: 4 servings
PREP TIME: 15 minutes
COOK TIME: 12 minutes

 Pizza for breakfast! This dish is super easy to make; you can throw it together, pop it in the oven, and walk away. Add extra veggies or other meats as you'd like—the recipe is totally customizable.

1 tablespoon salted butter or olive oil, for greasing the dish

1 red bell pepper, diced

½ cup chopped pepperoni (about 2½ ounces)

¼ cup tomato sauce

5 ounces mozzarella cheese

8 large eggs

½ teaspoon dried oregano leaves

¼ cup sliced black olives (optional)

1. Preheat the oven to 400°F. Grease a large baking dish (or four 8-ounce ramekins) with the butter.

2. Layer the bell pepper, pepperoni, and tomato sauce in the bottom of the baking dish or ramekins.

3. Shred about a quarter of the mozzarella and slice the rest. Lay the sliced cheese over the top of the tomato sauce.

4. Crack all the eggs into the baking dish (or 2 eggs into each ramekin) and sprinkle the oregano and shredded cheese over the top. Top with the olives, if using.

5. If using ramekins, place them on a rimmed baking sheet to make it easier to remove them from the oven.

6. Bake for 10 minutes, or until the egg whites are just set. Then turn on the oven broiler and broil for 1 to 2 minutes so that the cheese topping is extra bubbly and delicious!

7. Serve immediately, being careful when handling the very hot baking dish.

MARINATED FLANK STEAK WITH TOASTED GARLIC

YIELD: 2 to 3 servings

PREP TIME: 10 minutes, plus 1 hour to marinate

COOK TIME: 20 minutes

 Get your steak marinating for tonight's dinner! The toasted garlic adds the most delicious flavor and crunch to the top of the steak.

FOR THE MARINADE:

¼ cup chopped green onions

¼ cup lime juice

2 tablespoons avocado oil

1 clove garlic, minced

½ teaspoon pink Himalayan salt

½ teaspoon ground black pepper

1 pound flank steak

2 tablespoons avocado oil

3 cloves garlic, thinly sliced

1. In a small bowl, whisk together all the ingredients for the marinade.

2. Pour the marinade into a resealable plastic bag and add the steak. Seal the bag and massage the marinade around the steak so that it is fully covered. Place in the refrigerator to marinate for at least 1 hour or up to overnight.

3. Remove the steak from the fridge 15 to 30 minutes before cooking to allow it to come to room temperature.

4. While the steak is coming to room temperature, set a large skillet over low heat and pour in the avocado oil. Add the garlic and cook until golden brown and toasted, 7 to 10 minutes.

5. Remove the toasted garlic to a paper towel–lined plate to drain and increase the heat to medium.

6. Place the steak and all of the marinade in the pan. Cook for 3 to 5 minutes on each side for medium doneness, or until cooked to your liking.

7. Remove the steak to a cutting board and tent with aluminum foil for at least 10 minutes before serving.

8. To serve, slice the steak thinly against the grain and top with the toasted garlic.

EVERYTHING CRUSTED PORK CHOPS

YIELD: 4 servings

PREP TIME: 5 minutes

COOK TIME: 12 minutes

  I just happened to have the idea for crusting pork chops in everything bagel seasoning while writing this book. I am so glad I did, because the crust and the flavor it creates are out of this world! Not only do these chops taste amazing, but you can make them in about 15 minutes.

¼ cup grated Parmesan cheese (about 1 ounce)

¼ cup everything bagel seasoning

4 boneless pork chops, about ¾ inch thick (about 1½ pounds)

1 tablespoon avocado oil, plus more for frying

1. Place the Parmesan cheese and seasoning in a shallow dish and mix together.

2. Brush the pork chops with the oil, then lay the chops in the cheese mixture to coat both sides.

3. Pour enough oil into a large nonstick skillet to cover the bottom. Heat the oil over medium heat.

4. When the oil is hot, carefully add the chops (see Tip) and fry for 5 to 6 minutes on each side, turning carefully so the coating doesn't come off. When done, the internal temperature of the chops should be 140°F.

5. Remove the chops to a serving dish and let rest for at least 5 minutes before slicing and serving.

> **TIP:** When placing a cut of meat in a pan that contains hot oil, make sure to set the edge closest to you down first, laying the rest of the meat down gently away from your body. Doing so greatly reduces the chance of hot oil splattering you.

PERFECT BAKED SALMON

YIELD: 4 servings
PREP TIME: 5 minutes
COOK TIME: 30 minutes

Although salmon is a fatty fish, if overcooked it can dry out. To combat this tendency and to add a smoky flavor, I like to top the salmon with strips of bacon. The fat in the bacon bastes the fish as it cooks and keeps everything nice and moist. You can use this method for any size fillet; just lay a few slices over most of the fish, especially on thinner areas, which tend to dry out faster.

Another method to employ for perfectly baked fish is to cook it in foil packets. This bake/steam combo slows down the cooking and keeps the fish moist. You cut the fillet into individual portions and create a little pouch of foil for each serving. The leftovers taste delicious served cold over a salad the next day!

1 (1½-pound) salmon fillet

½ teaspoon smoked or pink Himalayan salt

4 strips bacon, cut in half crosswise

Chopped fresh dill, for garnish (optional)

Tartar Sauce (page 77), for serving (optional)

INGREDIENT SPOTLIGHT:

Salmon is a superfood and is fairly high in fat compared to other proteins. I prefer wild-caught salmon for numerous reasons, including taste. Being from Seattle, I am a bit of a fish snob. When buying fillets, I choose sockeye or king salmon that is either fresh or was flash-frozen right after being caught. You can always ask the fishmonger to help you make a good selection.

1. Preheat the oven to 350°F.

2. Cut four 9-inch squares of aluminum foil. Then cut the salmon into four equal-sized pieces and place each piece on a foil square.

3. Sprinkle the salmon with the salt and top each piece with two half-strips of bacon. You want to cover most of the top of each piece of fish with the bacon.

4. Fold the foil loosely over each piece of salmon to create a packet. Place the packets on a rimmed baking sheet.

5. Bake for 25 to 30 minutes, depending on the thickness of the salmon pieces. Check for doneness after 25 minutes by opening a packet carefully, inserting a fork into the thickest part of the fish, and twisting. If the fish flakes easily, it is done; if it doesn't come apart easily or is a darker pink inside, refold the packet and continue cooking.

6. Once the fish is fully cooked, open the packets, remove and discard the bacon, and garnish the salmon with fresh dill, if using. Serve with tartar sauce, if desired, and enjoy!

SALT AND PEPPER CHUCK STEAK WITH BLUE CHEESE BUTTER

YIELD: 4 servings

PREP TIME: 30 minutes (not including time to make blue cheese butter)

COOK TIME: 15 minutes

  Chuck steak is an often overlooked cut of beef that is very budget-friendly. If you love steak but can't afford the higher price tag, look for chuck steak. You can have steak any night of the week, and it's delicious when cooked to medium-rare with some very basic seasonings! Letting the steak sit in the seasonings at room temperature for about a half-hour makes a huge difference in the flavor of the finished dish.

This recipe calls for 1½ pounds of boneless steak, which feeds four people, but it may be easier to find two 12-ounce steaks than one larger chuck steak.

1½ pounds boneless chuck steak

1 teaspoon pink Himalayan salt

½ teaspoon ground black pepper

2 tablespoons salted butter, for the pan

¼ cup Beyond Basic Blue Cheese Butter (page 75)

1. Pat the steak dry, then season on both sides with the salt and pepper. Let sit at room temperature for 30 minutes.

2. Preheat a cast-iron skillet over medium heat for 5 minutes, then add the butter and let it heat up for about 1 minute.

3. Carefully place the steak in the hot pan (see Tip, page 228). Depending on the thickness, 4 to 5 minutes per side should produce a medium-rare steak, and 6 minutes per side will be closer to medium doneness.

4. Once the steak is cooked to your liking, remove it to a cutting board and tent with aluminum foil for 10 to 15 minutes before serving.

5. Top the steak with the blue cheese butter and enjoy!

MARINATED FRIED CHICKEN STRIPS

YIELD: 2 servings

PREP TIME: 15 minutes, plus 30 minutes to marinate

COOK TIME: 20 minutes

The secret to this recipe is the pickle juice! Your chicken strips won't taste like pickles, but they will stay moist and tender when you fry them. They reheat beautifully in the oven or in a toaster oven.

1 pound boneless, skinless chicken breasts or thighs, cut into strips

½ cup dill pickle juice (from a jar of pickles; see Tip)

Avocado oil, for frying

1 large egg

1 tablespoon heavy cream (or coconut milk for dairy-free)

1 tablespoon water

⅓ cup crushed pork rinds

⅓ cup grated Parmesan cheese (about 1¼ ounces) (or additional crushed pork rinds for dairy-free)

1. Place the chicken strips and pickle juice in a resealable plastic bag and place in the refrigerator to marinate for at least 30 minutes.

2. Pour about ¼ inch of oil into a large heavy-bottomed pan. Warm the oil over medium heat.

3. In a shallow bowl, mix together the egg, heavy cream, and water.

4. In a second shallow bowl, combine the pork rinds and Parmesan cheese.

5. Dip each marinated chicken strip into the egg mixture and shake off the excess, then dip it into the dry mixture, fully coating the chicken.

6. Working in batches, carefully place the breaded chicken strips in the hot oil (see Tip, page 228). Fry until the coating is medium brown, 3 to 5 minutes on each side. Serve warm.

TIP: If I am not making my own pickles, which I do about 99 percent of the time, I love to get a jar of traditionally fermented pickles from my local supermarket. The juice is great for marinating chicken and other meats, and the pickles are high in probiotics. Waste not, want not!

REVERSE SEAR
TRI-TIP ROAST

YIELD: 4 to 6 servings
PREP TIME: 15 minutes
COOK TIME: 1 hour 15 minutes

Tri-tip is an amazing roast because it is as tender as a steak. The reverse sear method used in this recipe gives you a perfectly seared outside and a medium-rare inside. Use an oven-safe thermometer to keep tabs on the internal temperature of the roast as it cooks.

1 (1¾- to 2-pound) tri-tip roast

1 tablespoon mayonnaise

1 teaspoon pink Himalayan salt

½ teaspoon smoked paprika

½ teaspoon garlic powder

½ teaspoon onion powder

¼ teaspoon Chinese five-spice powder

2 tablespoons avocado oil, for the pan

1. Preheat the oven to 250°F.

2. Using a silicone basting brush, cover all sides of the roast with the mayonnaise.

3. In a small bowl, mix together the salt and spices, then cover the roast with the spice mixture.

4. Place the roast on a rimmed baking sheet or roasting pan and cook for 45 minutes to 1 hour, until the internal temperature is 110°F. (The meat will not be fully cooked at this point.) Remove from the oven.

5. Heat the avocado oil in a large skillet over medium-high heat. When hot, sear the roast for 5 to 7 minutes on each side. The internal temperature should be between 120°F and 130°F for medium-rare.

6. Let the meat rest for at least 15 minutes before slicing and serving. Note that a tri-tip roast has grain going in two directions; you want to cut against the grain into thin slices.

CRISPY BAKED CHICKEN

OPTION

An oldie but a goodie! I have been making a variation of this recipe since I was in college. I use chicken thighs because the dark meat is a little fattier and more flavorful. The extra fat also gives you a little wiggle room when cooking; chicken thighs won't dry out as quickly and easily as chicken breasts. Using a wire rack ensures that the chicken will become crispy on all sides.

The combination of finely grated Parmesan cheese and spices makes for the best breading around. You can use any sort of spice mix you like here; I love taco seasoning or a mesquite rub. If you opt for taco seasoning, note that most brands found in stores contain hidden carbs, like brown rice or potato flour. Skip those versions in favor of something that contains just herbs and spices.

¼ cup finely grated Parmesan cheese (about 1 ounce) (or crushed pork rinds for dairy-free)

2 tablespoons spice mix of choice

4 bone-in, skin-on chicken thighs

2 tablespoons avocado oil

1. Preheat the oven to 375°F. Line a rimmed baking sheet with parchment paper and set a wire rack on top.

2. In a shallow bowl, combine the Parmesan cheese and spice mix.

3. Take a chicken thigh and give it a generous brushing of oil on all sides. Press the chicken into the spice mixture, making sure the entire thigh is coated. Place the coated chicken on the wire rack. Repeat with the remaining thighs.

4. Bake for 35 to 40 minutes, until the coating is dark brown and a thermometer inserted into the thickest part of a thigh reads 165°F. Let rest for at least 5 minutes before serving.

LAMB RIB CHOPS WITH MUSHROOMS

YIELD: 2 servings

PREP TIME: 10 minutes

COOK TIME: 15 minutes

OPTION

Lamb rib chops are a special treat at my house. They are a smaller cut, so incredibly tender, and they cook up very quickly. In this recipe, you roll the edges in breading, pan-fry them, and then top them with buttery mushrooms for a fancy-feeling dinner!

4 lamb rib chops (about 1 pound)

Pink Himalayan salt and ground black pepper

¼ cup crushed pork rinds

¼ teaspoon garlic powder

¼ teaspoon ground dried thyme

¼ teaspoon pink Himalayan salt

Leaves from 1 (5-inch) sprig fresh rosemary, chopped

2 tablespoons salted butter or avocado oil

8 ounces cremini mushrooms, sliced

¼ cup chopped shallots

Chopped fresh parsley, for garnish (optional)

1. Season the chops generously on both sides with salt and pepper and set aside.

2. Mix together the pork rinds, garlic powder, thyme, salt, and rosemary in a shallow dish. Then heat the butter in a medium-sized skillet over medium heat.

3. Roll the edges of each chop in the crumb mixture.

4. Carefully place the chops in the hot skillet (see Tip, page 228). Cook for about 4 minutes per side for medium-rare chops, then remove the chops to a platter to rest.

5. Add the mushrooms and shallots to the skillet. Toss them in the pan juices and cook until soft, about 7 minutes.

6. To serve, top the chops with the mushrooms and shallots. Garnish with chopped parsley, if desired.

SIMPLE BAKED COD

YIELD: 4 servings

PREP TIME: 10 minutes

COOK TIME: 10 minutes

Many people are afraid to cook fish. Don't be! This recipe is similar to my Perfect Baked Salmon (page 230), as it uses the foil packet method to cook the fish slightly more slowly so it stays tender.

1 (1½-pound) cod fillet

1 small shallot, thinly sliced

¼ cup (½ stick) salted butter (or butter-flavored olive oil or coconut oil for dairy-free)

2 tablespoons chopped fresh chives

1. Preheat the oven to 350°F.

2. Cut four 9-inch square pieces of aluminum foil. Then cut the cod fillet into four equal-sized servings and place each piece on a foil square.

3. Place some sliced shallots and a tablespoon of butter on top of each piece of cod.

4. Loosely fold the foil over each piece of fish to create a packet. Place the packets on a rimmed baking sheet.

5. Bake for 10 minutes, then check for doneness by carefully opening one foil packet. Gently insert a fork into the thickest part of the cod and twist. If the fish flakes easily, it is done. If it does not flake and is still raw in the middle, close the packet and bake for another 3 to 5 minutes, then check the fish again.

6. Open the packets and sprinkle the fish with the chives. Serve!

CABBAGE, SAUSAGE, AND PEPPER SHEET PAN DINNER

YIELD: 4 large servings

PREP TIME: 10 minutes

COOK TIME: 30 minutes

  Sheet pan dinners are the best for busy nights; plus, you end up with a good amount of leftovers. If you are feeding a crowd, you can make two pans!

3 green bell peppers, seeded and cut into strips

½ head cabbage, cut into wedges

¼ cup olive oil

1 teaspoon pink Himalayan salt

1 teaspoon ground coriander

½ teaspoon garlic powder

½ teaspoon onion powder

1½ pounds mild Italian sausage links, cut into bite-sized chunks

1. Preheat the oven to 350°F and line a rimmed baking sheet with parchment paper.

2. Spread the bell pepper strips and cabbage wedges on the lined baking sheet. Drizzle the olive oil over the vegetables.

3. Evenly sprinkle the salt, coriander, garlic powder, and onion powder over the vegetables. Toss gently to coat. Distribute the sausage chunks among the vegetables.

4. Bake until the sausage is cooked through, about 30 minutes. Serve immediately.

PERFECT ROAST BEEF

YIELD: 8 servings

PREP TIME: 10 minutes

COOK TIME: about 3 hours

  Eye of round is an inexpensive cut, but if you know how to cook it correctly, it makes the best roast beef. I serve this roast hot for dinner, then slice it thinly for leftovers for the week. Because the meat is very lean, make sure to add a little extra fat to the meal, such as mayonnaise mixed with freshly grated horseradish, or any of your favorite keto sauces.

1 (3-pound) beef eye of round roast

2 tablespoons prepared yellow mustard

1½ teaspoons pink Himalayan salt

1 teaspoon smoked paprika

½ teaspoon ground black pepper

¼ teaspoon Chinese five-spice powder

1. Preheat the oven to 500°F.

2. Brush the mustard in a thin layer all over the roast.

3. In a small bowl, mix together the salt and spices. Sprinkle the seasoning mixture over the roast, pressing it into the mustard so it sticks to the meat.

4. Place the roast in a Dutch oven or roasting pan. Bake, uncovered, for 21 minutes, then turn the oven off. Leave the roast in the oven, without opening the door, for 2½ hours.

5. After 2½ hours, check the internal temperature of the roast with a meat thermometer. I find that 130°F is about perfect. If the meat has not reached temperature, turn the oven back on to 200°F and check the roast every 10 minutes until an internal temperature of 130°F is achieved.

6. Slice the roast thinly and serve.

TIP: You can make this recipe with a larger or smaller roast if you'd like. Cook the meat for 7 minutes per pound before turning off the oven.

RIB-EYE STEAK WITH SHALLOTS AND GARLIC

YIELD: 2 servings

PREP TIME: 10 minutes

COOK TIME: 13 minutes

  Rib-eye is my absolute favorite type of steak. It's tender and fatty, and all it needs is a little sear in a cast-iron skillet and an easy dressing of some garlic, shallots, and butter. In this case, simple wins out. There is no need to be fussy when the steak is the star of the show!

1 (1-pound) boneless rib-eye steak

Pink Himalayan salt and ground black pepper

2 tablespoons salted butter

1 shallot, diced

1 clove garlic, minced

Chopped fresh parsley, for garnish (optional)

1. Generously season the steak on both sides with salt and pepper. Let sit at room temperature for 15 to 30 minutes. Before cooking, pat the steak dry with a paper towel.

2. In a cast-iron skillet or other heavy-bottomed pan, melt the butter over medium heat.

3. Add the shallot and garlic and sauté for about 3 minutes, until the shallot is soft. Remove from the pan and set aside.

4. Increase the heat to medium-high and carefully add the seasoned steak. Cook for about 4 minutes, until a nice dark brown crust has formed. Flip the steak and cook for another 4 minutes for medium-rare, or until cooked to your liking.

5. Remove the steak to a serving dish and let rest for about 10 minutes before cutting in half to serve. Top with the garlic and shallot mixture and garnish with parsley, if desired.

GREENS AND HAM BAKED EGGS

YIELD: 4 small servings

PREP TIME: 10 minutes

COOK TIME: 15 minutes

 Baked eggs are a favorite for lazy weekend mornings and quick dinners at my house. Everyone gets their own ramekin and digs right in! These eggs go great with a side of bacon or Habanero Brussels Sprouts (page 156).

1 tablespoon salted butter, for greasing the ramekins

1 cup cubed ham steak (about 5 ounces)

1 cup arugula

¼ cup shredded mozzarella cheese (about 1 ounce)

¼ cup heavy cream

4 large eggs

¼ cup chopped green onions

Pink Himalayan salt and ground black pepper

¼ cup shredded Parmesan cheese (about 1 ounce) (optional)

1. Preheat the oven to 375°F. Grease four 8-ounce ramekins with the butter and place on a rimmed baking sheet.

2. In each ramekin, layer the ham, arugula, and mozzarella.

3. Pour the heavy cream evenly into the ramekins, then crack an egg into each dish.

4. Top with the green onions and a sprinkle of salt and pepper, then add the Parmesan cheese, if using.

5. Bake for 10 to 15 minutes, until the egg whites are just set.

6. Serve, being careful when handling the hot ramekins.

EVERYDAY ROASTED CHICKEN

YIELD: 4 to 6 servings

PREP TIME: 10 minutes

COOK TIME: 45 minutes

OPTION

This chicken wins all the awards for an easy weeknight meal. First, you spatchcock, or butterfly, the chicken, meaning you cut out the spine and then flatten out the chicken so it cooks more quickly and evenly. I recommend a good pair of kitchen shears for this job (see page 66). Spatchcocking also makes the roasted chicken easier to carve.

¼ cup (½ stick) salted butter (or lard, coconut oil, or butter-flavored coconut oil for dairy-free), softened

5 cloves garlic, minced

2 tablespoons chopped fresh parsley

1 (3- to 5-pound) whole chicken, spatchcocked

1 teaspoon pink Himalayan salt

1. Preheat the oven to 400°F. Line a rimmed baking sheet with parchment paper and set a wire rack on top.

2. Place the butter, garlic, and parsley in a small bowl and mix well.

3. Place the spatchcocked chicken on the wire rack and create a pocket between the skin and the meat down both sides of the breast bone.

4. Put half of the butter mixture in each pocket. Spread the butter down onto the legs and wings by pressing it down the pockets. Sprinkle the chicken skin with the salt.

5. Roast for 45 minutes, or until the internal temperature in the thickest part of the chicken is 160°F.

6. Remove the chicken to a platter. Tent with aluminum foil and allow to rest for at least 10 minutes, then carve and serve.

BUTTER-BASTED NEW YORK STRIP STEAK

YIELD: 2 servings

PREP TIME: 5 minutes

COOK TIME: 15 minutes

  Nothing is simpler than a New York strip steak cooked in butter with a few aromatics. Butter basting is the process of spooning the melted butter from the hot pan over the top of the steak over and over again as you cook it. It imparts a delicious flavor and cooks the steak more evenly because you are heating both sides of the steak at once.

1 large or 2 small New York strip steaks

Pink Himalayan salt and ground black pepper

2 tablespoons salted butter

1 shallot, chopped

3 cloves garlic, roughly chopped

1. Pat the steak dry and season generously on both sides with salt and pepper.

2. Place the butter, shallot, and garlic in a small skillet over medium-high heat. Once the butter is melted, add the steak.

3. As the steak cooks, tilt the pan slightly to one side to gather the melted butter. With a spoon, ladle the hot butter over the steak. Continually baste the steak with the butter as it cooks. Depending on the thickness, the steak should be cooked medium-rare at 5 to 6 minutes per side.

4. Serve the steak with the butter, shallot, and garlic from the pan spooned over the top.

THE BEST EVER GRILLED CHEESE

YIELD: 4 servings

PREP TIME: 3 minutes (not including time to make bread)

COOK TIME: 15 minutes

 I warned you about this grilled cheese, right?! It is simply the best! Use my Cinnamon Bread and any kind of cheese you love. A few suggestions: blue, Brie, cheddar, mozzarella, or a combination!

2 tablespoons salted butter, softened

8 slices Cinnamon Bread (page 98)

2 tablespoons grated Parmesan cheese

6 ounces cheese of choice, sliced

TIP: If you are preparing these sandwiches for a crowd, which I highly recommend, remove the hot sandwiches to a cookie sheet or oven-safe platter, cover with aluminum foil, and place in a preheated 200°F oven to keep them warm. Seriously, preprepped grilled cheeses make a good party great!

1. Butter one side of each slice of bread.

2. Divide the Parmesan cheese evenly among the slices of bread, sprinkling it onto the buttered side. Press the cheese into the butter so it sticks to the bread.

3. In a large skillet over medium-low heat, place 4 slices of bread buttered side down. Top each piece with sliced cheese and a second slice of bread, buttered side up.

4. Cook for 5 minutes, or until the cheese is mostly melted. Carefully flip the sandwiches and cook for another 3 to 5 minutes, until the bread is golden brown on the second side and the cheese inside is fully melted.

5. Remove to a plate and slice in half, if desired. Serve immediately.

PORK BELLY

YIELD: 4 servings

PREP TIME: 10 minutes, plus time to chill overnight

COOK TIME: 1 hour 30 minutes

  Pork belly is one of the fattiest cuts of meat you can get. It takes a bit of time to get right, but well-cooked pork belly is worth the wait. If you find that you like it, bake multiple 1-pound pork bellies at a time to store in the fridge, slice, and fry up until crispy, as needed. Pork belly is great with a fried egg for breakfast, in salads (as pictured here), or on its own.

1½ teaspoons pink Himalayan salt

¼ teaspoon ground cinnamon

¼ teaspoon ground cumin

¼ teaspoon Chinese five-spice powder

1 pound pork belly

1. Combine the salt and spices in a small bowl. Sprinkle the spice mixture on all sides of the pork belly.

2. Place the pork belly on a plate and cover with plastic wrap. Place in the refrigerator to chill overnight.

3. When ready to cook the pork belly, preheat the oven to 450°F and line a rimmed baking sheet with parchment paper. Set a wire rack on top of the lined baking sheet.

4. Place the chilled pork belly, fat side up, on the rack. Bake for 30 minutes, then reduce the oven temperature to 275°F and bake for 1 hour, or until tender.

5. Remove from the oven and let cool completely. Once cool, wrap the pork belly tightly in plastic wrap and refrigerate for at least a few hours, until chilled through, or for up to 2 days.

6. Thickly slice the chilled pork belly as needed. Brown the slices in a skillet over medium-high heat until crispy.

CHICKEN CORDON BLEU

YIELD: 4 servings

PREP TIME: 15 minutes

COOK TIME: 45 minutes

Chicken cordon bleu was one of my favorite meals as a child. Here, I've upgraded it slightly by replacing lean ham with fattier prosciutto. In addition, wrapping the cheese in the prosciutto prevents the cheese from leaking out of the chicken!

⅓ cup crushed pork rinds

⅓ cup grated Parmesan cheese (about 1¼ ounces)

¼ cup poultry seasoning

4 slices prosciutto

4 slices Swiss cheese (about 2 ounces) (make them small to fit inside the chicken breast halves)

4 boneless, skinless chicken breast halves

2 tablespoons mayonnaise

TIP: Switch up the flavor profile of this dish by changing out the poultry seasoning for any other spice blend you love. My Smoky Taco Seasoning (page 79) works great here!

1. Preheat the oven to 350°F. Line a rimmed baking sheet with parchment paper and set a wire rack on top.

2. In a shallow dish, combine the pork rinds, Parmesan cheese, and poultry seasoning. Set aside.

3. Lay a slice of prosciutto on a clean work surface and place a slice of Swiss cheese at one end. Wrap the prosciutto around the cheese.

4. Carefully cut each chicken breast horizontally along one side to create a pocket. Insert the prosciutto-wrapped cheese into the pocket.

5. Use a silicone basting brush to coat both sides of the chicken breasts with the mayonnaise. Roll each stuffed breast in the pork rind mixture and place on the wire rack.

6. Bake for 40 to 45 minutes, until the juices run clear and there is no pink remaining in the thickest part of the chicken. The internal temperature should be 160°F at the thickest part.

7. Serve immediately.

FLANK STEAK WITH CHARRED GREEN ONIONS

YIELD: 4 servings

PREP TIME: 35 minutes

COOK TIME: 15 minutes

 This summer meal comes together in a flash and can easily be doubled or tripled to feed a crowd. You can season the steak and prepare the vegetables ahead of time and throw everything on the grill once your guests arrive!

1½ pounds flank steak

Pink Himalayan salt and ground black pepper

FOR THE CHARRED GREEN ONIONS:

1 bunch green onions (5 to 7), trimmed

5 tablespoons olive oil, divided

¼ teaspoon pink Himalayan salt

1 small shallot, roughly chopped

2 cloves garlic, roughly chopped

1 tablespoon red wine vinegar

¼ teaspoon red pepper flakes

1. About 15 minutes prior to cooking, remove the steak from the refrigerator and season generously on both sides with salt and pepper.

2. Preheat a heavy-bottomed pan or an outdoor grill to medium-high heat.

3. Marinate the green onions: In a large bowl, toss the onions in 2 tablespoons of the oil, the salt, shallot, and garlic. Set aside.

4. Lay the steak in the preheated pan or on the grill and cook for 4 to 8 minutes per side for medium-rare, depending on the thickness of the steak, or until cooked to your liking.

5. Meanwhile, char the green onions: Transfer the onions and their marinade to a small skillet over medium heat and cook until tender and slightly charred, 3 to 5 minutes.

6. Remove the steak from the pan or grill, tent with aluminum foil, and let rest for at least 15 minutes before thinly slicing against the grain.

7. Just before serving, toss the charred green onions in the remaining 3 tablespoons of olive oil, the red wine vinegar, and the red pepper flakes. Serve the onions over the sliced steak.

BUFFALO BAKED CHICKEN

YIELD: 4 servings

PREP TIME: 5 minutes, plus 30 minutes to marinate

COOK TIME: 40 minutes

   A very simple preparation but a family favorite. Hot sauce makes an amazing marinade due to its salt content; it also keeps the chicken very tender when baked. I like to use boneless chicken thighs for easy slicing, but you can use bone-in thighs if you prefer. This chicken is great as the base of a meal or on top of a salad or pizza!

6 boneless or bone-in, skin-on chicken thighs

⅓ cup hot sauce, such as Frank's RedHot

1. Place the chicken thighs and hot sauce in a shallow dish or resealable plastic bag. Make sure that the sauce covers the thighs. Place in the refrigerator to marinate for at least 30 minutes, or preferably overnight.

2. When ready to cook the chicken, preheat the oven to 375°F. Line a rimmed baking sheet with parchment paper and set a wire rack on top.

3. Place the marinated chicken on the rack. Bake for 30 to 40 minutes, until the internal temperature in the thickest part of a thigh is 160°F. Let rest for about 5 minutes before serving.

STEAK TACOS

YIELD: 4 servings

PREP TIME: 10 minutes (not including time to cook steak)

COOK TIME: 20 minutes

OPTION

This recipe is ideal for leftover steak—as if there is such a thing. But if you ever happen to have some leftover steak on hand, chop it up small and make this awesome taco filling. It is very simple, yet delicious on a cool, crisp lettuce wrap. I love making these tacos with hanger steak.

4 strips bacon

1 green bell pepper, diced

½ medium yellow or white onion, diced

1½ pounds hanger or flank steak, cooked and diced

1 cup shredded cheese of choice, such as cheddar or pepper Jack (omit for dairy-free, or use a dairy-free cheese)

Butter lettuce leaves, for taco "shells"

1. In a large skillet over medium-low heat, fry the bacon until crispy, about 6 minutes. Remove to a plate and set aside.

2. Add the green pepper, onion, and steak to the skillet. Sauté over medium heat for about 7 minutes, until the vegetables are soft and the liquid released from the vegetables has cooked off.

3. Top the mixture in the skillet with the cheese and let it melt for about 1 minute.

4. Crumble the bacon. Scoop the taco filling into the lettuce leaves, sprinkle with the crumbled bacon, and enjoy.

DESSERTS

Lemon Macaroons | *270*

Strawberry Cream Ice Pops | *272*

Creamy Lemon Ice Cream | *274*

Lime Curd | *276*

Strawberry Jam Parfaits | *278*

Macadamia Nut Clusters | *280*

Chocolate-Covered Bacon Ice Cream | *282*

Toasted Coconut Pudding | *284*

Keto Caramel Sauce | *286*

White Chocolate Peppermint Swirl Ice Cream | *288*

Candied Pecans | *290*

Chocolate Chip Cookies | *292*

Peanut Butter Tarts | *294*

Dairy-Free Spiced Chocolate Coconut Ice Cream | *296*

Butter Pecan Pudding | *298*

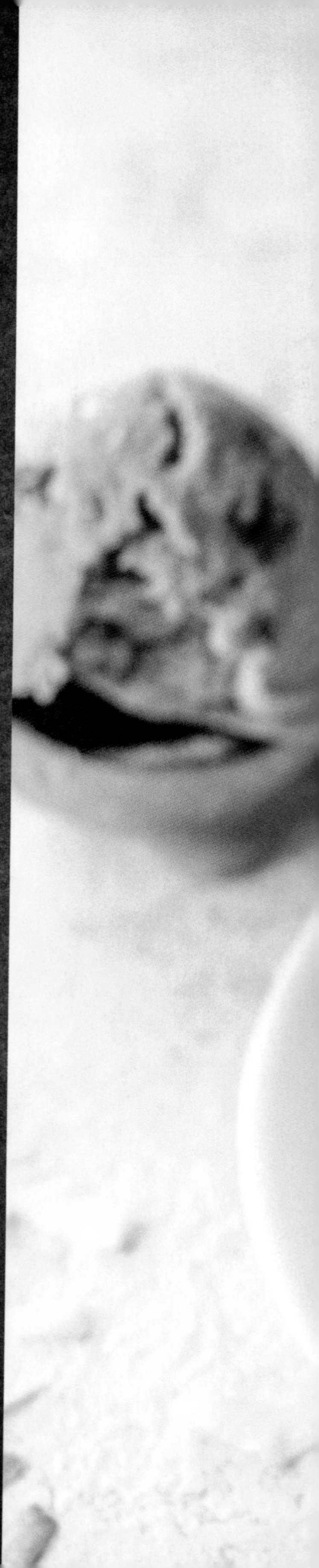

LEMON MACAROONS

YIELD: 20 to 25 cookies
(2 per serving)

PREP TIME: 25 minutes

COOK TIME: 15 minutes

 Macaroons are absolutely delicious and very easy to make. This recipe uses a homemade keto-fied sweetened condensed milk that gives the coconut stacks the slightly sticky texture of the original recipe. These cookies are very low in carbs and high in fat, almost like fat bombs, but perhaps even more delicious!

1 tablespoon salted butter

1 cup heavy cream

½ teaspoon unflavored liquid stevia

1 large egg white

1 tablespoon granulated erythritol

8 ounces unsweetened shredded coconut

2 tablespoons lemon juice

½ teaspoon pink Himalayan salt

TIP: Anytime you are directed to line a baking sheet with parchment paper, you can also use a silicone baking mat. It's a little more work to clean, but it saves you from using so much parchment.

1. Melt the butter in a medium-sized saucepan over medium-low heat. Add the heavy cream and stevia. Simmer gently until the liquid has reduced by about one-third, 15 to 20 minutes.

2. Meanwhile, in a large mixing bowl, beat the egg white and erythritol until white and very foamy. Gently fold in the coconut, lemon juice, salt, and reduced sweetened cream.

3. Preheat the oven to 350°F and line a rimmed baking sheet with parchment paper.

4. Scoop up a rounded tablespoon of the dough and squeeze it into a tightly packed mound, then place on the lined baking sheet. Repeat with the remaining dough, making a total of 20 to 25 cookies.

5. Bake for 12 to 15 minutes, until the tops are golden brown.

6. Let cool on the baking sheet for at least 10 minutes before eating. Cooling the cookies further in the refrigerator will help them firm up a bit more. Store in the refrigerator for up to 1 week.

STRAWBERRY CREAM ICE POPS

YIELD: 4 ice pops (1 per serving)

PREP TIME: 5 minutes, plus time to freeze overnight

  (N)

Summer is all about cool treats. These creamy berry ice pops are just like the ones you probably remember eating as a kid!

2 cups halved fresh strawberries (about 9 ounces)

½ cup water

3 tablespoons heavy cream (or coconut cream or full-fat coconut milk for dairy-free), divided

1 teaspoon vanilla extract

Pinch of pink Himalayan salt

SPECIAL EQUIPMENT:
4 (4-ounce) ice pop molds

1. Put the berries, water, 2 tablespoons of the cream, the vanilla extract, and salt in a blender and blend until smooth, about 1 minute.

2. Pour the blended mixture equally into 4 ice pop molds.

3. Divide the remaining tablespoon of cream evenly among the molds.

4. Freeze the pops overnight before serving.

CREAMY LEMON ICE CREAM

YIELD: 1 quart (½ cup per serving)

PREP TIME: 10 minutes

CHURN TIME: 25 minutes

A refreshing and delicious ice cream flavor. You've had lemon sorbet before, but a creamy lemon ice cream? This is another amazing hot weather treat!

2 cups heavy cream

½ cup nut milk of choice

½ cup lemon juice

1 large egg yolk

1 teaspoon unflavored liquid stevia

1 teaspoon lemon extract or grated lemon zest

1 drop yellow food coloring (optional)

SPECIAL EQUIPMENT:

ice cream maker

1. In a large bowl, whisk together all the ingredients.

2. Pour the mixture into an ice cream maker and churn according to the manufacturer's instructions, about 25 minutes.

3. Serve the ice cream immediately or, if you would like it to be slightly firmer, freeze it in an ice cream storage container for about 2 hours. If it's frozen longer than that, the ice cream will harden quite a bit. Leave the container on the counter for 15 to 20 minutes to soften slightly and use an ice cream scoop that has been run under hot water to make scooping easier. Store in the freezer for up to 2 weeks.

NOTE: To make this ice cream dairy-free and nut-free, use three 13½-ounce cans of full-fat coconut milk instead of the heavy cream and nut milk and increase the number of egg yolks to three.

LIME CURD

YIELD: 2 cups (½ cup per serving)

PREP TIME: 15 minutes, plus 2 hours to chill

COOK TIME: 10 minutes

 Have you ever made curd before? It's a slightly sweet, citrusy, creamy bite of heaven. If you've tried making it, you know it can be a total pain: cooking the mixture to the right temperature, straining out the egg bits . . . way too many steps. Worry no more! This super simplified recipe turns out the smoothest, creamiest curd. Use a countertop blender or a stick blender here—either one will work.

You can easily substitute other citrus flavors for the lime juice; however, lime is less tart than lemon, so you may want to increase the sweetener if you go with lemon juice.

⅔ cup lime juice (3 to 4 large limes)

2 large eggs

2 large egg yolks

6 tablespoons (¾ stick) salted butter, cubed

⅓ cup granulated erythritol

Grated lime zest, for garnish (optional)

1. Put the lime juice, whole eggs, egg yolks, butter, and erythritol in a blender and blend until smooth, about 1 minute. (If you are using a stick blender, the mixture may not get 100 percent smooth and may look a bit curdled. This is totally fine and normal.)

2. Pour the mixture into a heavy saucepan and set over medium-low heat. Cook, stirring continuously, for 7 to 10 minutes, until the curd mixture coats the back of a spoon or reaches 170°F to 175°F on a candy thermometer.

3. Pour the curd into a storage container and cover with plastic wrap, laying the plastic directly on the surface of the curd to prevent a skin from forming. Place in the refrigerator to chill for at least 2 hours, until cold.

4. Serve chilled and garnished with grated lime zest, if desired. Store in the refrigerator for up to 3 days.

STRAWBERRY JAM PARFAITS

YIELD: 4 parfaits (1 per serving)

PREP TIME: 10 minutes
(not including time to make
curd or jam

 Love lime curd but don't want to eat it plain? Or need a fancier dessert for a dinner party? This is my go-to recipe for such occasions. I love that I can make these parfaits the day before and just keep them lightly covered with plastic wrap in the fridge until serving time.

½ cup heavy cream

1 teaspoon vanilla extract

Liquid stevia, to taste (optional)

1 batch Lime Curd (page 276)

¼ cup Roasted Strawberry Jam (page 82)

1. In a chilled mixing bowl, use a hand mixer to whip the heavy cream with the vanilla extract and stevia, if using, until soft peaks form.

2. In each of four serving dishes, layer ½ cup of the lime curd and then 1 tablespoon of the jam. Top with equal amounts of the whipped cream.

3. Store covered with plastic wrap in the refrigerator for up to 1 day.

MACADAMIA NUT CLUSTERS

YIELD: 20 clusters
(2 per serving)

PREP TIME: 10 minutes,
plus 1 hour 30 minutes to chill
(not including time to make
caramel sauce)

 A delicious and crunchy fat bomb! You can easily substitute another type of nut in this recipe, but if you do, the clusters will be lower in fat. These make a really fun treat to give as a gift to your best keto pal.

30 roasted salted macadamia nuts, halved (about 2 ounces)

¼ cup Keto Caramel Sauce (page 286)

¼ cup sugar-free chocolate chips

Coarse salt (optional)

1. Line a cookie sheet with parchment paper. Place 20 clusters of 3 macadamia nut halves each on top.

2. Top each cluster with a dollop of caramel sauce. Place the cookie sheet in the refrigerator to chill for at least 30 minutes.

3. Melt the chocolate chips according to the package directions, or place the chocolate chips in a small glass bowl and set the bowl over a pan of simmering water to slowly melt the chocolate.

4. When the chocolate is fully melted and easy to work with, drizzle some over each chilled nut cluster. Top each cluster with a pinch of coarse salt, if desired.

5. Put the cookie sheet back in the refrigerator or in the freezer for at least 1 hour, until the clusters have set. Store the clusters in the refrigerator for up to 1 week or in the freezer for up to 2 weeks.

CHOCOLATE-COVERED BACON ICE CREAM

YIELD: 1 quart (½ cup per serving)

PREP TIME: 15 minutes

COOK TIME: 10 minutes

CHURN TIME: 30 minutes

  The key to this ice cream is to cook the bacon until it is very crispy but not burned. Even slightly charred bacon will ruin the flavor of the ice cream. Make sure to add the chocolate-covered bacon to the ice cream in the last 10 minutes of churning; otherwise, all the good bits will end up at the bottom.

4 strips bacon

1 tablespoon unsweetened cocoa powder

1 tablespoon confectioner's-style erythritol (see Notes)

1½ teaspoons ground cinnamon, divided

2 large eggs

2 teaspoons vanilla extract

1 teaspoon unflavored liquid stevia

2 cups heavy cream

1 cup whole milk

SPECIAL EQUIPMENT:

ice cream maker

NOTES: To make this ice cream dairy-free, use three 13½-ounce cans of full-fat coconut milk instead of the heavy cream and milk and add an extra egg yolk.

If you have only granulated erythritol on hand, you can pulse it in a blender a few times to get the powdered texture needed for this recipe.

1. Cook the bacon in a medium-sized skillet over medium-low heat until very crispy, about 10 minutes.

2. While the bacon is cooking, put the cocoa powder, erythritol, and ½ teaspoon of the cinnamon in a shallow dish and mix together. Set aside.

3. Crack the eggs into a large bowl and whisk.

4. Add the vanilla extract, stevia, and remaining teaspoon of cinnamon to the eggs and mix well with the whisk. Set aside in the refrigerator while you prepare the bacon bits.

5. Remove the crispy bacon from the skillet and, while it is still hot, chop it into small pieces. Place the bacon bits in the cocoa mixture and toss to coat well; the oil and heat from the bacon will make the cocoa mixture stick to the bacon. Set aside.

6. Remove the egg mixture from the refrigerator and mix in the heavy cream and milk. Pour into an ice cream maker and churn for 20 minutes.

7. At the 20-minute mark, add the cocoa-covered bacon bits. Churn for 10 more minutes.

8. Serve the ice cream immediately or, if you would like it slightly firmer, freeze in an ice cream storage container for about 2 hours. If it's frozen longer than that, the ice cream will harden quite a bit. Leave the container on the counter for 15 to 20 minutes to soften slightly and use an ice cream scoop that has been run under hot water to make scooping easier. Store in an airtight container in the freezer for up to 2 weeks.

TOASTED COCONUT PUDDING

YIELD: 4 servings

PREP TIME: 10 minutes, plus 3 hours to chill

COOK TIME: 5 minutes

   Sometimes I need a creamy treat, but I am done with dairy for the day. If you are avoiding dairy but love a creamy dessert, this just slightly sweetened coconut pudding fits the bill. It doesn't set as firm as store-bought pudding, but it does thicken up in the fridge.

2 tablespoons water

1 tablespoon unflavored gelatin

2 cups full-fat coconut milk

10 drops unflavored liquid stevia

½ teaspoon vanilla extract

Whipped coconut cream, for topping (optional)

½ cup unsweetened coconut flakes, toasted, for garnish

1. In a medium-sized mixing bowl, stir together the water and gelatin; a paste will form.

2. Bring the coconut milk just to a simmer in a small saucepan over medium heat. Once simmering, pour the milk into the bowl with the gelatin paste and stir well until the gelatin is dissolved. Add the stevia and vanilla extract and mix well.

3. Pour the pudding into four small serving dishes, cover with plastic wrap, and place in the refrigerator to chill until set, about 3 hours. Depending on the brand of coconut milk you used, the pudding may separate. After 1 hour of chilling, stir to reincorporate the ingredients before the pudding sets completely.

4. When ready to serve the pudding, toast the coconut flakes in a dry skillet over medium heat, shaking the pan to toss the coconut occasionally, until golden brown, 3 to 5 minutes. Top each serving of pudding with whipped coconut cream, if desired, and the toasted coconut.

KETO CARAMEL SAUCE

YIELD: ⅓ cup (2 tablespoons per serving)

PREP TIME: 5 minutes

COOK TIME: 15 minutes

  Every ice cream sundae needs a drizzle of caramel sauce! This version is very lightly sweetened. The trick is to make sure the butter is well browned; that is what gives the caramel sauce its color and flavor. The cooking will go slightly faster if you use a wider pan. To prevent the sauce from separating, add the cream a little at a time while whisking continuously.

¼ cup (½ stick) salted butter

½ cup heavy cream

6 drops unflavored liquid stevia

Pink Himalayan salt

NOTE: You may need to melt this sauce slightly to make it pourable for use in a recipe. To do so, fill a bowl with hot water and place the jar of caramel sauce in the water. Stir the sauce as it warms.

1. In a large saucepan over medium-low heat, brown the butter for about 5 minutes. Whisk gently as it cooks so that it browns evenly.

2. Slowly add the heavy cream while whisking. Then add the stevia and a pinch of salt. Keep whisking until the sauce is a blond caramel color and slightly thick, 5 to 10 minutes.

3. Pour the caramel sauce into a glass jar or other heat-safe container; it will thicken further as it cools. When cool, top with another pinch of salt. Store in the refrigerator for up to 2 weeks.

WHITE CHOCOLATE PEPPERMINT SWIRL ICE CREAM

YIELD: 1 quart (½ cup per serving)

PREP TIME: 10 minutes

CHURN TIME: 25 minutes

OPTION OPTION

The key to super creamy ice cream is super cold ingredients. Make sure to keep everything very cold and combine the ingredients right before you pour the mixture into the ice cream maker.

1 cup heavy cream

1 cup nut milk of choice

2 large eggs

1½ teaspoons peppermint extract

1 teaspoon vanilla extract

1 teaspoon unflavored liquid stevia

1 drop red food coloring (optional)

FOR THE WHITE CHOCOLATE SWIRL:

3 ounces cacao butter, finely chopped

¼ cup confectioner's-style erythritol

SPECIAL EQUIPMENT:

ice cream maker

1. In a large bowl, whisk together all the ice cream ingredients.

2. Pour the mixture into an ice cream maker and churn for 15 minutes.

3. While the ice cream churns, make the white chocolate swirl: Heat a small saucepan of water over medium-low heat. Place a heat-safe bowl over the saucepan and put the cacao butter and erythritol in the bowl. Stir until fully melted and smooth.

4. After 15 minutes of churning, slowly pour the white chocolate swirl into the ice cream maker. Churn for 5 to 10 more minutes, until the mixture has increased in size.

5. Serve the ice cream immediately or, if you would like it slightly firmer, freeze in an ice cream storage container for about 2 hours. If it's frozen longer than that, the ice cream will harden up quite a bit. Leave the container on the counter for 15 to 20 minutes to soften slightly and use an ice cream scoop that has been run under hot water to make scooping easier. Store in an airtight container in the freezer for up to 2 weeks.

NOTE: To make this ice cream dairy-free and nut-free, use three 13½-ounce cans of full-fat coconut milk instead of the heavy cream and nut milk and add an extra egg yolk.

CANDIED PECANS

YIELD: 4 servings

PREP TIME: 5 minutes

COOK TIME: 50 minutes

 Candied nuts are one of our staple snacks during the holidays; we give them as gifts and always have a bowl of them for sharing at parties. I also like to use them for topping salads year-round. You can substitute your favorite nuts for the pecans; just make sure to keep an eye on them in the oven, as smaller nuts or seeds will need less roasting time. These are keto candied nuts, so they are less sweet than traditional versions, but they do the trick, and your taste buds will thank you.

¼ cup granulated erythritol

1 large egg white

1 tablespoon water

1 teaspoon ground cinnamon

Pinch of pink Himalayan salt

2 cups raw pecan halves

1. Preheat the oven to 250°F and line a rimmed baking sheet with parchment paper.

2. In a shallow bowl, mix the erythritol, egg white, water, cinnamon, and salt.

3. Add the pecans to the bowl and toss to coat. The erythritol mixture will be a bit thick and grainy, so make sure to give the nuts a good stir so that all of them are coated.

4. Spread the nuts in a single layer on the lined baking sheet. Bake for 50 minutes, until dark brown. Store in the freezer for up to 1 month.

CHOCOLATE CHIP COOKIES

OPTION

Enjoy these simple nut-free keto chocolate chip cookies anytime. I keep mine in the freezer because to me, a cookie is best served ice cold!

¾ cup (1½ sticks) salted butter (or ⅔ cup melted coconut oil for dairy-free)

300 g (about 2½ cups) sunflower seed flour (see Ingredient Spotlight)

¾ cup granulated erythritol

2 teaspoons pink Himalayan salt

1½ teaspoons baking soda

20 drops unflavored liquid stevia

2 teaspoons vanilla extract

1 large egg

1 large egg yolk

1 cup sugar-free chocolate chips

INGREDIENT SPOTLIGHT:

For best results, I always weigh my sunflower seed flour rather than measure it by volume.

1. Preheat the oven to 375°F. Line a rimmed baking sheet with parchment paper.

2. In a small saucepan, brown the butter over medium-low heat, whisking until it turns golden brown. This should yield about ⅔ cup of browned butter. (If using coconut oil, skip this step.)

3. In a large bowl, whisk together the flour, erythritol, salt, and baking soda. Add the stevia, vanilla extract, egg, and egg yolk and mix with a spoon or an electric mixer.

4. Once fully combined, fold in the chocolate chips.

5. Drop rounded tablespoons of the dough onto the lined baking sheet, making a total of about 20 cookies. If you like crispier cookies, flatten the dough slightly with a fork or spatula.

6. Bake for 15 minutes, or until medium brown.

7. Let the cookies cool on the baking sheet for at least 15 minutes because they are very fragile after baking. Then remove the cookies to a wire rack and let cool completely. Store in the freezer for up to 1 month.

PEANUT BUTTER TARTS

My husband loves chocolate and peanut butter more than any other dessert. What he doesn't love is overly sweet keto desserts. This treat is hardly sweet at all, and it's perfect to split over coffee after dinner.

FOR THE CRUST:

30 g (¼ cup) sunflower seed flour

2 tablespoons unsweetened cocoa powder

2 tablespoons melted salted butter (or melted coconut oil for dairy-free)

5 drops unflavored liquid stevia

FOR THE FILLING:

⅓ cup smooth unsweetened peanut butter or nut butter of choice, room temperature

1 tablespoon heavy cream (or coconut cream or full-fat coconut milk for dairy-free)

15 drops unflavored liquid stevia

¼ teaspoon vanilla extract

Whipped cream, for topping (optional)

SPECIAL EQUIPMENT:
4 mini tart pans with removable bottoms

1. Preheat the oven to 350°F.

2. In a medium-sized bowl, mix together all the ingredients for the crust.

3. Press equal portions of the crust mixture into four mini tart pans and bake for 10 minutes. Allow the crusts to cool for 10 to 15 minutes.

4. Meanwhile, in another medium-sized bowl, mix together all of the ingredients for the filling.

5. Once the crusts are cool, fill with the peanut butter mixture. Top with whipped cream, if desired. Store in the refrigerator for up to 3 days.

DAIRY-FREE SPICED CHOCOLATE COCONUT ICE CREAM

YIELD: 1 quart (½ cup per serving)

PREP TIME: 10 minutes

CHURN TIME: 25 minutes

 This is a delicious ice cream for all the dairy-free folks out there. One thing to note: because the fat content is slightly lower than that of the other ice cream recipes, this ice cream will freeze much harder. Set the container on the counter for at least 30 minutes before scooping.

3 (13½-ounce) cans full-fat coconut milk

3 large egg yolks

2 tablespoons unsweetened cocoa powder

1 teaspoon unflavored liquid stevia

1 teaspoon vanilla extract

1 teaspoon ground cinnamon

½ teaspoon ground cloves

¼ teaspoon ground nutmeg

Toasted unsweetened coconut flakes, for garnish (optional)

SPECIAL EQUIPMENT:

ice cream maker

1. In a large bowl, whisk together all the ingredients.

2. Pour the mixture into an ice cream maker and churn according to the manufacturer's instructions, about 25 minutes.

3. Serve the ice cream immediately or, if you would like it slightly firmer, freeze in an ice cream storage container for about 2 hours. If frozen longer than that, the ice cream will harden up quite a bit. Leave the container on the counter for 30 minutes to soften slightly and use an ice cream scoop that has been run under hot water to make scooping easier. Store in the freezer for up to 2 weeks.

BUTTER PECAN PUDDING

YIELD: 4 servings

PREP TIME: 10 minutes
(not including time to make
caramel sauce)

COOK TIME: 10 minutes, plus
3 hours to chill

 Butter pecan is one of my mom's favorite ice cream flavors. I was inspired to make it a pudding instead of ice cream since homemade ice cream needs to sit out for quite a while before it is scoopable. I like to serve desserts like this at family dinners because you can make it the night before and then serve it the next day. Entertaining made easy!

1 cup plus 2 tablespoons water, divided

1½ teaspoons unflavored gelatin

1 cup heavy cream

1½ teaspoons vanilla extract

15 drops unflavored liquid stevia

Pinch of pink Himalayan salt

FOR SERVING:

¼ cup Keto Caramel Sauce (page 286)

½ cup chopped pecans, toasted

1. Put 2 tablespoons of the water in a small dish. Sprinkle in the gelatin and whisk until a smooth, thick paste forms.

2. Warm the heavy cream, remaining 1 cup of water, vanilla extract, stevia, and salt in a medium-sized saucepan over medium-low heat, about 10 minutes.

3. Add the gelatin mixture to the saucepan and whisk until combined. Pour the pudding into a large mixing bowl.

4. Cover the bowl with plastic wrap and place in the refrigerator to chill for 3 hours or until ready to serve.

5. Before serving, whip the pudding in the bowl with a whisk or an electric mixer, then divide among four serving dishes. Top with the caramel sauce and toasted pecans.

DRINKS

Drinking Chocolate | *302*

Mocha Coffee | *303*

Raspberry Smash | *304*

Strawberry Creme | *305*

Blackberry Lime Slushies | *306*

Orange Cranberry Spritzer | *307*

Peppermint Italian Soda | *308*

Strawberry Basil Sparkling Punch | *309*

Cinnamon Cream Coffee | *310*

Lemonade Slushies | *311*

Ginger Lime Soda | *312*

Sparkling Green Tea Elixir | *313*

DRINKING CHOCOLATE

YIELD: 2 small servings

PREP TIME: 5 minutes

COOK TIME: 10 minutes

Drinking chocolate is such a decadent treat. Luckily, it doesn't need to be super sweet. This drink can be enjoyed hot or cold. It is very rich, so the two servings are small.

½ cup heavy cream (or full-fat coconut milk for dairy-free)

½ cup nut milk of choice

3 to 6 drops unflavored liquid stevia

1 ounce dark chocolate (100% cacao), chopped

1 tablespoon unsweetened cocoa powder

⅛ teaspoon vanilla extract

Pinch of ground nutmeg

Pinch of pink Himalayan salt

1. In a medium-sized saucepan over medium-low heat, gently whisk together all the ingredients. Continue whisking until the chocolate is melted and the mixture is nice and smooth, about 10 minutes. Check for chocolate pieces sticking to the bottom of the pan as you whisk.

2. If serving hot, pour into two glass mugs and enjoy immediately; if serving cold, pour into an airtight storage container and then place in the refrigerator to chill before enjoying.

MOCHA COFFEE

YIELD: 1 serving

PREP TIME: 10 minutes (including time to brew coffee; not including time to make Drinking Chocolate)

OPTION

Here's a simple way to use drinking chocolate: mix it with a cup of hot coffee, creating a delicious sugar-free mocha. If you normally use cream in your coffee, this is the perfect substitute. If your drinking chocolate is cold, it will make the hot coffee the perfect temperature. For a more decadent treat, top it with some whipped cream!

2 to 4 tablespoons Drinking Chocolate (page 302)

1 cup brewed coffee, hot

Whipped cream, for topping (optional)

Pour the drinking chocolate into a large mug and pour the hot coffee over the top. Stir vigorously or use a milk frother to mix well. Top with whipped cream, if desired, and enjoy!

RASPBERRY SMASH

   Apple cider vinegar can be a healthy tonic to get extra probiotics into your gut. This drink not only tastes deliciously tangy but is good for you to boot!

10 fresh raspberries

2 tablespoons apple cider vinegar

2 cups sparkling mineral water, chilled

1. In a small bowl, use a kraut smasher or fork to mash the raspberries with the vinegar. Let macerate for at least 5 minutes.

2. Split the smash between two tall glasses and top with the sparkling water; the mixture will foam, so pour carefully.

STRAWBERRY CREME

YIELD: 2 servings

PREP TIME: 5 minutes

OPTION

Enjoy this blended drink instead of a high-calorie, high-sugar frappé from the nearest coffee shop. It's quicker to make than hitting the drive-through and stores well in the fridge for about a day. You can make it in the morning and have it at work midday!

10 ice cubes

10 frozen strawberries

½ cup nut milk of choice

2 tablespoons heavy cream (or coconut cream or full-fat coconut milk for dairy-free)

1 teaspoon vanilla extract

Whipped cream, for topping (optional)

Place all the ingredients in a blender and blend until smooth. Pour into two glasses and top with whipped cream, if desired.

BLACKBERRY LIME SLUSHIES

YIELD: 2 servings

PREP TIME: 5 minutes, plus time to freeze overnight

   This is such a fun drink to make, and it's perfect for a hot summer day. You can easily swap out the lime juice for lemon and the blackberries for raspberries, strawberries, or even blueberries. The options are endless!

14 fresh blackberries

⅔ cup lime juice

1½ cups club soda, chilled

5 to 8 drops unflavored liquid stevia

SPECIAL EQUIPMENT:

ice cube tray

1. Place a blackberry in each of 14 wells of an ice cube tray. Pour equal amounts of the lime juice into the wells and place the tray in the freezer overnight.

2. Put the frozen blackberry and lime juice cubes, club soda, and 5 drops of stevia in a blender and pulse until the mixture has a slushy consistency. Taste for sweetness and add up to 3 drops more stevia, if desired.

3. Pour into two glasses and serve immediately.

ORANGE CRANBERRY SPRITZER

YIELD: 2 servings

PREP TIME: 15 minutes

I was in Thanksgiving mode when I created this spritzer. Although cranberries and orange juice are not traditionally keto, you can use just a little of each to give this mocktail a holiday flavor. If you prefer to omit the orange juice, you can use water mixed with ½ teaspoon orange extract or a few drops of orange oil. This drink might be a tad bitter, so add a drop or two of stevia to sweeten it if you like. Cheers!

10 to 15 fresh or frozen cranberries

2 tablespoons orange juice

2 tablespoons water

2 cups club soda, chilled

Ice

Grated orange zest, for garnish (optional)

1. In a small saucepan, combine the cranberries, orange juice, and water. Cook over medium-low heat for 10 minutes. As the cranberries burst, smash them into the liquid with a fork so that they release their juices further.

2. Strain out the cranberry solids. Split the cranberry-infused juice between two glasses and top each with 1 cup of club soda.

3. Garnish with orange zest, if desired.

PEPPERMINT ITALIAN SODA

  This is my favorite holiday drink!

Ice

1 cup club soda, chilled

¼ teaspoon peppermint extract

1½ tablespoons heavy cream

Whipped cream, for topping (optional)

1. Fill a large glass about halfway with ice and pour the club soda over the ice.

2. Stir in the peppermint extract, then slowly pour in the heavy cream.

3. Top with whipped cream, if desired. Enjoy!

STRAWBERRY BASIL SPARKLING PUNCH

YIELD: 6 servings

PREP TIME: 5 minutes, plus 30 minutes to chill

   This lightly sweet sparkling punch combines the essence of berries and the herbiness of basil. The strawberries release more juice the longer you mash them and let them sit. You can easily multiply this recipe and serve it in a punch bowl for a holiday celebration. Other berries work well here, too; you can add more erythritol or stevia to taste with a more tart fruit.

½ cup chopped fresh strawberries (about 6 medium)

2 tablespoons chopped fresh basil

1 teaspoon granulated erythritol

Pinch of pink Himalayan salt

5 cups club soda, chilled

¼ teaspoon vanilla extract

Ice

1. Place the berries, basil, erythritol, and salt in a small bowl and mash well so that the fruit starts to release its juices.

2. Let the mixture sit for at least a half-hour so that the berries release more juices.

3. Strain the berry mixture into a punch bowl. Pour in the club soda and vanilla extract and stir well. Ladle into glasses filled halfway with ice to serve.

CINNAMON CREAM COFFEE

YIELD: 2 servings

PREP TIME: 5 minutes

OPTION

Make this creamer up to a week ahead of time and store it in the refrigerator. Use it when you want to add a little cinnamon kick to your morning coffee.

¼ cup heavy cream (or coconut cream or nut milk of choice for dairy-free)

1 teaspoon ground cinnamon

¼ teaspoon vanilla extract

2 cups brewed coffee, hot

1. Place the heavy cream, cinnamon, and vanilla extract in a small bowl and stir together. Let the mixture sit for at least 5 minutes to allow the flavors to combine.

2. Split the creamer evenly between two mugs and pour the hot coffee over the top.

LEMONADE SLUSHIES

YIELD: 2 servings

PREP TIME: 5 minutes, plus
time to freeze overnight

  This is my favorite drink recipe for summer! You can make it as sweet as you like by adjusting the amount of stevia. Keep a bag of frozen lemon juice cubes in the freezer all summer long for making these slushies in a flash.

Juice of 2 large lemons (about ¾ cup), or 1½ cups lemon juice ice cubes

1½ cups club soda, chilled

5 to 8 drops unflavored liquid stevia

SPECIAL EQUIPMENT:

ice cube tray

1. Pour the lemon juice into an ice cube tray and place the tray in the freezer overnight.

2. Place the frozen lemon juice cubes, club soda, and 5 drops of stevia in a blender and pulse until the mixture has a slushy consistency. Taste for sweetness and add up to 3 drops more stevia, if desired. Pulse again to combine.

3. Pour into two large glasses and serve immediately.

GINGER LIME SODA

YIELD: 2 servings

PREP TIME: 5 minutes, plus
1 hour to rest

   I make a double batch of this soda each week. I love to use mineral water to get extra electrolytes in, but it does have a slightly minerally flavor compared to club soda. You can use a combination of lemon and lime juice to switch things up.

1½ tablespoons lime juice

¼ teaspoon freshly grated ginger

3 drops unflavored liquid stevia

2 cups club soda or sparkling mineral water, chilled

1. In a small bowl, use a fork to muddle together the lime juice and ginger. Let sit for 1 hour to allow the flavors to combine.

2. Add the stevia to the lime juice mixture and stir to combine.

3. Split the mixture between two glasses and top with the club soda. Enjoy!

SPARKLING GREEN TEA ELIXIR

YIELD: 1 or 2 servings

PREP TIME: 10 minutes, plus 30 minutes to chill

  This is one of my favorite drinks to make while fasting. I omit the lemon during a fast, but for refreshing summer mocktails, I make sure to keep lemons on hand. This makes a great pitcher drink as well. The key is to brew the tea so that it is concentrated; boil ½ cup of water for every tea bag you plan to use. This recipe can serve one or two people depending on how strong you like the green tea flavor to be!

½ cup boiling water

1 bag green tea

Ice

1 lemon slice

1 to 2 cups sparkling mineral water or club soda, chilled

1. Pour the boiling water into a mug and insert the green tea bag. Steep according to the package directions, usually 2 to 3 minutes. Remove the tea bag.

2. Place the mug in the refrigerator to chill the tea for 30 minutes.

3. When ready to serve, put some ice in a glass along with the lemon slice. Pour the green tea over the ice and fill the glass with sparkling water.

ACKNOWLEDGMENTS

From Jimmy:

I simply cannot believe this is my seventh book with Victory Belt Publishing. I'm truly thrilled about this one because it is the long-awaited companion cookbook to the book I'm probably forever going to be most famous for—*Keto Clarity*. So, to everyone who has read that book, which helped kick off the keto revolution in earnest, thank you for all of your kind words about how it helped you understand low-carb, high-fat living.

To Victory Belt Publishing, you took a chance on me seven years ago as an unknown entity in the publishing world, and I think it's turned out pretty well for all of us. Thank you for always believing in me and giving me the platform to write books that are greatly impacting the lives of millions of people worldwide. I will forever be grateful to you.

To my coauthor, Heather, I am excited for your debut cookbook that epitomizes years of healing your body, honing your cooking skills, and making truly delicious and nutritious foods. Thank you for gifting us with some incredible recipes in this book that I know will quickly become favorites in keto kitchens around the world.

To the keto community, which didn't exist when I wrote *Keto Clarity,* thank you for showing such enthusiasm about the pursuit of nutritional ketosis. Not that long ago, I felt like a lone wolf out there trying to get the world to pay attention to this message. Now we are cumulatively changing the world one delicious bite of steak, eggs, and bacon at a time!

Finally, to my wife, Christine, you are my everything and why I work so hard every single day. I'm so grateful you are in my life, lovingly supporting me every step of the way (even when you think I'm crazy!) and being that steadfast lighthouse that I need in my life. We'll keep riding the wave now and forevermore, my dear. Buckle your seatbelt, because we are far from finished.

From Heather:

First, to my husband, George, my rock, who lifted me up throughout this process, put up with my experiments, and tried just about every recipe in the book!

To my parents, for giving me a life where an opportunity like this could be possible. Thank you for telling everyone you know about this book!

To my best friends, Liam and Jackie—thank you for your support in my journey and for always being available to talk when I needed you!

To my grandma Eileen, for letting me eat cheese whenever I wanted and for always sharing time in the kitchen with me!

To my grandma Myrtle, who taught me all about homemade bread and that we could only bake it when the house was warm. That was the beginning of my curiosity about how food worked.

To everyone in my life who has supported me, given me a job, or even just a kind word—thank you. None of this would be possible without you.

RECIPE INDEX

SAUCES AND BASICS

 **70**
Smoky Chimichurri

 **72**
Roasted Garlic
Two Ways

 **74**
Smoky Garlic
Burger Sauce

 **75**
Beyond Basic
Blue Cheese Butter

76
Mignonette Sauce
Three Ways

 **77**
Tartar Sauce

 **78**
Ranch Dressing

 **79**
Smoky Taco
Seasoning

 **80**
Maple Orange Butter

81
Lime-Marinated
Red Onions

 **82**
Roasted Strawberry
Jam

 **83**
Blue Cheese Dressing

 **84**
Mustard Seed Aioli

 **85**
Buffalo Dill Sauce

 **86**
Nut-Free Pesto

 **87**
Berry Vinaigrette

 **88**
Caramelized Onions
Three Ways

 **90**
Crispy Mushrooms

 **92**
Psyllium Husk
Pizza Crust

 **94**
Drop Biscuits

 **96**
Seeded
Hamburger Buns

 **98**
Cinnamon Bread

APPETIZERS AND SNACKS

102
Spiced Seeds

104
Caramelized Onion Dip

106
Garlic Parmesan Chicken Wings

108
Smoky Chicken Pâté

110
Baked Brie

112
Vanilla Bacon–Stuffed Celery

114
Jalapeño Poppers with Strawberry Jam

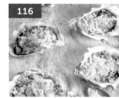

116
Lemon Oysters

118
Elote Chicken Wings

120
Cheesy Stuffed Meatballs

122
Lime Butter Shrimp

124
Bruschetta Mushrooms

126
Caprese Skewers

128
Onion Rings

130
Roasted Berries with Prosciutto

132
Salt and Vinegar Chicken Wings

134
Spiced Nuts Three Ways

136
Prosciutto Meat Cups

SOUPS, SALADS, AND SIDES

140
Avocado Shrimp Salad

142
Mushroom Bisque

144
Truffle Garlic–Roasted Broccoli

146
Southwest Chicken Salad

148
Instant Pot Chicken and Rice Soup

150
Stovetop Green Beans

152
Diner Roasted Radishes

154
Wasabi Broccoli Slaw

156
Habanero Brussels Sprouts

158
Steak Salad

160
Hot Spinach and Bacon Salad

162
George's Soup

164
Grilled Romaine Salad

166
Breakfast Cobb Salad

168
Hot and Smoky Wedge Salad

170
Taco Soup

172
Lime Slaw

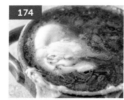
174
French Onion Soup

176
Arugula Caesar Salad

BURGERS AND PIZZA

180
Triple Onion Burgers

182
Balsamic Onion, Truffle, and Arugula Burgers

184
Southwest Burgers

186
Fontina Burgers

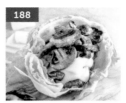
188
Rosemary, Mushroom, and Swiss Burgers

190
Garlic Tomato Burgers

192
Onion Horsey Burgers

194
Asian-Style Burgers

196
Crispy Mushroom and Blue Cheese Burgers

198
Jalapeño Popper Pizza

200
Spicy Chicken Pizza

202
Prosciutto Arugula Pizza

204
White Pizza

206
Sausage and Provolone Pizza

208
Blue Cheese and Sausage Pizza

MAIN DISHES

212

Keto Pot Roast

214

Roast Leg of Lamb

216

Slow Cooker
Rich Beef Shanks

218

Tri-Tip and Broccoli
Bowls

220

Marinated Pork Loin

222

Chicken, Bacon,
and Ranch–Stuffed
Peppers

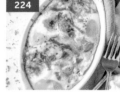
224

Pizza Baked Eggs

226

Marinated Flank Steak
with Toasted Garlic

228

Everything Crusted
Pork Chops

230

Perfect Baked Salmon

232

Salt and Pepper
Chuck Steak with Blue
Cheese Butter

234

Marinated Fried
Chicken Strips

236

Reverse Sear
Tri-Tip Roast

238

Crispy Baked Chicken

240

Lamb Rib Chops with
Mushrooms

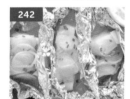
242

Simple Baked Cod

244

Cabbage, Sausage,
and Pepper Sheet Pan
Dinner

246

Perfect Roast Beef

248

Rib-Eye Steak with
Shallots and Garlic

250

Greens and Ham
Baked Eggs

252

Everyday
Roasted Chicken

254

Butter-Basted New
York Strip Steak

256

The Best Ever
Grilled Cheese

258

Pork Belly

260

Chicken
Cordon Bleu

262

Flank Steak with
Charred Green Onions

264

Buffalo Baked Chicken

266

Steak Tacos

DESERTS

270 Lemon Macaroons

272 Strawberry Cream Ice Pops

274 Creamy Lemon Ice Cream

276 Lime Curd

278 Strawberry Jam Parfaits

280 Macadamia Nut Clusters

282 Chocolate-Covered Bacon Ice Cream

284 Toasted Coconut Pudding

286 Keto Caramel Sauce

288 White Chocolate Peppermint Swirl Ice Cream

290 Candied Pecans

292 Chocolate Chip Cookies

294 Peanut Butter Tarts

296 Dairy-Free Spiced Chocolate Coconut Ice Cream

298 Butter Pecan Pudding

DRINKS

302 Drinking Chocolate

303 Mocha Coffee

304 Raspberry Smash

305 Strawberry Creme

306 Blackberry Lime Slushies

307 Orange Cranberry Spritzer

308 Peppermint Italian Soda

309 Strawberry Basil Sparkling Punch

310 Cinnamon Cream Coffee

311 Lemonade Slushies

312 Ginger Lime Soda

313 Sparkling Green Tea Elixir

GENERAL INDEX

A

almonds
  Vanilla Bacon–Stuffed Celery, 112–113
anchovy paste
  Arugula Caesar Salad, 176–177
Anti-Inflammation Mix Spiced Nuts recipe, 134–135
appetizers and snacks
  Baked Brie, 110–111
  Bruschetta Mushrooms, 124–125
  Caprese Skewers, 126–127
  Caramelized Onion Dip, 104–105
  Cheesy Stuffed Meatballs, 120–121
  Elote Chicken Wings, 118–119
  Garlic Parmesan Chicken Wings, 106–107
  Jalapeño Poppers with Strawberry Jam, 114–115
  Lemon Oysters, 116–117
  Lime Butter Shrimp, 122–123
  Onion Rings, 128–129
  Prosciutto Meat Cups, 136–137
  Roasted Berries with Prosciutto, 130–131
  Salt and Vinegar Wings, 132–133
  Smoky Chicken Pâté, 108–109
  Spiced Nuts Three Ways, 134–135
  Spiced Seeds, 102–103
  Vanilla Bacon–Stuffed Celery, 112–113
arugula
  Arugula Caesar Salad, 176–177
  Avocado Shrimp Salad, 140–141
  Balsamic Onion, Truffle, and Arugula Burgers, 182–183
  Fontina Burgers, 186–187
  Greens and Ham Baked Eggs, 250–251
  Lime Butter Shrimp, 122–123
  Prosciutto Arugula Pizza, 202–203
Arugula Caesar Salad recipe, 176–177
Asian-Style Burgers recipe, 194–195

Avocado Shrimp Salad recipe, 140–141
avocados
  Avocado Shrimp Salad, 140–141
  Breakfast Cobb Salad, 166–167
  Southwest Chicken Salad, 146–147
  Steak Salad, 158–159

B

bacon
  Balsamic Onion, Truffle, and Arugula Burgers, 182–183
  Breakfast Cobb Salad, 166–167
  Chicken, Bacon, and Ranch–Stuffed Peppers, 222–223
  Chocolate-Covered Bacon Ice Cream, 282–283
  Habanero Brussels Sprouts, 156–157
  Hot and Smoky Wedge Salad, 168–169
  Hot Spinach and Bacon Salad, 160–161
  Jalapeño Popper Pizza, 198–199
  Perfect Baked Salmon, 230–231
  Smoky Chicken Pâté, 108–109
  Steak Tacos, 266–267
  Taco Soup, 170–171
  Vanilla Bacon–Stuffed Celery, 112–113
Baked Brie recipe, 110–111
baking mat, 67, 270
baking sheet, 67
Balsamic Onion, Truffle, and Arugula Burgers recipe, 182–183
Banting, William, "Letter on Corpulence," 17
basil
  Blue Cheese and Sausage Pizza, 208–209
  Caprese Skewers, 126–127
  Garlic Tomato Burgers, 190–191
  Nut-Free Pesto, 86
  Roasted Strawberry Jam, 82
  Strawberry Basil Sparkling Punch, 309

beef
  Asian-Style Burgers, 194–195
  Balsamic Onion, Truffle, and Arugula
    Burgers, 182–183
  Butter-Basted New York Strip Steak,
    254–255
  Cheesy Stuffed Meatballs, 120–121
  Crispy Mushroom and Blue Cheese
    Burgers, 196–197
  Flank Steak with Charred Green Onions,
    262–263
  Fontina Burgers, 186–187
  Garlic Tomato Burgers, 190–191
  Keto Pot Roast, 212–213
  Marinated Flank Steak with Toasted Garlic,
    226–227
  Onion Horsey Burgers, 192–193
  Perfect Roast Beef, 246–247
  Prosciutto Meat Cups, 136–137
  Reverse Sear Tri-Tip Roast, 236–237
  Rib-Eye Steak with Shallots and Garlic,
    248–249
  Rosemary, Mushroom, and Swiss Burgers,
    188–189
  Salt and Pepper Chuck Steak with Blue
    Cheese Butter, 232–233
  Slow Cooker Rich Beef Shanks, 216–217
  Southwest Burgers, 184–185
  Steak Salad, 158–159
  Steak Tacos, 266–267
  Taco Soup, 170–171
  Triple Onion Burgers, 180–181
  Tri-Tip and Broccoli Bowls, 218–219
beef bone broth
  French Onion Soup, 174–175
  Keto Pot Roast, 212–213
  Mushroom Bisque, 142–143
  Taco Soup, 170–171
bell peppers
  Cabbage, Sausage, and Pepper Sheet Pan
    Dinner, 244–245
  Chicken, Bacon, and Ranch–Stuffed
    Peppers, 222–223
  George's Soup, 162–163
  Pizza Baked Eggs, 224–225
  Sausage and Provolone Pizza, 206–207
  Steak Tacos, 266–267

berries
  Roasted Berries with Prosciutto, 130–131
Berry, Ken
  about, 12
  Moments of Clarity, 17, 25, 31
Berry Vinaigrette recipe, 87
The Best Ever Grilled Cheese recipe, 256–257
Beyond Basic Blue Cheese Butter recipe, 75
  Crispy Mushroom and Blue Cheese
    Burgers, 196–197
  Salt and Pepper Chuck Steak with Blue
    Cheese Butter, 232–233
Blackberry Lime Slushies recipe, 306
blending hot liquids, 142
blood sugar, testing, 19
blue cheese
  Beyond Basic Blue Cheese Butter, 75
  Blue Cheese and Sausage Pizza, 208–209
  Blue Cheese Dressing, 83, 168–169
  buying, 75
  Grilled Romaine Salad, 164–165
  Hot and Smoky Wedge Salad, 168–169
  Steak Salad, 158–159
Blue Cheese and Sausage Pizza recipe,
  208–209
Blue Cheese Dressing recipe, 83
  Hot and Smoky Wedge Salad, 168–169
bone broth. See beef bone broth; chicken
  bone broth
breads
  Cinnamon Bread, 98–99
  Drop Biscuits, 94–95
  Psyllium Husk Pizza Crust, 92–93
  Seeded Hamburger Buns, 96–97
breakfast
  keto diet example, 29
  low-fat diet example, 28
Breakfast Cobb Salad recipe, 166–167
breakfast sausage
  Breakfast Cobb Salad, 166–167
  George's Soup, 162–163
Brie cheese
  Baked Brie, 110–111
broccoli
  Tri-Tip and Broccoli Bowls, 218–219
  Truffle Garlic–Roasted Broccoli, 144–145
  Wasabi Broccoli Slaw, 154–155
  White Pizza, 204–205

broiling pizzas, 198
Bruschetta Mushrooms recipe, 124–125
Brussels sprouts
    Habanero Brussels Sprouts, 156–157
Buffalo Baked Chicken recipe, 264–265
Buffalo Dill Sauce recipe, 85
burgers
    Asian-Style Burgers, 194–195
    Balsamic Onion, Truffle, and Arugula
        Burgers, 182–183
    Crispy Mushroom and Blue Cheese
        Burgers, 196–197
    Fontina Burgers, 186–187
    forming patties, 180
    Garlic Tomato Burgers, 190–191
    Onion Horsey Burgers, 192–193
    Rosemary, Mushroom, and Swiss Burgers,
        188–189
    Southwest Burgers, 184–185
    Triple Onion Burgers, 180–181
butter
    Beyond Basic Blue Cheese Butter, 75
    Maple Orange Butter, 80
butter lettuce
    for burgers, 180
    Steak Tacos, 266–267
Butter Pecan Pudding recipe, 298–299
Butter-Basted New York Strip Steak recipe,
    254–255

C

cabbage
    for burgers, 180
    Cabbage, Sausage, and Pepper Sheet Pan
        Dinner, 244–245
    Lime Slaw, 172–173
Cabbage, Sausage, and Pepper Sheet Pan
    Dinner recipe, 244–245
cacao butter
    White Chocolate Peppermint Swirl Ice
        Cream, 288–289
Camembert cheese
    Cheesy Stuffed Meatballs, 120–121
Candied Pecans recipe, 290–291
Caprese Skewers recipe, 126–127
Caramelized Onion Dip recipe, 104–105
    Onion Horsey Burgers, 192–193

Caramelized Onions Three Ways recipe,
    88–89
    Caramelized Onion Dip, 104–105
    Triple Onion Burgers, 180–181
carbohydrates
    refined, 21
    sensitivity to, 18–19
cast-iron skillet, 64
cauliflower
    Chicken, Bacon, and Ranch–Stuffed
        Peppers, 222–223
    Instant Pot Chicken and Rice Soup,
        148–149
celery
    Vanilla Bacon–Stuffed Celery, 112–113
cheddar cheese
    Asian-Style Burgers, 194–195
    Balsamic Onion, Truffle, and Arugula
        Burgers, 182–183
    Chicken, Bacon, and Ranch–Stuffed
        Peppers, 222–223
    Onion Horsey Burgers, 192–193
    Southwest Burgers, 184–185
    Steak Tacos, 266–267
    Triple Onion Burgers, 180–181
cheese. *See also specific types*
    The Best Ever Grilled Cheese, 256–257
    Breakfast Cobb Salad, 166–167
    Steak Tacos, 266–267
cheese grater, 64
Cheesy Stuffed Meatballs recipe, 120–121
chicken
    Buffalo Baked Chicken, 264–265
    Chicken, Bacon, and Ranch–Stuffed
        Peppers, 222–223
    Chicken Cordon Bleu, 260–261
    Crispy Baked Chicken, 238–239
    Elote Chicken Wings, 118–119
    Everyday Roasted Chicken, 252–253
    Garlic Parmesan Chicken Wings, 106–107
    Instant Pot Chicken and Rice Soup,
        148–149
    Marinated Fried Chicken Strips, 234–235
    protein in, 24
    Salt and Vinegar Wings, 132–133
    Southwest Chicken Salad, 146–147
    Spicy Chicken Pizza, 200–201

Chicken, Bacon, and Ranch–Stuffed Peppers
    recipe, 222–223
chicken bone broth
    George's Soup, 162–163
    Instant Pot Chicken and Rice Soup,
      148–149
    Mushroom Bisque, 142–143
    Taco Soup, 170–171
Chicken Cordon Bleu recipe, 260–261
chicken livers
    Smoky Chicken Pâté, 108–109
chimichurri
    Smoky Chimichurri, 70–71
chocolate
    Chocolate Chip Cookies, 292–293
    Drinking Chocolate, 302
    Macadamia Nut Clusters, 280–281
Chocolate Chip Cookies recipe, 292–293
Chocolate-Covered Bacon Ice Cream recipe,
    282–283
Cholesterol Clarity (Moore and Westman), 8
chopping hot peppers, 198
cilantro
    Asian-Style Burgers, 194–195
    Avocado Shrimp Salad, 140–141
    Jalapeño Poppers with Strawberry Jam,
      114–115
    Lime Butter Shrimp, 122–123
    Lime Slaw, 172–173
    Southwest Burgers, 184–185
    Southwest Chicken Salad, 146–147
cinnamon
    Candied Pecans, 290–291
    Chocolate-Covered Bacon Ice Cream,
      282–283
    Cinnamon Bread, 98–99
    Cinnamon Cream Coffee, 310
    Dairy-Free Spiced Chocolate Coconut Ice
      Cream, 296–297
    Pork Belly, 258–259
    Spiced Nuts Three Ways, 134–135
Cinnamon Bread recipe, 98–99
    The Best Ever Grilled Cheese, 256–257
Cinnamon Cream Coffee recipe, 310
cleaning mushrooms, 124
club soda
    Blackberry Lime Slushies, 306
    Ginger Lime Soda, 312

Lemonade Slushies, 311
Orange Cranberry Spritzer, 307
Peppermint Italian Soda, 308
Sparkling Green Tea Elixir, 313
Strawberry Basil Sparkling Punch, 309
cocoa powder
    Chocolate-Covered Bacon Ice Cream,
      282–283
    Dairy-Free Spiced Chocolate Coconut Ice
      Cream, 296–297
    Drinking Chocolate, 302
    Peanut Butter Tarts, 294–295
coconut
    Dairy-Free Spiced Chocolate Coconut Ice
      Cream, 296–297
    Lemon Macaroons, 270–271
    Toasted Coconut Pudding, 284–285
coconut cream
    Cinnamon Cream Coffee, 310
    Peanut Butter Tarts, 294–295
    Strawberry Creme, 305
    Toasted Coconut Pudding, 284–285
coconut milk
    Chocolate-Covered Bacon Ice Cream,
      282–283
    Creamy Lemon Ice Cream, 274–275
    Dairy-Free Spiced Chocolate Coconut Ice
      Cream, 296–297
    Drinking Chocolate, 302
    Mushroom Bisque, 142–143
    Peanut Butter Tarts, 294–295
    Strawberry Cream Ice Pops, 272–273
    Strawberry Creme, 305
    Toasted Coconut Pudding, 284–285
    White Chocolate Peppermint Swirl Ice
      Cream, 288–289
cod
    Simple Baked Cod, 242–243
coffee
    Cinnamon Cream Coffee, 310
    Mocha Coffee, 303
Cole, Will
    about, 11
    Moments of Clarity, 23, 33
Cotija cheese
    Elote Chicken Wings, 118–119
cranberries
    Orange Cranberry Spritzer, 307

cream cheese
    Jalapeño Popper Pizza, 198–199
    Jalapeño Poppers with Strawberry Jam,
        114–115
    Roasted Berries with Prosciutto, 130–131
    Vanilla Bacon–Stuffed Celery, 112–113
Creamy Lemon Ice Cream recipe, 274–275
Crispy Baked Chicken recipe, 238–239
Crispy Mushroom and Blue Cheese Burgers
    recipe, 196–197
Crispy Mushrooms recipe, 90–91
    Arugula Caesar Salad, 176–177
    Crispy Mushroom and Blue Cheese
        Burgers, 196–197
cucumbers
    Mignonette Sauce Three Ways, 76

D
Dairy-Free Spiced Chocolate Coconut Ice
    Cream recipe, 296–297
Dairy-Free Week 1 meal plan, 52–53
Dairy-Free Week 2 meal plan, 54–55
Dairy-Free Week 3 meal plan, 56–57
Dairy-Free Week 4 meal plan, 58–59
deep breathing exercises, 40
deglazing, 162
dessert
    keto diet example, 29
    low-fat diet example, 28
dietary fat myth, 31
Dietary Guidelines for Americans, 17
dill
    Breakfast Cobb Salad, 166–167
    Buffalo Dill Sauce, 85
    Lime Butter Shrimp, 122–123
dill pickle juice
    Marinated Fried Chicken Strips, 234–235
dill pickles
    Tartar Sauce, 77
Diner Roasted Radishes recipe, 152–153
dinner
    keto diet example, 29
    low-fat diet example, 28
dressings. See also sauces
    Berry Vinaigrette, 87
    Blue Cheese Dressing, 83
    Ranch Dressing, 78

Drinking Chocolate recipe, 302
    Mocha Coffee, 303
drinks
    Blackberry Lime Slushies, 306
    Cinnamon Cream Coffee, 310
    Drinking Chocolate, 302
    Ginger Lime Soda, 312
    Lemonade Slushies, 311
    Mocha Coffee, 303
    Orange Cranberry Spritzer, 307
    Peppermint Italian Soda, 308
    Raspberry Smash, 304
    Sparkling Green Tea Elixir, 313
    Strawberry Basil Sparkling Punch, 309
    Strawberry Creme, 305
Drop Biscuits recipe, 94–95
Dutch oven, 64

E
eggs
    Breakfast Cobb Salad, 166–167
    Candied Pecans, 290–291
    Chocolate Chip Cookies, 292–293
    Chocolate-Covered Bacon Ice Cream,
        282–283
    Cinnamon Bread, 98–99
    Creamy Lemon Ice Cream, 274–275
    Dairy-Free Spiced Chocolate Coconut Ice
        Cream, 296–297
    Drop Biscuits, 94–95
    Greens and Ham Baked Eggs, 250–251
    Lemon Macaroons, 270–271
    Lime Curd, 276–277
    Marinated Fried Chicken Strips, 234–235
    Onion Rings, 128–129
    Pizza Baked Eggs, 224–225
    Psyllium Husk Pizza Crust, 92–93
    Seeded Hamburger Buns, 96–97
    White Chocolate Peppermint Swirl Ice
        Cream, 288–289
electric mixer, 65
electric pressure cooker, 65
Elote Chicken Wings recipe, 118–119
Emmerich, Maria, *The Ketogenic Cookbook,* 8
equipment, kitchen, 64–67
erythritol
    Candied Pecans, 290–291

Chocolate Chip Cookies, 292–293
Chocolate-Covered Bacon Ice Cream, 282–283
Cinnamon Bread, 98–99
Lemon Macaroons, 270–271
Lime Curd, 276–277
Strawberry Basil Sparkling Punch, 309
White Chocolate Peppermint Swirl Ice Cream, 288–289
essential oils, 40
Everyday Roasted Chicken recipe, 252–253
Everything Crusted Pork Chops recipe, 228–229
exercise, 40

F

"Fat: The New Health Paradigm" study, 27
fat-free, 28–29
fats. *See also* high fat
monounsaturated, 30
saturated, 30
fatty proteins, 24
FBOMB nut butter products, 27
fermented vegetables, 21
fish and seafood
Avocado Shrimp Salad, 140–141
Lemon Oysters, 116–117
Lime Butter Shrimp, 122–123
Perfect Baked Salmon, 230–231
Simple Baked Cod, 242–243
Fix Your Diet, Fix Your Diabetes (Hampton), 13
Flank Steak with Charred Green Onions recipe, 262–263
Fontina Burgers recipe, 186–187
foods
sources for, 34
whole, 35
French Onion Soup recipe, 174–175

G

garlic
Butter-Basted New York Strip Steak, 254–255
Everyday Roasted Chicken, 252–253
Flank Steak with Charred Green Onions, 262–263
George's Soup, 162–163
Habanero Brussels Sprouts, 156–157
Instant Pot Chicken and Rice Soup, 148–149
Marinated Flank Steak with Toasted Garlic, 226–227
Rib-Eye Steak with Shallots and Garlic, 248–249
Roast Leg of Lamb, 214–215
Roasted Garlic Two Ways, 72–73
Slow Cooker Rich Beef Shanks, 216–217
Smoky Garlic Burger Sauce, 74
Tri-Tip and Broccoli Bowls, 218–219
White Pizza, 204–205
Garlic Parmesan Chicken Wings recipe, 106–107
garlic salt, 102
Garlic Tomato Burgers recipe, 190–191
gelatin
Butter Pecan Pudding, 298–299
Roasted Strawberry Jam, 82
Toasted Coconut Pudding, 284–285
George's Soup recipe, 162–163
ginger
Ginger Lime Soda, 312
Marinated Pork Loin, 220–221
Tri-Tip and Broccoli Bowls, 218–219
Ginger Lime Soda recipe, 312
glass measuring cups, 65
glass storage containers/jars, 65
goat cheese
Roasted Berries with Prosciutto, 130–131
golden flax meal
Cinnamon Bread, 98–99
Psyllium Husk Pizza Crust, 92–93
grains, whole, 21
grater, 64
green beans
Stovetop Green Beans, 150–151
green leafy nonstarchy vegetables, 20
green onions
Flank Steak with Charred Green Onions, 262–263
Greens and Ham Baked Eggs, 250–251
Hot Spinach and Bacon Salad, 160–161
Jalapeño Poppers with Strawberry Jam, 114–115
Marinated Flank Steak with Toasted Garlic, 226–227
Southwest Chicken Salad, 146–147

green onions *(continued)*
    Steak Salad, 158–159
    Tri-Tip and Broccoli Bowls, 218–219
    Wasabi Broccoli Slaw, 154–155
green tea
    Sparkling Green Tea Elixir, 313
Greens and Ham Baked Eggs recipe, 250–251
Grilled Romaine Salad recipe, 164–165
Gruyère cheese
    French Onion Soup, 174–175

H

Habanero Brussels Sprouts recipe, 156–157
ham
    Greens and Ham Baked Eggs, 250–251
Hampton, Tony
    about, 13
    Moments of Clarity, 18, 21, 23, 33, 36, 40
handheld electric mixer, 65
healthy lifestyle choices, as a Keto Clarity
    concept, 14–15
heavy cream
    Butter Pecan Pudding, 298–299
    Chocolate-Covered Bacon Ice Cream,
      282–283
    Cinnamon Cream Coffee, 310
    Creamy Lemon Ice Cream, 274–275
    Drinking Chocolate, 302
    Greens and Ham Baked Eggs, 250–251
    Keto Caramel Sauce, 286–287
    Lemon Macaroons, 270–271
    Lime Butter Shrimp, 122–123
    Marinated Fried Chicken Strips, 234–235
    Mushroom Bisque, 142–143
    Onion Rings, 128–129
    Peanut Butter Tarts, 294–295
    Peppermint Italian Soda, 308
    Ranch Dressing, 78
    Strawberry Cream Ice Pops, 272–273
    Strawberry Creme, 305
    Strawberry Jam Parfaits, 278–279
    White Chocolate Peppermint Swirl Ice
      Cream, 288–289
    White Pizza, 204–205
high fat
    about, 27
    dietary fat myth, 31

as a Keto Clarity concept, 14–15
low-fat/fat-free, 28–29
monounsaturated fats, 30
saturated fats, 30
taste, 31
high-intensity interval training (HIIT), 40
horseradish
    Fontina Burgers, 186–187
    Onion Horsey Burgers, 192–193
horseradish root, 186
Hot and Smoky Wedge Salad recipe, 168–169
hot liquids, blending, 142
hot peppers, chopping, 198
hot sauce
    Buffalo Baked Chicken, 264–265
    Buffalo Dill Sauce, 85
    Mignonette Sauce Three Ways, 76
Hot Spinach and Bacon Salad recipe, 160–161
hot tub, 40

I

ice cream
    Chocolate-Covered Bacon Ice Cream,
      282–283
    Creamy Lemon Ice Cream, 274–275
    Dairy-Free Spiced Chocolate Coconut Ice
      Cream, 296–297
    Strawberry Cream Ice Pops, 272–273
    White Chocolate Peppermint Swirl Ice
      Cream, 288–289
ice cream maker, 65
iceberg lettuce
    for burgers, 180
    Hot and Smoky Wedge Salad, 168–169
infrared sauna, 40
immersion blender. *See* stick blender
Instant Pot, 65
Instant Pot Chicken and Rice Soup recipe,
    148–149
Instant Pot recipes
    Caramelized Onions Three Ways, 88–89
    French Onion Soup, 174–175
    Garlic Parmesan Chicken Wings, 106–107
    Instant Pot Chicken and Rice Soup,
      148–149
    Marinated Pork Loin, 220–221
    Roasted Garlic Two Ways, 72–73

Italian sausage
    Blue Cheese and Sausage Pizza, 208–209
    Cabbage, Sausage, and Pepper Sheet Pan
        Dinner, 244–245
    Sausage and Provolone Pizza, 206–207

J

Jacobson Salt Co., 102
jalapeño peppers
    Jalapeño Popper Pizza, 198–199
    Jalapeño Poppers with Strawberry Jam,
        114–115
    Taco Soup, 170–171
Jalapeño Popper Pizza recipe, 198–199
Jalapeño Poppers with Strawberry Jam recipe,
    114–115
jam
    Roasted Strawberry Jam, 82

K

Keto Caramel Sauce recipe, 286–287
    Butter Pecan Pudding, 298–299
    Macadamia Nut Clusters, 280–281
Keto Clarity (Moore and Westman), 8, 10, 15
Keto Clarity, concepts of, 14–15
The Keto Cure (Nally and Moore), 8
Keto Pot Roast recipe, 212–213
The Ketogenic Cookbook (Moore and
    Emmerich), 8
Ketotarian (Cole), 11
kimchi
    Asian-Style Burgers, 194–195
kitchen scale, 65
kitchen shears, 66
kitchen tools and equipment, 64–67
knives, 66
kraut smasher, 66

L

lamb
    Lamb Rib Chops with Mushrooms, 240–241
    Roast Leg of Lamb, 214–215
Lamb Rib Chops with Mushrooms recipe,
    240–241
leeks
    Sausage and Provolone Pizza, 206–207

Lemon Macaroons recipe, 270–271
Lemon Oysters recipe, 116–117
Lemonade Slushies recipe, 311
lemons
    Arugula Caesar Salad, 176–177
    Blue Cheese Dressing, 83
    Creamy Lemon Ice Cream, 274–275
    Lemon Macaroons, 270–271
    Lemon Oysters, 116–117
    Lemonade Slushies, 311
    Mignonette Sauce Three Ways, 76
    Ranch Dressing, 78
    Roast Leg of Lamb, 214–215
    Sparkling Green Tea Elixir, 313
    Stovetop Green Beans, 150–151
    Tartar Sauce, 77
    Wasabi Broccoli Slaw, 154–155
"Letter on Corpulence" (Banting), 17
lettuce. *See also specific types*
    Crispy Mushroom and Blue Cheese
        Burgers, 196–197
    Garlic Tomato Burgers, 190–191
    Onion Horsey Burgers, 192–193
    Rosemary, Mushroom, and Swiss Burgers,
        188–189
    Southwest Burgers, 184–185
    Triple Onion Burgers, 180–181
Lies My Doctor Told Me (Berry), 12
lifestyle factors
    about, 39
    exercise, 40
    sleep, 39
    strategies for complementing diet, 40
    stressors, 41
light therapy, 40
Lime Butter Shrimp recipe, 122–123
Lime Curd recipe, 276–277
    Strawberry Jam Parfaits, 278–279
Lime Slaw recipe, 172–173
Lime-Marinated Red Onions recipe, 81
    Grilled Romaine Salad, 164–165
    Hot and Smoky Wedge Salad, 168–169
    Steak Salad, 158–159
limes
    Avocado Shrimp Salad, 140–141
    Blackberry Lime Slushies, 306
    Breakfast Cobb Salad, 166–167
    Ginger Lime Soda, 312

limes *(continued)*
    Lime Butter Shrimp, 122–123
    Lime Curd, 276–277
    Lime Slaw, 172–173
    Lime-Marinated Red Onions, 81
    Marinated Flank Steak with Toasted Garlic,
        226–227
    Marinated Pork Loin, 220–221
    Mignonette Sauce Three Ways, 76
    Southwest Burgers, 184–185
Livin' La Vida Low-Carb (blog), 7
The Livin' La Vida Low-Carb Show (podcast), 7
loaf pan, 66
Love You Foods, LLC, 27
low-carb
    about, 17–18
    fermented vegetables, 21
    green leafy nonstarchy vegetables, 20
    as a Keto Clarity concept, 14–15
    refined carbohydrates, 21
    sensitivity to carbs, 18–19
    whole grains, 21
Lowery, Ryan
    about, 12
    Moments of Clarity, 19, 39, 41
low-fat, 28–29
lunch
    keto diet example, 29
    low-fat diet example, 28

M

Macadamia Nut Clusters recipe, 280–281
macronutrients, 62–63
Maple Orange Butter recipe, 80
maple syrup
    Maple Orange Butter, 80
marinara sauce
    Blue Cheese and Sausage Pizza, 208–209
    Sausage and Provolone Pizza, 206–207
Marinated Flank Steak with Toasted Garlic
    recipe, 226–227
Marinated Fried Chicken Strips recipe,
    234–235
Marinated Pork Loin recipe, 220–221
mascarpone cheese
    Caramelized Onion Dip, 104–105
massage, 40

mayonnaise
    Blue Cheese Dressing, 83
    Buffalo Dill Sauce, 85
    Mustard Seed Aioli, 84
    Ranch Dressing, 78
    Tartar Sauce, 77
meal plans
    about, 43
    Dairy-Free Week 1, 52–53
    Dairy-Free Week 2, 54–55
    Dairy-Free Week 3, 56–57
    Dairy-Free Week 4, 58–59
    Week 1, 44–45
    Week 2, 46–47
    Week 3, 48–49
    Week 4, 50–51
meals, savoring, 36
measuring cups, 65
meat, searing, 212. *See also specific types*
Mignonette Sauce Three Ways recipe, 76
milk, whole. *See also* coconut milk; nut milk
    Chocolate-Covered Bacon Ice Cream,
        282–283
mindful meditation, 40
mint/mint flavor
    Peppermint Italian Soda, 308
    Roast Leg of Lamb, 214–215
    White Chocolate Peppermint Swirl Ice
        Cream, 288–289
Mocha Coffee recipe, 303
moderate protein
    about, 23
    fatty proteins, 24
    fulfilling body's protein needs, 24
    as a Keto Clarity concept, 14–15
    quality, 25
    types of protein, 25
monounsaturated fats, 30
Moore, Christine
    food sources for, 34
    Real Food Keto, 8, 33, 35
Moore, Jimmy
    Cholesterol Clarity, 8
    food sources for, 34
    Keto Clarity, 8, 10, 15
    The Keto Cure, 8
    The Ketogenic Cookbook, 8

personal story of, 7–8
Real Food Keto, 8, 33, 35
mozzarella cheese
    Blue Cheese and Sausage Pizza, 208–209
    Bruschetta Mushrooms, 124–125
    Caprese Skewers, 126–127
    Garlic Tomato Burgers, 190–191
    Greens and Ham Baked Eggs, 250–251
    Jalapeño Popper Pizza, 198–199
    Jalapeño Poppers with Strawberry Jam,
        114–115
    Pizza Baked Eggs, 224–225
    Prosciutto Arugula Pizza, 202–203
    Sausage and Provolone Pizza, 206–207
    Spicy Chicken Pizza, 200–201
    White Pizza, 204–205
Mushroom Bisque recipe, 142–143
mushrooms
    Bruschetta Mushrooms, 124–125
    cleaning, 124
    Crispy Mushrooms, 90–91
    Keto Pot Roast, 212–213
    Lamb Rib Chops with Mushrooms, 240–241
    Mushroom Bisque, 142–143
    Rosemary, Mushroom, and Swiss Burgers,
        188–189
    Spicy Chicken Pizza, 200–201
Mustard Seed Aioli recipe, 84
    Triple Onion Burgers, 180–181

N

The New Atkins for a New You (Westman), 13
nonstick skillet, 66
nut milk
    Cinnamon Cream Coffee, 310
    Creamy Lemon Ice Cream, 274–275
    Drinking Chocolate, 302
    Strawberry Creme, 305
    White Chocolate Peppermint Swirl Ice
        Cream, 288–289
Nut-Free Pesto recipe, 86
nutrient density, 37
nuts. *See also* nut milk
    Butter Pecan Pudding, 298–299
    Candied Pecans, 290–291
    Spiced Nuts Three Ways, 134–135
    Vanilla Bacon–Stuffed Celery, 112–113

O

olives
    Pizza Baked Eggs, 224–225
Onion Horsey Burgers recipe, 192–193
Onion Rings recipe, 128–129
onions. *See also* green onions
    Avocado Shrimp Salad, 140–141
    Balsamic Onion, Truffle, and Arugula
        Burgers, 182–183
    Blue Cheese Dressing, 83
    Buffalo Dill Sauce, 85
    Caprese Skewers, 126–127
    Caramelized Onions Three Ways, 88–89
    Cheesy Stuffed Meatballs, 120–121
    French Onion Soup, 174–175
    George's Soup, 162–163
    Grilled Romaine Salad, 164–165
    Instant Pot Chicken and Rice Soup,
        148–149
    Keto Pot Roast, 212–213
    Lime-Marinated Red Onions, 81
    Mushroom Bisque, 142–143
    Mustard Seed Aioli, 84, 180–181
    Onion Rings, 128–129
    Slow Cooker Rich Beef Shanks, 216–217
    Smoky Chicken Pâté, 108–109
    Southwest Burgers, 184–185
    Steak Salad, 158–159
    Steak Tacos, 266–267
    Taco Soup, 170–171
    Triple Onion Burgers, 180–181
    White Pizza, 204–205
Orange Cranberry Spritzer recipe, 307
oranges
    Maple Orange Butter, 80
    Orange Cranberry Spritzer, 307
Oura Ring, 39
OXO brand, 67
oysters
    Lemon Oysters, 116–117

P

parchment paper, 66, 270
Parmesan cheese
    Arugula Caesar Salad, 176–177
    The Best Ever Grilled Cheese, 256–257
    Chicken Cordon Bleu, 260–261

Parmesan cheese *(continued)*
 Crispy Baked Chicken, 238–239
 Everything Crusted Pork Chops, 228–229
 Garlic Parmesan Chicken Wings, 106–107
 Greens and Ham Baked Eggs, 250–251
 Lemon Oysters, 116–117
 Marinated Fried Chicken Strips, 234–235
 Nut-Free Pesto, 86
 Onion Rings, 128–129
 Prosciutto Meat Cups, 136–137
 Psyllium Husk Pizza Crust, 92–93
 Spicy Chicken Pizza, 200–201
 Truffle Garlic–Roasted Broccoli, 144–145
 White Pizza, 204–205
parsley
 Smoky Chimichurri, 70–71
 Tartar Sauce, 77
peanut butter
 Peanut Butter Tarts, 294–295
Peanut Butter Tarts recipe, 294–295
pecans
 Butter Pecan Pudding, 298–299
 Candied Pecans, 290–291
Pecorino Romano cheese
 Arugula Caesar Salad, 176–177
pepper Jack cheese
 Steak Tacos, 266–267
Peppermint Italian Soda recipe, 308
pepperoni
 Pizza Baked Eggs, 224–225
Perfect Baked Salmon recipe, 230–231
Perfect Roast Beef recipe, 246–247
pesto, 86
Pizza Baked Eggs recipe, 224–225
pizza stone, 66
pizza
 Blue Cheese and Sausage Pizza, 208–209
 Jalapeño Popper Pizza, 198–199
 Pizza Baked Eggs, 224–225
 Prosciutto Arugula Pizza, 202–203
 Psyllium Husk Pizza Crust, 92–93
 Sausage and Provolone Pizza, 206–207
 Spicy Chicken Pizza, 200–201
 White Pizza, 204–205
Pork Belly recipe, 258–259
pork rinds
 Chicken Cordon Bleu, 260–261
 Crispy Baked Chicken, 238–239

Everything Crusted Pork Chops, 228–229
Lamb Rib Chops with Mushrooms, 240–241
Lemon Oysters, 116–117
Marinated Fried Chicken Strips, 234–235
Marinated Pork Loin, 220–221
Onion Rings, 128–129
Prosciutto Meat Cups, 136–137
portabella mushrooms, for burgers, 180
poultry scissors, 66
prayer, 40
pressure cooker, 65
pressure cooker recipes
 Caramelized Onions Three Ways, 88–89
 French Onion Soup, 174–175
 Garlic Parmesan Chicken Wings, 106–107
 Instant Pot Chicken and Rice Soup,
  148–149
 Roasted Garlic Two Ways, 72–73
prosciutto
 Chicken Cordon Bleu, 260–261
 Garlic Tomato Burgers, 190–191
 Prosciutto Arugula Pizza, 202–203
 Prosciutto Meat Cups, 136–137
 Roasted Berries with Prosciutto, 130–131
 Stovetop Green Beans, 150–151
Prosciutto Arugula Pizza recipe, 202–203
Prosciutto Meat Cups recipe, 136–137
proteins
 fatty, 24
 types of, 25
 whey, 25
provolone cheese
 Sausage and Provolone Pizza, 206–207
Psyllium Husk Pizza Crust recipe, 92–93
 Blue Cheese and Sausage Pizza, 208–209
 Jalapeño Popper Pizza, 198–199
 Prosciutto Arugula Pizza, 202–203
 Sausage and Provolone Pizza, 206–207
 Spicy Chicken Pizza, 200–201
 White Pizza, 204–205
psyllium husks
 Cinnamon Bread, 98–99
 Psyllium Husk Pizza Crust, 92–93
 Seeded Hamburger Buns, 96–97
pumpkin seeds
 Spiced Seeds, 102–103
 Wasabi Broccoli Slaw, 154–155

R

radishes
    Asian-Style Burgers, 194–195
    Avocado Shrimp Salad, 140–141
    Breakfast Cobb Salad, 166–167
    Diner Roasted Radishes, 152–153
    Keto Pot Roast, 212–213
Ranch Dressing recipe, 78
    Chicken, Bacon, and Ranch–Stuffed
        Peppers, 222–223
    Southwest Chicken Salad, 146–147
Raspberry Smash recipe, 304
real food
    about, 33
    food sources, 34
    as a Keto Clarity concept, 14–15
    nutrient density, 37
    savoring meals, 36
    whole foods, 35
Real Food Keto (Moore and Moore), 8, 33, 35
A Real Food Journey (blog), 10
A Real Food Journey (podcast), 9
recipes. *See also specific recipes and
    categories of recipes*
    kitchen tools and equipment for, 64–67
    macronutrients not included, 62–63
red peppers, roasted
    Blue Cheese and Sausage Pizza, 208–209
red wine
    George's Soup, 162–163
refined carbohydrates, 21
Reverse Sear Tri-Tip Roast recipe, 236–237
Rib-Eye Steak with Shallots and Garlic recipe,
    248–249
rimmed baking sheet, 67
Roast Leg of Lamb recipe, 214–215
Roasted Berries with Prosciutto recipe,
    130–131
Roasted Garlic Two Ways recipe, 72–73
Roasted Strawberry Jam recipe, 82
    Berry Vinaigrette, 87
    Jalapeño Poppers with Strawberry Jam,
        114–115
    Strawberry Jam Parfaits, 278–279
romaine lettuce
    Arugula Caesar Salad, 176–177
    Breakfast Cobb Salad, 166–167
    Grilled Romaine Salad, 164–165

rosemary
    Keto Pot Roast, 212–213
    Lamb Rib Chops with Mushrooms, 240–241
    Mushroom Bisque, 142–143
    Rosemary, Mushroom, and Swiss Burgers,
        188–189
Rosemary, Mushroom, and Swiss Burgers
    recipe, 188–189
Rushin, Heather, personal story of, 9–10

S

salad greens
    Breakfast Cobb Salad, 166–167
    Southwest Chicken Salad, 146–147
    Steak Salad, 158–159
salads
    Arugula Caesar Salad, 176–177
    Avocado Shrimp Salad, 140–141
    Breakfast Cobb Salad, 166–167
    Grilled Romaine Salad, 164–165
    Hot and Smoky Wedge Salad, 168–169
    Hot Spinach and Bacon Salad, 160–161
    Lime Slaw, 172–173
    Southwest Chicken Salad, 146–147
    Steak Salad, 158–159
    Wasabi Broccoli Slaw, 154–155
salmon
    Perfect Baked Salmon, 230–231
salt, types of, 110
Salt and Pepper Chuck Steak with Blue Cheese
    Butter recipe, 232–233
Salt and Vinegar Wings recipe, 132–133
saturated fats, 30
saucepans, 67
sauces
    Berry Vinaigrette, 87
    Beyond Basic Blue Cheese Butter, 75
    Blue Cheese Dressing, 83
    Buffalo Dill Sauce, 85
    Keto Caramel Sauce, 286–287
    Maple Orange Butter, 80
    Mignonette Sauce Three Ways, 76
    Mustard Seed Aioli, 84
    Nut-Free Pesto, 86
    Ranch Dressing, 78
    Roasted Garlic Two Ways, 72–73
    Roasted Strawberry Jam, 82

sauces (continued)
    Smoky Chimichurri, 70–71
    Smoky Garlic Burger Sauce, 74
    Tartar Sauce, 77
Sausage and Provolone Pizza recipe, 206–207
scale, 65
scissors, 66
seafood. See fish and seafood
searing meat, 212
Seeded Hamburger Buns recipe, 96–97
    Asian-Style Burgers, 194–195
    Balsamic Onion, Truffle, and Arugula
        Burgers, 182–183
    Crispy Mushroom and Blue Cheese
        Burgers, 196–197
    Fontina Burgers, 186–187
    Garlic Tomato Burgers, 190–191
    Onion Horsey Burgers, 192–193
    Rosemary, Mushroom, and Swiss Burgers,
        188–189
    Southwest Burgers, 184–185
    Triple Onion Burgers, 180–181
sesame seeds
    Seeded Hamburger Buns, 96–97
    Tri-Tip and Broccoli Bowls, 218–219
shallots
    Butter-Basted New York Strip Steak,
        254–255
    Flank Steak with Charred Green Onions,
        262–263
    Fontina Burgers, 186–187
    Lamb Rib Chops with Mushrooms, 240–241
    Mignonette Sauce Three Ways, 76
    Rib-Eye Steak with Shallots and Garlic,
        248–249
    Sausage and Provolone Pizza, 206–207
    Simple Baked Cod, 242–243
    Smoky Chimichurri, 70–71
    Stovetop Green Beans, 150–151
    White Pizza, 204–205
shopping lists
    about, 43
    Dairy-Free Week 1 meal plan, 53
    Dairy-Free Week 2 meal plan, 55
    Dairy-Free Week 3 meal plan, 57
    Dairy-Free Week 4 meal plan, 59
    Week 1 meal plan, 45
    Week 2 meal plan, 47
    Week 3 meal plan, 49
    Week 4 meal plan, 51
shrimp
    Avocado Shrimp Salad, 140–141
    Lime Butter Shrimp, 122–123
side dishes. See also salads; soups
    Diner Roasted Radishes, 152–153
    Habanero Brussels Sprouts, 156–157
    Lime Slaw, 172–173
    Stovetop Green Beans, 150–151
    Truffle Garlic–Roasted Broccoli, 144–145
    Wasabi Broccoli Slaw, 154–155
silicone baking mat, 67, 270
silicone spatulas, 67
Simple Baked Cod recipe, 242–243
skillet, 64, 66
sleep, 39
slow cooker recipes
    Caramelized Onions Three Ways, 88–89
    George's Soup, 162–163
    Slow Cooker Rich Beef Shanks, 216–217
Slow Cooker Rich Beef Shanks recipe,
    216–217
Smoky Chicken Pâté recipe, 108–109
Smoky Chimichurri recipe, 70–71
Smoky Garlic Burger Sauce recipe, 74
Smoky Taco Seasoning recipe, 79
    Chicken Cordon Bleu, 260–261
    Southwest Burgers, 184–185
    Southwest Chicken Salad, 146–147
    Spiced Nuts Three Ways, 134–135
    Taco Soup, 170–171
snacks. See also appetizers and snacks
    keto diet example, 29
    low-fat diet example, 28
soups
    French Onion Soup, 174–175
    George's Soup, 162–163
    Instant Pot Chicken and Rice Soup,
        148–149
    Mushroom Bisque, 142–143
    Taco Soup, 170–171
sour cream
    Blue Cheese Dressing, 83
    Caramelized Onion Dip, 104–105
    Ranch Dressing, 78
    Southwest Burgers, 184–185
Southwest Burgers recipe, 184–185

Southwest Chicken Salad recipe, 146–147
Sparkling Green Tea Elixir recipe, 313
sparkling mineral water
    Ginger Lime Soda, 312
    Raspberry Smash, 304
    Sparkling Green Tea Elixir, 313
spatchcocking, 252
spatulas, 67
Spiced Nuts Three Ways recipe, 134–135
Spiced Seeds recipe, 102–103
Spicy Chicken Pizza recipe, 200–201
Spicy Mix Spiced Nuts, 134–135
spinach
    Hot Spinach and Bacon Salad, 160–161
    Spicy Chicken Pizza, 200–201
splatter screen, 67
spoons, 67
Sriracha sauce
    Asian-Style Burgers, 194–195
Standard American Diet, 35
Steak Salad recipe, 158–159
Steak Tacos recipe, 266–267
stick blender, 67
stockpot, 67
storage containers/jars, 65
Stovetop Green Beans recipe, 150–151
strawberries
    Roasted Berries with Prosciutto, 130–131
    Roasted Strawberry Jam, 82
    Strawberry Basil Sparkling Punch, 309
    Strawberry Cream Ice Pops, 272–273
    Strawberry Creme, 305
Strawberry Basil Sparkling Punch recipe,
    309
Strawberry Cream Ice Pops recipe, 272–273
Strawberry Creme recipe, 305
Strawberry Jam Parfaits recipe, 278–279
stressors, 41
sunflower seed flour
    Chocolate Chip Cookies, 292–293
    Cinnamon Bread, 98–99
    Drop Biscuits, 94–95
    Peanut Butter Tarts, 294–295
    Seeded Hamburger Buns, 96–97
sunflower seeds
    Nut-Free Pesto, 86
    Spiced Seeds, 102–103
    Wasabi Broccoli Slaw, 154–155

Swiss cheese
    Chicken Cordon Bleu, 260–261
    Rosemary, Mushroom, and Swiss Burgers,
        188–189

T

Taco Soup recipe, 170–171
Tartar Sauce recipe, 77
    Perfect Baked Salmon, 230–231
taste, of healthy food, 31
thin spatula, 67
thyme
    French Onion Soup, 174–175
    Keto Pot Roast, 212–213
Toasted Coconut Pudding recipe, 284–285
tomato sauce
    Blue Cheese and Sausage Pizza, 208–209
    Pizza Baked Eggs, 224–225
    Sausage and Provolone Pizza, 206–207
tomatoes
    Bruschetta Mushrooms, 124–125
    Caprese Skewers, 126–127
    Garlic Tomato Burgers, 190–191
    George's Soup, 162–163
    Slow Cooker Rich Beef Shanks, 216–217
    Southwest Burgers, 184–185
    Taco Soup, 170–171
tools, kitchen, 64–67
Triple Onion Burgers recipe, 180–181
Tri-Tip and Broccoli Bowls recipe, 218–219
Truffle Garlic–Roasted Broccoli recipe,
    144–145

V

Vanilla Bacon–Stuffed Celery recipe, 112–113
vegetables
    fermented, 21
    green leafy nonstarchy, 20
vibration plate, 40
Vickery, Gus
    about, 11
    Moments of Clarity, 14, 27, 34, 37, 39, 41

W

Wasabi Broccoli Slaw recipe, 154–155
Week 1 meal plan, 44–45

Week 2 meal plan, 46–47
Week 3 meal plan, 48–49
Week 4 meal plan, 50–51
Westman, Eric
    about, 13
    Keto Clarity, 15
    Moments of Clarity, 17, 20, 30
whey protein, 25
whipped cream
    Mocha Coffee, 303
    Peppermint Italian Soda, 308
    Toasted Coconut Pudding, 284–285
whisk, 67
White Chocolate Peppermint Swirl Ice Cream
    recipe, 288–289
White Pizza recipe, 204–205
whole foods, 35
whole grains, 21
Wintry Mix Spiced Nuts, 134–135
wire rack, 67
wooden spoons, 67

Z

zucchini
    Cheesy Stuffed Meatballs, 120–121
    Prosciutto Meat Cups, 136–137